A NOBLE CAUSE

A NOBLE CAUSE

AMERICAN BATTLEFIELD VICTORIES IN VIETNAM

DOUGLAS NILES

BERKLEY CALIBER, NEW YORK

An imprint of Penguin Random House LLC
375 Hudson Street, New York, New York 10014

This book is an original publication of Penguin Random House LLC.

Library of Congress Cataloging-in-Publication Data

Niles, Douglas.
A noble cause : American battlefield victories in Vietnam / Douglas Niles. — First edition.
p. cm.
Includes bibliographical references and index.
ISBN 978-0-425-27834-5 (hardback)
1. Vietnam War, 1961–1975—Campaigns.   2. Vietnam War, 1961–1975—United States.
3. Battles—Vietnam—History—20th century.   4. Courage—Vietnam—History—20th
century.   5. Soldiers—United States—History—20th century.   6. Soldiers—Vietnam
(Republic)—History.   7. United States—Armed Forces—History—Vietnam War,
1961–1975.   8. Vietnam (Republic)—Armed Forces—History.   I. Title.
DS558.2.N55 2015
959.704'342—dc23
2015022110

First edition: October 2015

PRINTED IN THE UNITED STATES OF AMERICA

10   9   8   7   6   5   4   3   2   1

Jacket design by Jerry Todd.
Jacket photos: "Helicopter" © sculpies / Shutterstock; "Soldiers" © rudall30 / Shutterstock.

Most Berkley Caliber Books are available at special quantity discounts for bulk purchases
for sales promotions, premiums, fund-raising, or educational use. Special books,
or book excerpts, can also be created to fit specific needs. For details,
write: SpecialMarkets@penguinrandomhouse.com.

This book is dedicated to the memories, and the legacies, of the 58,300 men and women whose names are engraved on the Vietnam Veterans Memorial Wall in Washington, DC.

CONTENTS

MAPS

ACKNOWLEDGMENTS

A number of good people have helped put a human face on the stories in this book. In particular, Master Sergeant Scott E. McClellan USMC (Retired) shared in detail his experiences and photos from his time as a young Marine arriving with the first wave of American combat troops, in the summer of 1965. Don Franzene willingly discussed his experiences as a draftee in the United States Army of 1969. Good friends and smart people, including Steve Winter, Hedi Lauffer, Patrick Seghers, Kevin Dockery, and Timothy Brown, looked over important parts of the manuscript and offered perceptive comments and critiques. I am grateful to Bill Fawcett, who provided me with the opportunity to write the book, and Tom Colgan of Berkley Caliber, who saw the project through to completion and publication. The contributions of the editorial and production staff at Berkley Caliber have been great, most especially the work of copyeditor Martin Karlow, and managing editor Pam Barricklow, who caught and corrected so many of my embarrassing errors. Naturally, any mistakes that may lurk in these pages are my responsibility alone. Finally, I couldn't have brought this book to completion without the love and support, both emotional and material, of my wonderful wife of the last thirty-eight years, Christine S. Niles.

Corps Tactical Zones in South Vietnam

CENTER OF MILITARY HISTORY, UNITED STATES ARMY

The United States is a country that is always looking to the future, moving forward with greater intensity, seeming to increase its national velocity with every passing decade, each succeeding generation. It is not surprising, then, that as we begin to pass the 50-year anniversary mark of America's involvement in Vietnam, the image of the Vietnam War grows ever more blurry and unfocused in our collective rearview mirror.

The veterans who fought in that war, and who survived to come home, are in their sixties now—at least, the youngest of them are. And this, like all wars, was a conflict fought primarily by young men, each of whom was affected, some profoundly, by his tour of duty. Many Vietnam veterans have spent their adulthood living with the uncomfortable perception that the war that asked so much of them was not a successful war, that it is the first war that America "lost."

And of course, that outcome is not in doubt, in the sense that the Communist forces achieved their objective of a single nation, controlled by Hanoi, and the United States did not prevent that from happening. It is one of the universal truths of war, even if a little counterintuitive, that it is not the winner that decides when the conflict is over. It is the losing side that must make that bitter decision. In the early 1970s, the United States of America, as a true representative democracy, collectively decided that fighting the war was no longer worth paying the toll it was costing—most notably, the toll in American lives. The toll in American unity had also been high, and both costs would have continued to soar so long as young men were being drafted and sent to Vietnam to face the very real threat of dying there.

Almost all wars are asymmetrical, in the sense that the opposing sides are not usually fighting for the same goals. For example, one nation might be fighting for its survival, while its foe may be fighting to gain territory and treasure. In this regard, the Vietnam War was more asymmetrical than most. The North Vietnamese and the insurgent Viet Cong in the south were fighting to attain national unity—and doing so under the banner of the Communist cause. They had the backing, and the doctrinal and material support, of the USSR and Communist China, very much a pair of uneasy bedfellows but united in their opposition to America and its allies. The South Vietnamese, conversely, were fighting for the very survival of their unsteady democracy. They had the backing of the United States, not just in material support, but also through the direct aid of American combat units and eventually the shedding of much American blood.

The U.S.A., in a national sense, had a lot less at stake in the war than either North or South Vietnam, as it was not remotely threatened by the Vietnamese. America *was* threatened, however, by the specter of communism—a much graver threat to the entire free world in the 1960s than many younger Americans currently understand. The "domino theory" was held up as gospel, in that if South Vietnam fell to communism, then the rest of Southeast Asia would inevitably follow. History disproved the theory: although Laos and Cambodia, inextricably tied to the fate and future of Vietnam, were caught up and tossed chaotically in the wake of the Vietnam War, other more populous Southeast Asian nations including Thailand, Malaysia, and Indonesia remained stout pillars in the anti-Communist world.

The American men who fought in Vietnam (and the American men and women who supported the combat soldiers) were not the ones who failed to achieve victory. In what has been a national disgrace, the veterans who fought in Vietnam—either because they believed in the fight against communism, or because they were drafted into the military and chose to follow the law that required them to serve (or both)—have borne a completely disproportionate share of the blame for America's military performance in Vietnam. While in the vast majority of cases, these soldiers did their best to improve the lives, and the futures, of the South Vietnamese people they were there to defend, too many of them came home to antipathy and scorn.

In Vietnam, the United States Army and the United States Marine Corps both performed with exceptional effectiveness in battles against veteran, well-armed foes. The North Vietnamese Army was a professional organization composed of experienced officers, seasoned by a successful war of independence against the French, passionately committed to the cause of national unity. The Viet Cong insurgents were also veteran fighters, who, for a decade, had been waging war against the national government of South Vietnam. By the time America arrived in strength, the VC had carved out large pieces of territory that were effectively free of government control, where the Army of South Vietnam did not even dare to venture.

President Johnson, in 1965, made the decision to send American combat forces to Vietnam. Because he was not at heart a warlike man, and because he was haunted by the disastrous consequences of the massive Chinese intervention, fifteen years earlier, in the Korean War, he put restrictions on his military to try to prevent the conflict from escalating. Those restrictions included strict limits on where the United States could employ its overwhelming airpower, and banned American forces from operating in Cambodia and Laos, leaving those countries as untouchable sanctuaries for battered, but not destroyed, enemy forces. These two factors combined to create an unwinnable war.

While in Vietnam, the American military fought an impressive sequence of significant battles, and they won the vast majority of those battles. They introduced revolutionary new concepts to warfare, most notably the use of large numbers of helicopters to give combat formations unprecedented mobility. United States' soldiers fine-tuned tactics used by their forefathers, including the traditional American reliance on overwhelming support by artillery and, as in more recent wars, the effective use of direct strikes by aircraft to aid the efforts of the men on the ground. In the end, as always, it would be the individual "grunt," the Army infantryman and the Marine rifleman, who would win the battle with his M16, his bayonet, hand grenades, and the unflinching support of his fellow soldiers to the right and left.

The cost of the war to America is well known. The tally of men and women lost has been carved into black marble on our national mall. The Vietnam War would cost Lyndon Johnson his optimism, his presidency, and most of his legacy. The lives of the war's survivors, in many cases, were scarred deeply. Some of them were disabled by physical wounds. The health of others was weakened or destroyed by the impact of chemical poisons widely used, and too poorly understood, at the time. Dark memories have caused too many to remain silent about their experiences there, or have festered to overshadow futures, families, and lives.

But it is a mistake to think of Vietnam as some kind of hopeless lost cause. Albeit at a terrible cost, the United States let the Communist bloc know that they could not attack American allies with impunity—that at some point the forces of the "free world" would line up against them and fight. Those forces fought in Vietnam, and quite possibly that willingness to fight led the USSR to consider, very carefully, the impact of further aggressive actions in Europe and elsewhere in the world. During, and after, the Vietnam War, both the Soviet Union and China chose to accept the status quo rather than risk another military confrontation with the United States and its allies.

It is even possible that when the Berlin Wall came tumbling down in 1989, and the satellite subject governments of the Soviet Union toppled like—one has to say—"dominoes," one of the causes of that collapse was America's willingness to stand and fight in Vietnam. Perhaps that noble, if unsuccessful, struggle did have a significant impact on the course of world history through the rest of the 20th century, and beyond.

With the advantage of years, of historical perspective, and with a reflection on subsequent events far removed from Vietnam, perhaps the image of the war in America's rearview mirror may become just a little brighter, and more clear.

FIRST TO FIGHT

OPERATION STARLITE AND
THE UNITED STATES MARINES

We intend to convince the Communists that we cannot be
defeated by force of arms or by superior power. They are
not easily convinced.

PRESIDENT LYNDON BAINES JOHNSON,
PRESS CONFERENCE, 28 JULY 1965

By the spring of 1965, the South Vietnamese Army—or the Army of the
Republic of Vietnam (ARVN)—was so heavily engaged with the Viet Cong
rebels of their own country, and with the invading North Vietnamese
Army (NVA), also known as the People's Army of Vietnam (PAVN), that
the south was losing the equivalent of a battalion of soldiers every week.
Often posted at remote bases and camps, surrounded by either unpopulated terrain or villages and hamlets sympathetic to the enemy, the ARVN
units were often subject to violent, intense attacks. The Viet Cong had
practically made an art form of laying and executing ambushes against
relief columns that would invariably be dispatched to the threatened outposts along readily predictable routes.

At the time, American involvement in Vietnam was limited to a robust
Special Forces presence, mainly through the United States Army's legendary
Green Berets. These skilled and independent-minded soldiers were advising
and training the ARVN, and had established a number of camps throughout
the country in an attempt to monitor much of South Vietnam's rugged and

roadless interior. But it was clear that Special Forces would not be enough to stem the tide of Communist North Vietnam's aggression.

The senior American soldier in the country was General William Westmoreland, commander of the headquarters known as the Military Assistance Command—Vietnam (MACV). Recognizing that the situation was a true crisis, and that South Vietnam would fall sooner rather than later without significant American assistance, Westmoreland requested such support from President Lyndon Baines Johnson. Armed with the freedom to act granted to him by Congress in the Gulf of Tonkin Resolution, which had been signed the previous summer following a minor clash between United States Navy destroyers and North Vietnamese torpedo boats, Johnson quickly agreed. Even as he made plans to organize and move to South Vietnam an army force of over 100,000 men, the president took immediate steps to deploy America's most combat-ready military force: the United States Marines.

COMING ASHORE

By March, the 3rd Battalion, 9th Marine Regiment (3/9) had been aboard ships near the South Vietnamese coast for the previous two months; these would be the first Marines to land. Other units had completed training in Thailand, or would be moved from bases in Okinawa, Hawaii, and California. Before long, some 5,000 men of the USMC would be in position in country to protect the base at Da Nang, and to expand their missions as the war developed.

When the initial Marines rolled toward Red Beach at Da Nang, on March 8, 1965, they did so in a style that would have made their predecessors from World War II and Korea feel right at home: they deployed into landing craft and amphibious tractors from their sea transport ships, and rode right up onto the sand beach, a few miles south of the large airfield that would become the center of USMC presence in South Vietnam for the next eight years.

Of course, what happened after the landing was a little less traditional. Instead of machine-gun and artillery fire, the Marines were met by a bevy

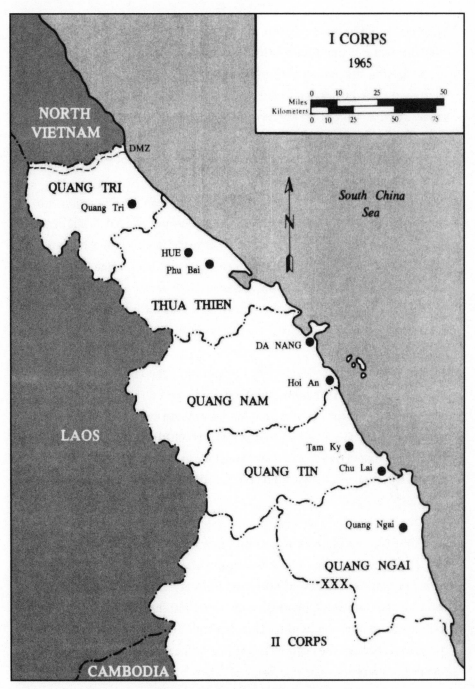

I Corps; USMC Operational Area

HISTORY AND MUSEUMS DIVISION, UNITED STATES MARINE CORPS

of pretty young Vietnamese women who insisted on draping flowered leis over the necks of the sodden leathernecks as soon as they emerged from the surf. After this not-altogether-unpleasant welcome to the country, the Marines boarded trucks and rode to the Da Nang air base. Cheering Vietnamese civilians lined the road for much of the way, and a banner proclaiming "Vietnam Welcomes the United States Marines" swung above the gate as the vehicles rumbled onto the post that would become one of America's primary bases for the rest of the war.

These Marines, the BLT 3/9 (battalion landing team, 3rd Battalion, 9th Marine Regiment), formed the vanguard of the unit that would initially be known as the 9th Marine Expeditionary Brigade (MEB) under Brigadier General Frederick Karch. A second formation, the 1/3 Marine battalion, flew into Da Nang from Okinawa. Although their arrival was a little more martial, in that snipers fired at the huge USAF C-130 transports that arrived at Da Nang every 30 minutes throughout the day, no hits were scored upon the transport planes.

On 9 March, 23 helicopters that would form the HMM-162 (Marine Medium Helicopter) squadron, took off from the carrier USS *Princeton*, which lay just over the horizon from the South Vietnamese coast. The choppers, which had been based in Vietnam for more than a year before a brief return to Okinawa, flew back to Da Nang to form the initial wave of USMC airpower in support of what would be a steadily increasing commitment of American strength.

Over the course of the next months following the initial landing at Da Nang, the Marine presence in country grew significantly. Fixed-wing aircraft of the VMA (Marine Attack Squadron) 311 and VMFA (Marine Fighter Attack Squadron) 542 arrived at the base. The Marine Expeditionary Brigade thus had the ability to support ground troops with helicopter transport as well as A4 and F4 ground-assault aircraft. In addition to the large base at Da Nang, a smaller air base near the city of Hue in the north of the country was fortified and expanded at Phu Bai, and a new base, with a quickly established airfield, was built south of Da Nang in Quang Tin province. This base, which was created in an area lacking an existing name, was located during a flyover by the Marine force commander, General Krulak. He called it "Chu Lai," using the letters in the Mandarin alphabet for his initials.

By the middle of May 1965, the US had deployed seven of the nine battalions of the 3rd Marine Division to Vietnam. These Marines were supported by an artillery regiment, transport troop, and a number of air-support squadrons. Though most of this strength remained centered in Da Nang, which was subject to continued harassment by the Viet Cong, both the northern base at Phu Bai and the southern installation, Chu Lai, had significant garrisons and well-established defensive perimeters. As a capstone to the initial deployment—and at least in part because the term *expeditionary* invoked in the Vietnamese unpleasant memories of the war against the French—the name of the Marine Expeditionary Brigade was changed to the III Marine Amphibious Force.

FITTING INTO A COUNTRY, AND A WAR

Throughout May, June, and July of 1965, the Marines struggled to define their role in the fight against the Viet Cong. The country of South Vietnam was divided into four so-called Corps areas for command purposes, with the I Corps in the north and the IV in the far south. The Marines would operate in the I Corps area, which was composed of the five northernmost provinces of the country. Initially, however, their efforts were constrained to simply defending the three bases where their aircraft and artillery units were concentrated. Through negotiations with the ARVN, each base was surrounded by a very small TAOR (tactical area of responsibility) in which the Marines were allowed to patrol.

Naturally, this restricted activity did not sit well with the typically aggressive commanders up through the USMC hierarchy. On 4 June, as Major General Lewis W. Walt took over command of the III MAF, the ceremony transferring the unit had to be held indoors at Da Nang, because American colors were still not allowed to be flown outside, where it was feared they might offend the sensibilities of the South Vietnamese.

Already frustrated by the restrictions created by the limited TAORs of

his units, Walt and the rest of the Marines were outraged by a highly pub-
licized VC attack on the Da Nang air base on 1 July. The base was hit by a
force of 85 enemy troops, combining a special operations company and a
mortar unit. An advance demolitions team dug a tunnel under the base's
outer-perimeter barbed-wire barrier and then punched through the inner
fence without being discovered, until a Marine sentry heard noise and
launched an illumination grenade at 0130.

This signaled the attackers to spring into action. Sappers threw satchel
charges at parked aircraft, destroying a fighter and two huge C-130s and
damaging several other aircraft. The attackers fled, and few casualties were
inflicted on either side, but the spectacular nature of the attack—and the
wide publicity it received—convinced the Marines that they would need to
leave their enclaves and carry the war to the enemy in order to prevent future
attacks. General William Westmoreland, CO of MACV (Military Assistance Command—Vietnam) and the senior American officer in country,
agreed, as did the ARVN commanders.

Almost immediately the Marines began to expand their TAOR, patrolling
aggressively well beyond the perimeters of their bases. As patrols pushed into
the jungle, however, the enemy simply seemed to melt away. Throughout July
and into early August, numerous patrols swept through the enlarged TAORs,
but no significant enemy presence could be located and brought to battle.

Meanwhile, on 28 July, President Johnson announced that the number
of American troops in Vietnam would be rapidly increased—to a level of
125,000—and that General Westmoreland would be given greater flexibility
in how those troops were employed. Still, the big question remained: How
could you battle an enemy if you couldn't find him?

FREED TO FIGHT

It was 6 August when General Walt was granted the authority to begin
offensive operations. In the Chu Lai area, a strong Viet Cong presence
identified as the 1st Viet Cong Regiment was suspected in the vicinity
south of the base. A month earlier, this force had attacked a hamlet about

20 miles south of Chu Lai, inflicting more than a hundred casualties on the ARVN defenders and capturing two large howitzers, among other weaponry. For weeks, Marines and ARVN patrols had been searching for the headquarters of the regiment, known to be located near the Phuoc Thuan Peninsula. Those patrols turned up tantalizing clues, but no hard proof—until a solid breakthrough unexpectedly materialized.

The intelligence windfall came in the form of a VC deserter who turned himself in to the South Vietnamese Army on 15 August. He claimed that the 1st Viet Cong Regiment had established a powerful base in the Van Tuong complex of villages. The location lay only some 12 miles south of the brand-new Marine base at Chu Lai. According to the deserter, who was personally interviewed by the ARVN area commander, General Thi, the regiment intended to stage a massive attack on the USMC installation. When the general found the deserter's tale credible, he reported the intelligence coup to General Walt.

Throughout July 1965, the intelligence branch, or S2, of the 3rd Marine Division had picked up background noise suggesting such an attack might be in the works. Thus far, however, the Marines had been unable to nail down a precise location for the VC regiment, which numbered some 1,500 experienced, motivated guerrilla fighters. Now the suspicions of attack had been confirmed, and the unit located.

General Walt decided to turn the tables on the VC, and so was born Operation Starlite, the first regimental-sized combat operation for the American military since the Korean War. (Initially termed Operation Satellite, the offensive was renamed after an electrical generator failed, and the clerk who was typing up the plan, working by candlelight, misread the term as Starlite.)

Operation Starlite followed an ambitious and somewhat complicated plan, especially considering that most of the young Marines would be new to combat, and that the battalion-sized offensive involved companies from no fewer than three different USMC regiments. On the other hand, the operation would benefit from the fact that the Marine units were bolstered by both officers and NCOs who had experienced jungle warfare in World War II, as well as some grueling fighting during the Korean War. Furthermore, the Marines were structured as a complete and independent fighting force, with their own air-transport and air-support elements, and benefited from a long history of cooperation with the United States Navy.

All of those elements would be employed as Operation Starlite was put into practice. The result would be a long day of battle, more days of mopping up, and a dramatic victory for the first large-unit American action of the Vietnam War.

With solid confirmation of the enemy's whereabouts, the planning for the attack proceeded quickly. The 1/7 Marines and the HQ of the 7th Marine Regiment had arrived in Chu Lai only days earlier. Although the 1st Battalion was assigned to the defense of the base, the regimental command staff was given command of the operation against the Viet Cong regiment, which would involve overland maneuver, air transport, and a beach landing.

General Walt demanded that a ship-based landing team be in place to support the operation, and such a force, the 3/7 Marines, was available in Subic Bay, the Philippines. Those troops, transported aboard the helicopter carrier USS *Iwo Jima*, could arrive off the coast of South Vietnam by 18 August, so that day was designated as the start of the operation. Fortunately, additional naval transport was nearby, enough to ensure the lift of the 3/3 from Chu Lai to the landing beaches. By the morning of 17 August, the plan was ready to be put into effect. Colonel Oscar Peatross, CO of the 7th Marines, would be in tactical command of the operation.

STARLITE BEGINS

Company M of the 3/3 made the initial movement, riding LVTs (Landing Vehicle, Tracked) along the coast from Chu Lai to a beach a few miles north of the Phuoc Thuan Peninsula. Debarking from their landing craft, the Marines marched some four miles inland, much of the move occurring after dark on the 17th. Despite some fog and confusion in the forested, somewhat hilly terrain, the company achieved its blocking position north of the Tra Bong River before dawn of 18 August. Here they dug in

and hunkered down; their mission was to prevent retreating VC from fleeing northward, away from the converging jaws of the main attack. Though
the move was initially noted by enemy scouts, the Marines had been making these kinds of excursions for several weeks now, so none of the VC
took the landing as the sign of any kind of imminent attack.

That unawareness vanished with the dawn as the rest of the 3/3 appeared
in landing craft off the beaches south of the peninsula, and air and artillery
bombardment commenced to soften up the three landing zones for the three
companies of the 2/4 that would make up the third prong of the triangular
offensive.

The transports carrying the amphibious force had sailed due east from
Chu Lai on the 17th, crossing the horizon so that they were out of sight of
land, before turning to the south and drawing close to the landing beaches.
In addition to Colonel Peatross, the amphibious force included Companies
K and I of the 3/3 and the battalion commander, Lieutenant Colonel Joseph
Muir. Company L would follow close behind as the battalion reserve.

A civilian hamlet, An Cuong (1) lay adjacent to the landing beach, so in
order to avoid civilian casualties the preliminary suppressing fire was limited to a series of strafing runs by the 20-mm cannon of Marine A-4 Skyhawks. (Another nearby village that would become involved in the battle
soon was named An Cuong (2); these numerical designations were common
in Vietnam, where several small clusters of huts would be separated by rice
paddies or forest, yet together would be regarded as a single village.) Aside
from a few snipers shooting from the trees, however, the landings proceeded
very much as planned.

The first wave of Marine infantry rode inside massive 40-ton AmTrac
amphibious landing vehicles. These behemoths, standing some 11 feet tall on
dry land, rumbled from the surf and drove quickly across the sand to approach
the tree line. Bow ramps dropped on each AmTrac, and the Marines—about
40 men per vehicle—came charging out to secure the beach. They quickly
advanced through An Cuong (1), but found no signs of the enemy.

Meanwhile, churning shoreward behind the AmTracs came a series of
landing craft carrying the Marines' potent fighting vehicles. A massive LCT

drew up onto the beach and disgorged five M48 main battle tanks, which at 50 tons would be the real heavyweights of this fight. Another brought up three M67 flame tanks in support, while still more delivered several of the unique Ontos recoilless rifle launchers. The latter looked strange but menacing, with a total of six long barrels, three to each side of the driver's turret. At nine tons, they were smaller than the tanks, but faster and more maneuverable. They scuttled along the beach, past local fishermen who continued to go about their daily routines, launching their boats and putting out to sea against the backdrop of the Marine landing.

Quickly the landing companies formed up and moved off the beach, except for Company L, which proceeded to establish a perimeter around the beach area. Company I swept through An Cuong (1) without resistance and continued inland. Company K shrugged off sniper fire from the right flank and proceeded north along the coast for about 2,000 yards, until it approached the first obstacle: a small hill. Heavy gunfire, including automatic rifles and machine guns, erupted from VC units entrenched on the hill, lashing the Marine unit, forcing the men to dive for cover. Mortar rounds thudded into the soft ground, exploding in blossoms of dirt and sand.

Company L was ordered forward to support the attack on the hill. Offshore, USN combat ships, most notably the light cruiser USS *Galveston*, armed with batteries of six-inch guns, pounded the hill with a crushing barrage. Amid searing heat, the Marines pressed the advance, and as always the battle became a struggle between individual troops. Marines with bayonets fixed leaped into the trenches, killing Viet Cong but suffering a number of fatal casualties on the way. But the Marines didn't falter, and by midafternoon they had reached the top of the hill and forced the enemy survivors to flee north.

The fighting raged with equal, perhaps even greater intensity on the third flank of the triangular battle. This part of Operation Starlite represented the first battalion-scale attack in USMC history in which all of the troops would be delivered to the battlefield by helicopter, and as it happened, the perils inherent in airmobile operation quickly became apparent.

The heliborne attack fell to the three rifle companies of the 2nd Battalion,

4th Marines. The men mounted bulky, green UH-34 helicopters at Chu Lai in the dawn mist, and flew at low altitude toward a series of three landing zones (LZ) that had been selected along the southwest boundary of the battlefield. These LZs were designated Red, White, and Blue, from the north to the south.

Fifteen minutes before the choppers arrived, big howitzers that had been moved into Company M's position, at the northern terminus of the battlefield just beyond the Tra Bong River, erupted with a barrage of 155-mm shells, pummeling each of the three LZs with a punishing series of explosive ordnance. Nearly two dozen A4 and F4 ground-attack aircraft delivered 18 tons of high-explosive bombs and napalm onto the ground to further soften up the three sites.

Company G of the 2/4 came down on LZ Red, and seemed to have the easiest time of it. They encountered only sporadic resistance from snipers, and quickly cleared two hamlets very near to the LZ. Within a few hours the company had moved north to link up with Company M, thus sealing off the northwest arc of the concentric battlefield.

Company E was assigned to LZ White, the middle of the three zones. The Marines there immediately took fire from a strong VC force posted on a ridgeline overlooking the landing zone. Mortar and machine-gun fire showered the freshly landed Americans, and it took a determined bayonet attack driving up and over the ridge before the VC were forced out of their position. Within a few hours the landing area was secure, and Company E was able to move out before noon, advancing to the northeast in an attempt to link up with Company G to the north and further tighten the noose around the 1st VC Regiment.

ORDEAL OF COMPANY H

It was at LZ Blue, the objective of Company H under the command of First Lieutenant Homer Jenkins, that the first perilous setbacks occurred. Landing Zone Blue occupied about the seven o'clock position on the ring of the roughly circular attacking formation. The LZ itself lay under the shadow of

Hill 43, just a couple of hundred yards to the east. The plan of advance had the company marching northeastward, where it would quickly encounter three small hamlets.

The first choppers swooped in and dropped off their Marines without incident, but by the time the second wave of helicopters approached, the VC had set up their fields of fire, and the enemy unleashed a murderous barrage from the top of the hill. As desperate pilots dropped to the ground and Marines sprinted out of the aircraft, Lieutenant Jenkins ordered his men to form a defensive perimeter around the LZ. At the same time, three well-armed US Army UH-1B Hueys arrived to deliver a series of withering bursts into the VC on the hill, pouring machine-gun and rocket fire from the sky to the ground.

Once Jenkins had all of his men assembled, he ordered one platoon to attack the hill, dispatching the other two toward the nearest hamlet, Nam Yen (3). Based on previous experience in the field, the officer not unreasonably expected the VC defenders to withdraw in the face of a Marine attack. What he did not realize, however, was that his LZ placed his company within rifle range of a VC battalion HQ; the enemy would not give up this position easily. Bullets hit home, dropping several men even before they had a chance to form up and move on the objectives.

Nevertheless, the double-pronged advance began immediately, spurred on by the nearness of the enemy firing positions. When the first Marines reached the base of the hill, however, they were driven to ground by a withering fusillade of small-arms and machine-gun fire—an outburst of firepower indicating a much larger defending force than the young lieutenant had imagined. At the same time, the platoons approaching Nam Yen (3) also encountered fierce opposition, as many of the innocent-looking huts were revealed to be fortified defensive positions; in several buildings, the walls flipped outward to reveal hidden machine-gun positions. Within minutes the lethal defensive fire halted progress against both objectives.

Reasoning that the elevation of the hill would provide the most advantageous position for his company, Jenkins determined to focus his strength against that objective. He recalled the two platoons from the fringe of the village and sent the full company against Hill 43. At the same time, he called for air support and reinforcements. Three battle tanks and three Ontos vehicles rumbled toward the hill from the beach at An Cuong (1), adding the tanks' main guns and machine guns, and the 18 recoilless rifles on the Ontos, to the Marine firepower.

Several waves of ground-attack jets roared over the hilltop, dropping bombs into the thick tropical growth, smashing trees, tearing up huge chunks of dirt, and pummeling the entrenched VC. Huey gunships added their firepower to the ordnance pouring into the hilltop. Still, the defensive fire remained savage as Company H crept through the broken ground, directing rifle fire at one objective after another. Well-aimed grenades flew through the air, exploding in VC trenches. As the Marines swept past one well-concealed heavy-machine-gun position, they counted many enemy dead in the foxhole and throughout the surrounding jungle.

After a long, brutal struggle, Jenkins and Company H finally drove the enemy from the hill. The lieutenant ordered the airstrikes to shift onto Nam Yen (3) and, with only a few minutes to rest and rehydrate, the now-battle-tested Marines marched down from the hill and formed up to move on the hamlet. Immediately beyond the first hamlet, An Cuong (2) formed the company's next objective. As his troops advanced, Jenkins received a radio message he interpreted to mean that both of the hamlets had been cleared by Marines of the 3/3 who had come over the beach.

Jenkins's picture of the situation was to prove erroneous because he couldn't know what was happening on the other side of the villages. Just east of An Cuong (2), Company I of the 3/3 had been driven to ground by the air attacks called in to support Jenkins's attack on Nam Yen (3), suffering several men wounded by friendly shrapnel. Captain Bruce Webb, CO of I Company, identified enemy fire coming from his left flank. Though that area lay in the 2/4 area of responsibility, he received permission from Colonel Peatross to change the axis of his attack in an effort to clear the hamlets and relieve some of the pressure faced by H Company of 2/4.

RELIEF COLUMNS

Several more tanks, M48 Pattons, rumbled up to join Company I in the attack, but they quickly found themselves blocked by a deep ditch, impassable to the huge, tracked vehicles. Captain Webb assigned a squad led by Corporal Robert O'Malley to mount the hulls of the tanks and ride along as they sought a passage around the south end of the trenchlike obstacle.

They quickly found trouble when a blistering volume of automatic rifle fire opened up on the tank section and its accompanying infantry. One Marine was killed instantly, while the rest of the foot soldiers dived for shelter behind and around the armored behemoths. No sooner had his men hit the ground, however, than O'Malley led them into the attack. Accompanied by another NCO, Lance Corporal Chris Buchs, the squad leader jumped into the trench. The two men killed eight VC before they had to stop to reload their M14s.

The young corporal continued to press the advance, suffering three wounds even as he killed many more VC. By the time his squad had cleared the trench, the fight in the hamlet had also been resolved, but O'Malley refused evacuation until all of his wounded Marines could be airlifted out—no easy task, as the choppers performing the medical evacuations continued to take heavy fire. The last aircraft was so badly damaged that it crash-landed aboard the USS *Iwo Jima*. O'Malley survived the crash, however, and would become the first Marine to be awarded the Congressional Medal of Honor for action in Vietnam.

As the fight in the trench raged, Company I advanced into An Cuong (2) without taking fire. Quickly the Marines began to spread out among the three dozen or so huts that made up the village. They were in the process of discovering trenches and fighting holes when a grenade tossed by a hidden VC flew into the midst of the company command group. The explosion killed Captain Webb and ignited a savage firefight. Enemy mortar shells exploded amid the advancing Marines as First Lieutenant Richard Purnell, company executive officer (XO), ordered all Company I platoons into the attack.

The VC ambush was lethal, but ultimately ineffective—perhaps because it had been sprung too late, after the Marines were already in the village. Small-arms fire and grenades from both sides chattered and banged as the men of I Company moved from hut to hut, killing more than 50 VC defenders before finally clearing the village of enemy troops. By around 1100, the hamlet was declared secure, and Purnell received orders to move Company I to the northeast, where it could join in securing the perimeter holding the retreating VC against the coast. That order was quickly modified, however, as a Huey gunship, disabled by enemy fire, crashed just northeast of An Cuong (2). Ordered to secure the crash site until survivors could be evacuated, Purnell detached two squads of riflemen and three tanks to guard the scene. The rest of I Company then moved out.

At the same time, Lieutenant Jenkins and H Company advanced from the crest of Hill 43, intending to move between the two hamlets and link up with the encircling Marines as they drove toward the sea. The company now had the added firepower of three Ontos and five tanks. However, under the impression that both hamlets had been cleared by Company I, the Marines marched into a deadly ambush. Machine guns and mortars opened up from the village, to the left and rear of the company. At the same time, another enemy strongpoint made itself known from atop Hill 30, a low elevation just to the northeast of both hamlets.

Finding themselves virtually surrounded by enemy guns, Jenkins's men dived to the ground and took whatever shelter they could find in the open patch of rice paddies they had been traversing. The big armored vehicles roared and slipped in the muddy terrain, tracks spinning as they vainly sought to maneuver. The best they could do in the face of the barrage was to form a tight circle and add their firepower to the small arms of the Marines who struggled to set up a defensive perimeter.

Clearly, the battle was no longer going according to plan. The position of Company H was perilous and, ultimately, untenable. Jenkins decided to fall back to LZ Blue, where he and his men had arrived at the battlefield. He called in artillery fire against Nam Yen (2) while Marine ground-attack fighters directed bombs and cannon fire against Hill 30. Under cover of this pounding bombardment, the company began to inch its way back to the landing zone.

The dangerous maneuver was further complicated when a medical evacuation helicopter arrived, coming to rest in the middle of the ragged formation and separating Jenkins's lead platoon from the rest of the company. That lone platoon quickly came under heavy VC fire. In perhaps the first lucky break of Company H's day, though, the detached platoon encountered the Company I tanks and squads that had been assigned to protect the downed Huey gunship (which had been repaired and flown out under its own power). The ad hoc formation fought its way into An Cuong (2), where the Marines took advantage of the fortifications abandoned by the VC to establish a strong defensive position.

After a running fight, Jenkins and Company H arrived at LZ Blue at around 1630. The lieutenant had fewer than 30 able-bodied riflemen remaining in his command. He was ordered to form a defensive perimeter at the landing zone, and learned that a convoy of reinforcements had been dispatched from the landing beach to his position. However, like so many other aspects of this company's battle, the relief did not materialize as planned—instead, the reinforcements were diverted to assist another beleaguered detachment that had found itself surrounded and very nearly cut to pieces.

SUPPLY CONVOY SIDETRACKED

Several hours earlier, around noon, a supply column consisting of five LVTs and three flame tanks, was dispatched to bring ammunition, water, and other essentials to Company I of the 3/3. At some point in the tangled network of trails and tracks that webbed around the multiple hamlets, the convoy made a wrong turn. With a tank in the lead, closely followed by an AmTrac, the rumbling formation found itself moving along a narrow trail with a rice paddy to one side and an impenetrable wall of foliage to the other.

With shocking suddenness, a barrage of grenade and recoilless rifle fire erupted against the vehicles. The convoy was attacked from both sides, and many of the vehicles suffered hits and damage. Backing into the hedgerow and thicket, the vehicles brought their weapons to bear across the rice paddy. Savage fire continued to erupt from all sides, and the Marines suffered numerous casualties. It quickly began to appear as if the whole detachment would be overrun. Unfortunately, the radio operator in one of the LVTs who was calling for help kept his microphone *talk* button depressed for a very long time, thwarting any and all attempts by HQ to get an exact fix on the besieged position.

The convoy CO, 1st Lieutenant Robert Cochran, did a remarkable job in organizing the lumbering vehicles into as much of a defensive position as possible, losing his life in the process. Staff Sergeant Jack Morino took over command, and held up the morale of the surrounded unit as the hours of daylight slipped away and it began to be clear that no relief would be forthcoming.

This was not for lack of effort, however. As Colonel Peatross, in the regimental CP (command post) followed the course of the battle, he feared that a major enemy counterattack was developing. This initiative suggested an enemy poised to drive a wedge between the supply convoy and the still-beleaguered Company H 2/4. (Peatross would later speculate that the ambushing VC force had been mustering to attack Company H, but that attack was disrupted by the inadvertent appearance of the supply convoy in the midst of the enemy position.)

Only one tank remained available for the relieving force, so the big M48 would take the lead of a new column that also included several Ontos and flame tanks. The weary neo-veterans of Company I, still under the command of 1st Lieutenant Purnell, had just returned to the regimental CP after their fierce fighting in the An Cuong (2) area. Since they had already fought through the terrain that the relief column would need to traverse, they were ordered back into the fray as the infantry component of the hastily assembled column.

A little after 1300, the file of armored vehicles, with Company I Marines riding atop the tank and Ontos, and inside the huge LVTs, moved out swiftly. Major Andrew Comer, executive officer of the 3/3 Battalion, commanded. Quickly traversing the coastal zone, the column rolled to the top of Hill 30 without notable opposition. As soon as the tank came over the crest, however, it took a hit from a recoilless rifle round and thudded to a stop. A fresh barrage of mortar and machine-gun fire lashed at the formation from both sides, almost immediately inflicting two dozen Marine casualties, including five dead. Airstrikes and artillery barrages in support of the column commenced almost immediately as Major Comer called in the support arms.

The pounding of guns, bombs, and rockets forced the VC to hunker down to a certain extent, but it did not eliminate the threat. Comer sent Company I forward to sweep through An Cuong (2), the hamlet where the company captain had perished just a few hours before. A detachment of riflemen, together with the disabled vehicles, remained behind to protect the wounded until choppers could arrive to evacuate them.

Entering the village again, initially finding only light opposition, the men of Company I encountered the two squads of their comrades who had been detached in the mission to protect the downed Huey. Those Marines were still accompanied by the platoon from H Company that had gotten separated during the withdrawal to LZ Blue. Comer sent the two squads of I Company back to Hill 30, the summit of which they reached after a stiff firefight; there they were evacuated with the wounded when the choppers began to arrive, while the separated platoon of H Company remained with the reinforcement column.

COMMITTING THE RESERVE

Colonel Peatross's reserve was the special landing force (SLF) consisting of the 3rd Battalion of the 7th Marines—the 7th representing the third of the three regiments contributing a company or two to Starlite. They remained aboard ships, including the LPH *Iwo Jima*, but had arrived off the coast during the morning hours. Late in the afternoon Peatross ordered Company L of the 3/7 into the battle. Helicopters carried the Marines directly to the regimental CP, which had been established about a half mile inland from the initial landing beach, at 1730. Company L, under the command of Captain Ronald Clark, immediately moved westward under orders to reinforce Major Comer's column and to continue the search for the still-

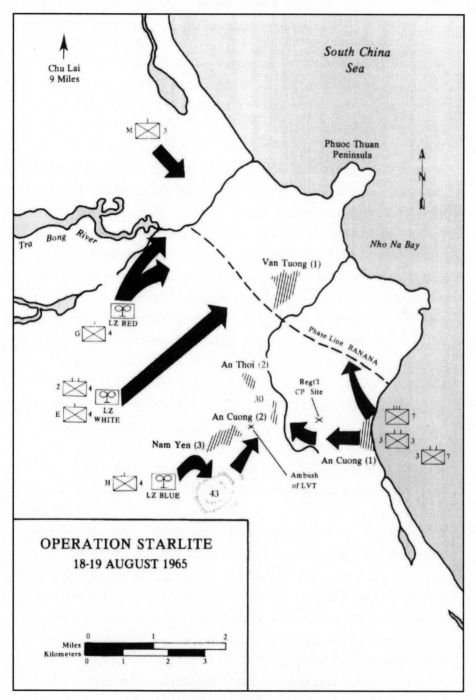

Operation Starlite Battle Map

HISTORY AND MUSEUMS DIVISION, UNITED STATES MARINE CORPS

lost, still-surrounded supply column. The command staff scraped up two tanks to accompany the fresh company.

Once again the open rice paddies around An Cuong (2) proved lethal to the young Marines. Even before it reached the hamlet, while crossing those exposed agricultural flats, Company L felt the impact of enfilading machine-gun and mortar fire. The men took shelter as best as they could, firing back with everything they had. By nightfall, the Viet Cong began to pull back, but in the short, intense firefight the company had suffered 18 serious casualties, four of them fatal.

Still, the presence of the third company in the area where Company H and Company I had battled for so much of the day proved decisive. The VC pulled back everywhere they were engaged, and an uneasy silence settled over the battlefield. In the thicket next to the rice paddy where the battered supply convoy still sheltered, desultory attacks continued through the hours of darkness, but the enemy proved disinclined to make any serious offensive forays.

OVERNIGHT INTERVAL

The long night of 18/19 August was brightened by a steady series of star shells fired from the batteries aboard the *Galveston*. The illumination was comforting to the weary Marines, who settled in to eat cold C rations—including delicacies such as beans and wieners, meatballs and beans, and ham and lima beans—and to catch a few nervous hours of sleep. The day had been particularly difficult for Company I, 3/4, which sustained casualties amounting to 53 wounded and 14 killed—out of the 177 men who had come ashore Green Beach near An Cuong (1). Company H of the 2/4 had also been severely mauled. Fortunately for the survivors, enough fresh reserves were available in the SLF battalion that those two companies would not have to resume the attack on the 19th.

The helicopter squadrons, HMM-361 and HMM-261, had also taken a pounding during the long day of fighting. The former flew from Chu Lai, and while the latter was based at Da Nang, some 50 minutes flight north of

Chu Lai, its aircraft made numerous sorties to the battlefield as well. Only one of the birds was destroyed during the day, but half of HMM-361's UH-34 "Seahorses" were declared unflyable by nightfall. Virtually all of them had taken hits from enemy ground fire. The Marine Corps official history notes that the VC marksmanship was somewhat deficient, in that most of the hits scored on the Marine choppers struck the tail booms, not the crew compartments or engines. Even so, many pilots and crew members were hit, but the machines were manned by replacement volunteers and continued flying. After the introduction of the SLF, the ship-borne helicopters of HMM-163 joined in the fray. More than 500 helicopter sorties would eventually be flown during the course of Operation Starlite.

As the veterans of the first day's battle rested and recovered, the two remaining companies of the SLF battalion arrived ashore. Company I, 3/7, reached the regimental headquarters by 1800 on the evening of the 18th, while Company M crossed the beach in the hours of darkness around midnight. By morning, these two fresh units were ready to join in the resumed offensive.

Two companies of the 3/7 were tasked with sweeping through the area of An Cuong (2) and relieving the supply convoy. The battered column had lost five of 23 men during the savage fighting of the previous afternoon, and only nine of the survivors remained fit for action when they were relieved. Still, they had survived a lethal, powerful ambush without being overrun. Some 60 VC bodies were discovered in the area of the convoy fight.

Shortly after rescuing the convoy survivors, the companies of the 3/7 joined the line with the remaining companies of the 3rd and 4th Battalions. Side by side, the Marine companies advanced northeastward, closing on the coast. Company M of the 3/3 remained in place, blocking any enemy withdrawal northward. The Viet Cong seemed to have vanished; at no point did they make a serious effort to stand and resist the American advance. Even so, the enemy remained dangerous; often individual or small groups of VC would appear from tunnels and other concealment after the Marines had passed, opening up on them from behind.

Nevertheless, by nightfall the Marines had swept all the way to the shore,

even clearing the small Phuoc Thuan Peninsula jutting into the South China
Sea. Suspecting that more enemy troops remained hidden, General Walt
decided to keep his Marines in the field for five more days. Over that time
numerous tunnels and fortified positions were destroyed by Marine engineers. Intelligence personnel determined that the hamlet of Van Tuong (1)
had been the HQ of the 1st VC Regiment. Protected by an extensive ring of
fortifications, and thoroughly booby-trapped with punji stick traps, the hamlet also contained communications equipment, supplies, and propaganda
leaflets. It was determined that the regiment consisted of two battalions, the
60th and the 80th. The 60th VC Battalion had been within rifle range of LZ
Blue, and had been virtually destroyed during the battle, while the 80th had
been very badly damaged.

OPERATIONAL ASSESSMENT

Operation Starlite represented a significant success for the United States
Marines. Naturally, a number of lessons were gleaned from the fighting, but
the overall efficacy of helicopter transport combined with amphibious
assault proved key to trapping an enemy force where it could be forced into
battle. The price of victory was high: 45 Marines lost their lives in the battle,
and more than 200 were wounded. In an enemy casualty ratio reminiscent
of the USMC battles against the Japanese during World War II, the Viet
Cong left 614 dead on the battlefield, while nine VC were taken prisoners.

One key to the Marine success was the flexibility allowed by the SLF
battalion available offshore as a reinforcement. Colonel Peatross was able
to bring the companies of the 3/7 into the battle quickly, deploying them
exactly where and when they were needed. The first company was delivered to the shore by helicopter transport, and the other two came over the
beach, one of them making a landing around midnight.

American firepower, both from the tubes of traditional artillery batteries and the crushing presence of airpower, proved its worth in this battle, and it would remain a key US advantage in virtually every subsequent
battle of the war. Advanced control of both elements, with spotters located

among the frontline troops and maintaining reliable, high-quality radio contact with their weapons to the rear, and in the air, allowed for an unprecedented level of accuracy. Additional spotters, both for artillery and airstrikes, observed the battlefield from helicopters, and could respond instantly to changes in the front lines below. The use of colored smoke, both to mark targets and to show the disposition of friendly forces, continually aided the delivery of explosive ordnance on target.

As a subset of this firepower advantage, American aircraft had advanced two weapons systems that had been tried in previous wars. Many of the helicopter gunships supporting the Marines (and, later, the Army) were equipped with rocket launchers, and could slam highly explosive rounds onto very precise targets. Also, the use of napalm—essentially jellied gasoline canisters that exploded into lethal, ground-cloaking infernos—proved to be a hellish, deadly weapon that would become greatly feared by the enemy.

The Vietnam War would be essentially an infantry war, but the presence of Marine Corps tanks at key locations proved decisive in Starlite. Armor would be used sparingly in this country with a very limited road net and highly rugged terrain off the beaten paths, but where it could be employed it would add another significant advantage to the American arsenal. Tanks and armored personnel carriers (APCs) would save a lot of lives, but they were not invulnerable. The Viet Cong and their regular-army allies in the North Vietnamese Army were well equipped with recoilless rifles, some up to a 75-mm bore, as well as handheld rocket launchers, and both of those weapons were capable of doing serious damage even to a main battle tank.

The inherent risks of airmobile tactics were revealed in the surprising proximity of the 60th VC Battalion to Landing Zone Blue. However, and despite the fact that helicopters make a lot of noise while they are approaching an LZ, the speedy insertion of airmobile troops generally gave an advantage of surprise to the attacker, since the soldiers could be dropped very suddenly into a position that the enemy, even when close, was not prepared to assault. Helicopters remained vulnerable to ground fire, and the Americans would lose a lot of them in this war, but the new generation of UH1 "Huey" choppers would prove to be exceptionally reliable and durable machines. Indeed, if there is an iconic image that remains in our memories of the Vietnam War, it is the picture of the redoubtable Huey helicopter.

The successful completion of the battle garnered a lot of positive publicity back in the United States. It was a clear-cut victory, and had been a large-unit action that involved spectacular uses of new technology and tactics. America's South Vietnamese allies, however, displayed some signs of ruffled feathers since, with the exception of two generals, none of the ARVN forces had been informed of the plan for Starlite. This secrecy had helped to achieve the surprise necessary for the operation's success, but in the future, international cooperation would require that more communication and shared planning take place between the two countries. Of course, all too often this communication would result in security failures and intelligence leaks, but it was a price that was necessary in coalition warfare.

The final lesson would be learned by the end of the year, a grim harbinger of the resiliency of this enemy, and an experience that would be repeated again and again throughout the war: despite the fact that it was surrounded and virtually annihilated during Operation Starlite, the 1st Viet Cong Regiment would be back.

TWO

AIR MOBILITY COMES OF AGE

THE IA DRANG CAMPAIGN AND
THE 1ST CAVALRY DIVISION (AIRMOBILE)

The Ia Drang campaign was to the Vietnam War what the
terrible Spanish Civil War of the 1930s was to World War
II: a dress rehearsal.

> LIEUTENANT GENERAL HAROLD MOORE (RET.),
> FROM THE PROLOGUE TO *WE WERE*
> *SOLDIERS ONCE . . . AND YOUNG* (1992)

Even as the Marines prepared to move out against the Viet Cong irregulars in the I Corps area, the United States' top military commanders were acknowledging that the mission to check Communist aggression in Southeast Asia would require a significant number of regular US Army units. Although untested in battle to this point, perhaps the most celebrated of those units was the division that had trained at Fort Benning, Georgia, in the use of helicopter operations.

Previously, rotary-wing aircraft had proven their use on the battlefield, at first as flying ambulances capable of moving casualties directly to the field hospitals and aid stations, then as stable platforms allowing aerial observation of the battle, and most recently as airborne attack elements, capable of firing machine guns and rockets directly into enemy positions. But helicopters were generally thought to be too slow and vulnerable to ground fire to be used practically on an active battlefield.

At least, that was the conventional wisdom, but it was not an opinion held universally. Early in 1963, at the behest of President Kennedy's secretary of defense, former Ford Motor Company president Robert S. McNamara, the United States Army had commissioned a new test formation. Although it was really only the size of a brigade, it had been dubbed the 11th Air Assault Division, and it had been placed in the hands of several young, maverick Army officers who believed in the concept of air mobility. Major General Harry W. O. Kinnard—the most senior of those mavericks, and a sincere believer in the concept—was placed in command of the test formation, and given leave to choose his subordinate officers from throughout the ranks of the Army.

Of course, like any new and revolutionary concept, especially in an organization as tradition bound as the United States Army, air mobility was not without its detractors. Most of the senior brass were dead set against the idea. They had a number of logical reasons for this resistance, even above and beyond the very real fear that helicopters lacked sufficient armor and durability to survive on a modern battlefield.

In addition to institutional conservatism and genuine concern about survivability, other reasons existed to explain the regular-army resistance to a new doctrine of air mobility. One of these echoed the objections raised during World War II when the Army introduced the then-revolutionary idea of airborne, namely paratroop, formations: the new units smacked of elitism, and threatened to draw resources and exceptional soldiers from the ranks of the Army as a whole, thus diluting it. There was some justification for this: as it happened, the airmobile division would prove to be tremendously expensive, and quite naturally would consume a great deal of the Army's helicopter resources.

A final reason went back to the age-old specter of interservice rivalry, most recently seen in the Key West Agreement of 1947, which attempted to clearly delineate the division of responsibilities between the good old United States Army and the very newfangled United States Air Force. Under that agreement, the Army was allowed to employ its own air units for reconnaissance and medical purposes, while all combat missions would fall under the purview of the Air Force. Most of the Army brass thought, not unreasonably, that the USAF would focus on strategic bombing and air superiority missions, giving short shrift to the transport and combat support of units engaged in ground combat.

However, with the full and enthusiastic support of a secretary of defense fully invested in the idea of air mobility, and fully committed to the use of combat helicopters by the United States Army, there was little to nothing that the forces of resistance in either branch of the service could do to stand in McNamara's way. Hence, the "airmobile division" trained and developed doctrine at Fort Benning, and prepared to go to war. And the new Bell Iroquois UH-1, forever to be known as the Huey, would be the harbinger of a new generation of exceptionally capable, robust, and reliable helicopters.

The test division's preparations included extensive planning in the areas of supply and logistics. Everyone acknowledged that the airmobile division would need a lot of helicopters, and that it would need an extensive support system to keep those aircraft maintained, repaired, and flyable. This would become a matter of ongoing tension throughout the war, a tension that the superior officers of the 11th Air Assault Division addressed by what they called the A-B-C maintenance concept. This concept decreed that the A level of maintenance would be handled integrally, at the battalion level, and would manage every aspect of support needed to return a helicopter to action within a four-hour window. The B level of maintenance was to be handled at the division level, and would address more serious issues that could nevertheless return an aircraft to service in a matter of a day or two. Only at the C level would the machine be removed from operations and transported to a depot for significant repair.

By the late summer of 1965, two airborne units—the Army's 173rd Airborne Brigade and the 1st Brigade, 101st Airborne Division—were already in Vietnam. However, both of these units relied on helicopters only for transport. The men would be carried to a landing zone somewhere near the area of operations where they would debark and march like standard infantry as they conducted operations. General Kinnard and his subordinate unit commanders, including Lieutenant Colonel Harold Moore, who had been one of Kinnard's original battalion commanders, had a much more aggressive plan for the use of helicopters in battle. By fall of 1965, they would get the chance to put those plans into action.

THE CENTRAL HIGHLANDS

The United States Marine Corps had responsibility for conducting the war in the northernmost area of South Vietnam, I Corps. As it encompassed the strategically important area around Saigon and the center of the country's government, III Corps was also a significant tactical zone, and would get a lot of attention from the Army's more traditional divisions and brigades. However, both General Westmoreland and the ARVN high command recognized the crucial significance of the II Corps area in between. The strategic heart of the II Corps area was known as the Central Highlands, and consisted of a rolling, heavily forested plateau that covered most of the ground between the Cambodian border and the coast.

At the west end of the Central Highlands rose the Chu Pong Massif, a sprawling mountainous region consisting of steep valleys, with some peaks towering more than two thousand feet above the plateau, and a rugged, roadless landscape that offered plenty of concealment to the Viet Cong, and to any infiltrating force of PAVN soldiers moving down the Ho Chi Minh Trail through Laos and Cambodia. By the summer of 1965, just such a force had arrived and begun to form a base in this most remote tangle of terrain.

In fact, a year earlier Hanoi had ordered a significant formation, the B3 Front, into the Highlands. Originally that force consisted of the 325th Division; when that division was broken up and dispatched to other parts of South Vietnam, the front commander, Major General Chu Huy Mân remained in the highlands, assembling a new force from units that continued to arrive between the end of 1964 and the summer of 1965. He had a number of potential targets for offensive, but his most ambitious objective was nothing short of a strike for the coast from his base in the Chu Pong Massif. If successful, his attack would cut South Vietnam in half, and seriously compromise the defense of the rest of the country.

Well aware of the danger, General Vinh Loc—commander of the entire II Corps area—had a number of units available to resist, including multiple battalions of South Vietnamese rangers, airborne troops, and marines, in addition to three regular-army regiments. More than a dozen Special Forces camps, often occupied by tribal garrisons under the tactical command of American Green Berets, dotted the rugged countryside. However, only one east-west road, Route 19, traversed the region. The provincial capital, Pleiku city, lay along this road and would form a key barrier to any attempt to move from the mountains to the coastline.

1ST CAVALRY DEPLOYS

By the end of June, the 11th Air Assault Division (Test) was deemed ready for battle, as a final series of training missions planned for the semitropical wilderness of Florida was canceled in order to mobilize the unit for combat. On July 1, the formation was designated the 1st Cavalry Division (Airmobile). The previous 1st Cavalry Division, in Korea, was now designated the 2nd Infantry Division; most of the 2nd Infantry personnel, who had been training at Fort Benning, were immediately absorbed into the airmobile force.

The soldiers of the 1st Cavalry Division (Airmobile) learned of their deployment to Vietnam from the television news, when President Johnson made an announcement during a July press conference. But even before that late-July declaration, it was obvious that something big was up at Fort Benning. Soldiers were coming in from all parts of the globe, including just about every helicopter pilot on the Army's roster. The new arrivals were processed through in a whirlwind, assigned to companies, quickly filling out the divisional organization. At the last minute, more than a hundred of the unit's members were recalled from a riot control mission in the Dominican Republic.

However, one political decision that would resonate throughout the Vietnam War began to make itself felt. The president and the secretary of defense had decided to conduct the conflict with an army of draftees, and would not call up the reserves, nor would they authorize extended terms of enlistment for the soldiers who had trained with the test division but were scheduled to return to civilian life in the near future. Consequently, when the division did deploy to Vietnam, it had to leave a number of crucial, well-trained members behind. Still, the division elements made their way to California, and were crammed aboard a small fleet of ancient transports, some of which had been modified with small flight decks so they could carry helicopters.

Last-minute adjustments were still being made on the Stateside docks when the first thousand men of the 1st Cavalry Division arrived in Vietnam. The group was heavily weighted toward officers and senior NCOs, but that didn't excuse them from pick and shovel duty as they scrambled to prepare a base large enough to be defended, and to hold nearly 500 helicopters. The site had been selected by assistant division commander Brigadier General John M. Wright. With an eye toward the Central Highlands, he had chosen a location along Highway 19, near a key pass. The closest town was An Khê, located about halfway between the provincial capital, Pleiku, and the coast.

For three weeks the advance party struggled to remove brush and trees, resulting in a broad clearing that became known as the "golf course." Most of the division arrived on September 21, and—finally assisted by a detachment of engineers—began to build the structures necessary to house, feed, and service a full division of airmobile troops. The camp was named in honor of US Army Major Don Radcliff, who had lost his life while piloting a helicopter gunship in support of the Marines battling at LZ Blue during Operation Starlite. Camp Radcliff quickly took shape, and the division was soon operational.

The "Air Cavalry" began its tour immediately, by conducting patrols on, and over, Highway 19. Initial operations in the area of An Khê included sweeps to drive the VC forces from the area, and to offer an umbrella of protection to the local citizens, who had, at first, fled from the clattering presence of the American helicopters. In a matter of weeks, the civilians had begun to return to their hamlets and farms.

ATTACK ON PLEI ME

The 1st Cavalry Division's command and intelligence staffs expected that their main opposition would come from the Viet Cong; they did not yet suspect the presence of General Mân's B3 Front, which had now reached the strength of a full division, including the 32nd, 33rd, and, by early November, the 66th PAVN Regiments. He also had the support of significant numbers of VC irregulars. The objective of General Mân's initial offensive was to be nothing less than Pleiku city, but he would pave the way for that attack by repeating a tactic that had proved remarkably effective in a number of battles over the previous year: he would surround and attack a Special Forces camp, and then ambush the ARVN convoy that would inevitably be dispatched to relieve the besieged outpost. Given the limited road network of the rural countryside, it was generally quite easy to predict the route that a relief force would take.

And this time, the initial attack would be made by two regiments of highly trained, well-equipped, and strongly motivated PAVN regulars. General Mân's target would be the Special Forces camp at Plei Me, which lay some 30 miles southwest of the provincial capital, and was connected to that base only by a rugged, narrow road, Route 6C. The camp itself was held by a garrison of 12 American Green Berets, 14 ARVN Special Forces soldiers, and a little more than 400 Humong tribesmen. About a quarter of this force was absent, conducting an operation eight or 10 miles to the northwest. Another 80 of the Humong were stationed outside of the camp, either as garrisons for a pair of listening posts or on station to conduct ambushes of enemy forces moving along the jungle trails.

The Humong, it should be noted, were an ethnic minority in the country, dwelling in isolated villages, and were viewed with at least an element of racist scorn by North and South Vietnamese alike. They were proud, warlike, and independent, however, and in the years from 1962 to 1965 they had established a close working relationship with many of the— equally proud and warlike—Green Berets who had been recruiting, arming, and training them. They were used to living in conditions most Vietnamese and Americans considered primitive, but they remained fiercely loyal, and coincidentally occupied some very strategic regions along the Vietnamese borders with Cambodia and Laos.

The attack commenced on 19 October at about 1900, which was just after sunset. The 33rd Regiment of the North Vietnamese Army opened the assault with an attack on one of the Humong detachments. Three hours later the NVA regulars hit the outpost to the southwest of the camp and at the same time commenced a barrage of the installation with mortars and recoilless rifles. By midnight the attack had expanded to include an onslaught against the northern perimeter of the camp. Within an hour, the NVA soldiers had penetrated the initial and secondary wire barriers surrounding Plei Me's perimeter.

These attacks involved two of the 33rd's battalions, with the third being held in reserve. Even so, General Mân's men maintained the pressure throughout the night and into the following dawn. By 0400, the first of more than a hundred airstrikes on 20 October roared onto the scene in support of the defenders, while the ARVN commander on the scene called for a reinforcement convoy. Before midnight on the 20th, General Vinh Loc—II Corps commander—had authorized a relief expedition to assemble in Pleiku.

That ARVN reinforcement was substantial, and included armored cavalry, a ranger battalion, and more. Still, it would take some time before the overland forces could be assembled and dispatched; as a result, the 5th Special Forces commander who had responsibility for the camp, Colonel William McKean, decided to send in an airborne contingent. His initial idea of a parachute drop into the camp was rejected as too dangerous, so he settled on dispatching 175 men—mostly ARVN rangers with a few US Special Forces troops, all under the command of Major Charles Beckwith—by helicopter. The initial relief force landed about five kilometers northeast of the besieged camp on the morning of 21 October. While the sporadic attacks continued on Plei Me, Beckwith's men made their way to the position, spending a night within earshot of the raging firefight. At dawn, he ordered his men to "run like hell" and they sprinted into the camp, with Beckwith, as senior officer, now taking command of the position.

General Vinh Loc knew that his overland relief column was likely to encounter an ambush, but he was reluctant to reinforce it further because he didn't want to denude the defense of Pleiku city, in the event the attack on the camp proved to be a ruse to trick him into doing just that. Fortunately, the 1st Cavalry Division (Airmobile), not too far to the east at An

Khê, was available to help protect the provincial capital. The Americans arriving at Pleiku allowed Vinh Loc to increase his reinforcement expedition to some 1,400 men.

General Kinnard was only too willing to dispatch his men toward the fighting, and began by sending his 2nd Battalion, 12th Cavalry—along with an artillery battery—to Pleiku. Some of the big 155-mm guns from that battery were transported by giant CH-54 "Flying Crane" helicopters to establish a forward fire support base (FSB) within range to support the relief convoy if and when it came under attack.

Indeed, General Mân had his entire 32nd Regiment in position to hit the reinforcement column as it made its way up Route 6C toward the camp. At about 1800 on 23 October, the front of the column, which consisted of M41 tanks and armored personnel carriers (APCs) was hammered by mortar and recoilless rifle fire. The armored vehicles swung off the road to both sides and returned fire with vigor. Close air-support bombing, strafing, and napalm attacks delivered by screaming F-100s forced the attackers into retreat.

The second part of the convoy suffered heavy losses as soft-skinned trucks carrying ammunition took lethal hits and exploded in blossoms of flame. With the aid of aggressive air support, these ARVN troops formed a tight perimeter and held on through the night. The 32nd North Vietnamese Army Regiment had suffered such heavy casualties during the evening and night of combat that it was forced to withdraw. Even so, the South Vietnamese convoy commander refused to proceed until more American artillery was positioned to support him. The relief convoy finally reached the Plei Me camp in the early afternoon of 25 October.

Plei Me had undergone steady, uninterrupted attacks for nearly six days by then. Supported by American artillery from the 1st Cavalry, and numerous bombing sorties by both Air Force and Navy aircraft, Beckwith's men had not just hung on, but had inflicted a great deal of punishment on the 33rd Regiment, battering all three of the unit's battalions and killing two of the battalion commanders. By evening on the 25th, General Mân was ready to order a withdrawal, pulling back about eight kilometers to the west, where the newly arrived 66th Regiment could replenish his two battle-scarred formations.

AIR CAV GOES TO WAR

Now that he occupied an advanced position in the Pleiku area, General Kinnard was reluctant to pull his airmobile division back to the coastal lowlands east of An Khê. He had chafed through a series of frustrating, exhausting sweeps that had failed to turn up any significant enemy forces in the Binh Dinh province, and with the relief of the Plei Me camp—and the evidence that the NVA was present in force in the Central Highlands, he strongly advocated that his division be "turned loose" to conduct aggressive, offensive operations. On 28 October, General Westmoreland relented, giving the division commander almost full independence to determine how and where the 1st Cavalry would be employed.

The reconnaissance element of the airmobile division was the 9th Cavalry, and soon helicopters from that squadron swept across the landscape around Plei Me. Unsure of the location of the main enemy base, they at first focused on areas north and northwest of the battlefield, and for several days encountered little to no signs of an enemy presence. By 1 November, General Mân had concentrated his three regiments on the eastern edge of the Chu Pong Massif, just as the air cavalry began to shift the focus of the aerial search patterns.

On the morning of the first day of November, elements of the 1st of the 9th Cavalry under the command of Major Robert Zion flew over the southernmost boundary of the 1st Cavalry Division's search zone. The scouts spotted a small group of enemy soldiers about 10 kilometers southwest of Plei Me, and Major Zion called in his Troop B rifle platoon to engage the enemy on the ground. After some light skirmishing and the capture of five prisoners, the platoon ran into a much larger NVA force that seemed determined to make a stand along a shallow streambed. Aggressively pressing the advance, the riflemen killed more than a dozen enemy soldiers and captured 15, in the process overrunning the field hospital of the 33rd Regiment and capturing medical supplies and a few documents. Many high-ranking officers, including General Vinh Loc, choppered in to inspect the battlefield, while the squadron helicopters spent the middle of the day evacuating the captured matériel and prisoners back to Pleiku.

The scout helicopters continued the search, however, and at 1410 discovered a significant enemy force moving toward the medical station from the northeast. First Battalion commander Colonel John Stockton quickly brought his rifle platoons from Troops A and C into the position, while aerial rocket and machine-gun fire from helicopter gunships delayed the enemy's advance. Troop B was hard-pressed until the reinforcements arrived, but the fresh rifle platoons and renewed fire from the gunships thwarted an enemy flanking attack and allowed the three platoons to hold the position.

Shortly thereafter Colonel Stockton received another three platoons from the brigade reserve, and he was able to go over to the attack. Threatening both flanks of the NVA force, he pushed the enemy into a precipitous withdrawal. By the next morning they had completely vanished from the area. The series of firefights on 1 November had been costly, with 11 cavalrymen slain and nearly 50 wounded; the 33rd Regiment, in turn, had suffered between 250 and 300 KIA, and lost not only the field hospital but a stash of documents that revealed NVA order-of-battle and route march information.

It was a start, but General Kinnard was seeking much bigger fish to fry.

PUSH TO THE BORDERLANDS

The discovery of the NVA medical outpost, as well as the presence of enemy soldiers farther west than had been expected, led the air cavalry to extend its presence toward the massif and the Cambodian border. Creating Landing Zone Mary just to the north of the Chu Pong Massif, Major Zion again sent the rifle platoons from Troops A, B, and C into action. Supported by the reconnaissance squadron, the riflemen dispersed from the LZ and set up ambushes along several of the trails they suspected would be used by moving enemy soldiers.

Though the air cav riflemen expected to encounter enemy columns withdrawing from the Plei Me area—that is, moving west—the first NVA soldiers to walk into an ambush were actually marching east, probably because they were newly arrived in country and looked to link up with one of the regiments. Obviously assuming they were on a safe trail, they talked

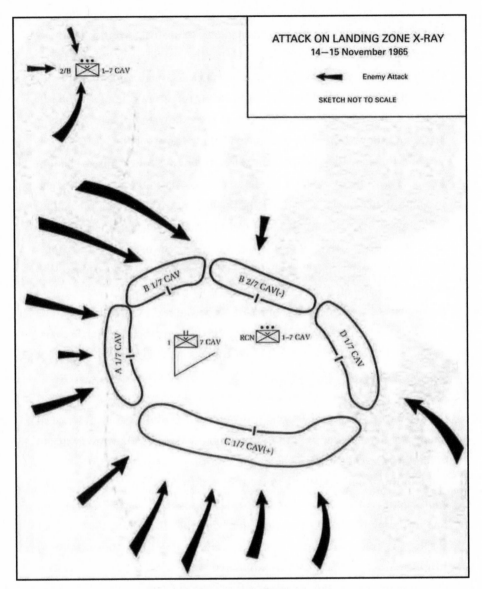

ATTACK ON LANDING ZONE X-RAY
14—15 November 1965

Enemy Attack

SKETCH NOT TO SCALE

2/B · · · 1–7 CAV

B 1/7 CAV

B 2/7 CAV(-)

A 1/7 CAV

1 · · 7 CAV

RCN · · · 1–7 CAV

D 1/7 CAV

C 1/7 CAV(+)

Battle at LZ X-Ray
CENTER OF MILITARY HISTORY, UNITED STATES ARMY

and joked as they walked, stopping to eat within earshot of the hidden Americans. They resumed the march, and the troopers allowed nearly a hundred of them to pass through the ambush. At that point, the troop commander, Captain Charles Knowlen, ordered the attack. Claymore mines, set along a football-field length of the trail, shredded the air and enemy soldiers with shrapnel while M16s set on full automatic further raked the NVA ranks. A large but unknown number of the enemy went down, but since Knowlen's men were still outnumbered by the survivors, he ordered his troop back to LZ Mary. Major Zion ordered the rest of his cavalrymen to rally there as well—and just in time, as a force numbering several companies of NVA infantry quickly pressed home an attack.

After a little more than an hour of battle, Zion faced the fact that his men were about to lose the position; at 2315 he made an emergency request for reinforcements. Though Colonel Stockton, at battalion HQ, didn't have the authority to commit new troops to the battle, he acted on his own responsibility to dispatch a company of the brigade reserve. The new men began to arrive shortly after midnight, and with the help of lethal fire from gunships, the cavalrymen fought off the attack throughout a furious night of battle. By dawn, the enemy had withdrawn. American losses were four killed and 25 wounded; enemy dead on the ground were counted at about 80 or 90. The NVA unit was determined to be the 8th Battalion of the 66th Regiment, confirming that a third regiment was in the area and bringing total enemy strength to the equivalent of a full division.

Another bloody day of fighting would follow on 6 November, when two companies of the 2nd Battalion, 8th Cavalry, fought a large force from the PAVN 33rd Regiment. This time the enemy force did not withdraw, but attempted to draw the Americans into a killing zone. The furious firefight left 26 cavalrymen killed and twice that many wounded, though as usual the enemy suffered even greater losses. Still, Colonel Clark's brigade had been through several lethal firefights, and was in serious need of rest and replenishments. Over the next few days, General Kinnard would replace Clark's unit with a fresh brigade-sized task force, composed of Colonel Harold Moore's 1st Battalion, 7th Cavalry; Lieutenant Colonel Robert McDade's

2nd of the 7th; Lieutenant Colonel Robert Tully's 2nd of the 5th Cavalry; and the 1st Battalion, 21st Artillery.

The airmobile division was just getting warmed up.

INTO THE IA DRANG VALLEY

On 9 November, the operational arm of the 1st Cavalry Division (Airmobile) became the 3rd Brigade, under the command of Colonel Thomas Brown. Following the encounters earlier in the month, General Kinnard, Colonel Brown, and the brigade's battalion commanders understood that they were facing a strong force of NVA regulars, and that the enemy base of operations lay to the west of Plei Me—right in the area at the base of the Chu Pong Massif. Brown decided to focus his initial searches in the rugged notch of the Ia Drang Valley, which ran along the north and northeast edge of the massif.

The brigade's operations section designated three search areas west of Plei Me, with the westernmost of these, LIME, occupying space on the foot of the Chu Pong Massif itself. Colonel Moore's 1st of the 7th Cavalry was ordered to take the first crack at finding the enemy concentrations. Moore, as well as every other soldier in the division, was well aware of the 7th Cavalry's infamous past—it was the regiment that, as horse cavalry in 1876, made the ill-fated attack against an overwhelming force of Sioux and Cheyenne warriors, resulting in the massacre of several hundred of the regiment's troops and its commander, General George Armstrong Custer. The parallel to this, another bold and mobile onslaught into a 20th-century version of "Indian Country" was too stark to ignore.

But Moore never hesitated, and never doubted that his well-trained, highly motivated troopers—and their aerial-support elements—were up to the task. The date for the first action was set for 14 November. After initial aerial patrols over the LIME search area suggested three possible landing spots, he personally conducted an overflight, following a circuitous route to keep his interest in certain locations secure from enemy discovery. He soon selected Landing Zone X-Ray as the only option that was large enough to allow eight or 10 helicopters to land at once. The LZ was a natural clearing surrounded by low trees, and lay within a rifle shot of the steep incline leading up several of the massif's fingerlike ridges.

Moore would have only 16 helicopters available to transport his battalion, and these UH-1D Hueys, though among the best and most reliable rotary-wing aircraft in the world, would each be able to carry only five troopers with their combat kits on this mission. The usual capacity of the Hueys on a combat deployment was eight men, but the thin air in the Central Highlands elevations decreased the machine's performance capabilities. Moore himself would land in the first chopper, and he ordered his command helicopter to station itself above the LZ, where the battalion operations and fire control officers could keep an eye on the action below, and order in accurate supporting fire at the very moment it was needed. The day before the initial landing, the 1st Battalion, 21st Artillery, set up a firing position at LZ Falcon, about 10 miles east of X-Ray, and close enough to provide accurate fire support.

Although Colonel Moore expected to encounter the enemy sooner rather than later, he did not know that three full battalions of PAVN regulars had gathered on the lower slopes of the massif, just above LZ X-Ray. This regimental-sized force numbered some 1,600 men, and was in excellent position to counterattack Moore's battalion of a little over 400 men. Air mobility was about to get its first true combat test.

BATTLE AT LANDING ZONE X-RAY

As the 16 helicopters carrying Moore's HQ and a portion of Captain John Herren's Company B took off from the Plei Me Camp on 14 November and flew toward Landing Zone X-Ray, the artillery at LZ Falcon commenced a 20-minute barrage, pulverizing X-Ray and its surrounding terrain. The sky was blue and the wind light, showing no signs of the northeast monsoon that was steadily pouring rain on the coast. One minute before the first Hueys arrived, multiple helicopter gunships raked the area surrounding the LZ with rocket and machine-gun fire. The 16 choppers met no resistance as they brought in the first group at 1048, with eight dropping just long enough to disgorge their troopers, then lifting off so that the second group of eight could land. In just a few minutes all 16 UH-1s were flying back to the marshaling base at Plei Me to collect the rest of Company B and the initial elements of Captain Ramon Nadal's A Company.

Moore and his men understood the precariousness of their position only too well: they were 80 men who would be all alone for at least the next 30 minutes, with no clear idea of what lay beyond the clearing where they had set down. Captain Herren wasted no time in sending out four small patrols to reconnoiter the immediate area, while holding the rest of his men near the battalion HQ, ready to defend the LZ or to serve as a fast-responding strike force.

The second lift of troopers, arriving at about 1130, and the third at 1210, brought the total force at the LZ up to 240 men, and Moore felt comfortable ordering Herren to take his company on a more aggressive, farther-ranging patrol. By the time the fourth lift of Hueys arrived, a little after 1330, no signs of resistance had been encountered, and the battalion had all of Companies A and B, and a good part of C, on the ground.

But Company B, starting up one of the massif's ridges that stretched so close to the LZ, had already run into trouble, and the period of easy, safe transport was about to come to a violent end. Herren's company advanced upward with his 1st Platoon on the left, 2nd on the right, and 3rd trailing as the company reserve. Both of the advance platoons soon ran into enemy sniper fire. Soon intense volleys from automatic weapons pinned down the 1st Platoon, and Herren ordered 2nd Lieutenant Henry Herrick, the 2nd Platoon leader, to come to the 1st's assistance. While beginning this maneuver, Herrick and his men observed enemy soldiers retreating along a well-used trail. The troopers pursued too aggressively, and within minutes additional sprays of bullets coming from hidden NVA soldiers in several directions halted the progress of the 2nd Platoon. Before they knew what was happening, the unit was completely cut off from the rest of Company B and LZ X-Ray.

Informed of Company B's predicament, Moore immediately perceived that his battalion faced a real danger of annihilation. With Herren's men completely occupied in trying to relieve their surrounded platoon, the colonel ordered Company A to move forward to support B Company's left flank. One platoon moved into position just in time to hammer an NVA force that was trying to outflank Herren's men. Still, the enemy rallied, using a dry creek bed that ran between the LZ and the beginning of the massif's upward slope to get between the two companies.

Though only about 75 yards from his beleaguered platoon, Herren was forced to pull the rest of his company back in order to maintain integrity with the battalion. They cleared the enemy out of the dry creek bed and used it as a makeshift trench to anchor the line. As the attackers were spreading out from the northwest around to the west and the southwest, and clearly growing in strength, Moore finally had his companies deployed with B on the right, A in the middle, and C filling in and extending the line on the left; the overall position was a semicircle, still open to the east and northeast, two directions where, as yet, the enemy had not yet attacked. Furthermore, the colonel had no reserves, and the entire LZ was now being raked by enemy small-arms fire and an occasional rocket-propelled grenade (RPG).

The next wave of choppers came in at 1442, and was met by a fusillade of fire from NVA troops near the landing zone and on the heights just to the west. The first eight Hueys brought in the rest of Company C, but the other eight had to abort their landings in the face of the lethal fire. No sooner had those newly arrived troopers joined up with their company than a wave of NVA attackers hit the battalion's position from the south. Now the howitzers set up at LZ Falcon really began to prove their worth as they poured in accurate barrages, often just a few yards in front of the company's position, to help shatter the impetus of the latest attack.

In the confusion of the raging firefight, the eight Hueys that had failed to land in the previous lift returned and deposited some of Captain Louis Lefebvre's D Company. Under fire even as they left the choppers, the men scattered into the nearest cover they could find—which happened to be a slight depression in the ground occupying a crucial gap between A and C Companies. Almost immediately an enemy force tried to push through there, only to be stopped by the new arrivals. Several men were wounded, including Captain Lefebvre, but they slammed closed a gap that otherwise might have proven to be a fatal flaw in Moore's desperate quasi-perimeter. Since the left flank of Company C remained essentially hanging in the air, the colonel subsequently ordered Company D, now under the command of Staff Sergeant Carl Palmer, to secure that flank and curl around to refuse attack from the north. The X-Ray perimeter was now defended around about 75 percent of a full circle, with only the northern sector—which as yet remained free of enemy activity—unmanned.

However, Herrick's platoon of B Company remained surrounded and isolated from the rest of the squadron. The lieutenant and his second-in-command had died in the early, desperate defense of the encircled detachment, which held a small perimeter barely 25 yards in diameter. The new platoon leader was Staff Sergeant Clyde Savage, and he did not hesitate to call in artillery barrages that landed harrowingly close to his own position. This fire support from the batteries at LZ Falcon, as well as from helicopter gunships, provided just enough punishment on aspiring attackers to allow the surrounded troopers to hold their line while collecting their casualties in the middle of the circle.

Colonel Moore's next decision was to send a force up the slope to try to retrieve the beleaguered platoon. He sent Company A and the other two platoons of Company B directly out of the battalion perimeter in a straightforward rush toward 2/B's position. Following a very close barrage, the relief force broke from the dry creek bed and began to work its way forward. Before they had gone a hundred yards, the concentrated fire of more than 100 NVA soldiers, well dug in and determined to hold, assailed the rescue party in a hailstorm of shooting. The Americans pressed hard, creeping from bits of cover to whatever other scant protection they could find, but further advance seemed impossible. As the artillery barrage continued upward, beyond the entrenched enemy, several North Vietnamese rushed forward, savagely attacking in hand-to-hand combat.

Leading the 2nd Platoon of A Company, 2nd Lieutenant Walter Marm found his men out in front of the relief expedition, but pinned down by several well-placed NVA machine guns. Marm exposed himself but destroyed one defensive strongpoint with a well-placed burst from his

M72 light antitank weapon (LAW). The young lieutenant then charged a second machine-gun nest, wiping it out with a hand grenade—and suffering a bad wound to the face in the process.

With the relief force pinned down and unable to advance any farther, Moore reluctantly ordered the men back to the perimeter. They retreated in good order, bringing their casualties with them. The wounded, including 2nd Lieutenant Marm, would quickly be evacuated by helicopter, while the artillery barrage that was protecting the isolated platoon continued unabated as midafternoon moved toward evening.

Although he no longer faced the threat of immediate annihilation, Colonel Moore knew that he needed more men, both to close his perimeter—still undefended to the north—and to stiffen his existing positions, all of which had been decimated by heavy casualties. Colonel Brown, 3rd Brigade commander, agreed to send a company from the 2nd Battalion immediately. Fully cognizant of Moore's perilous position, he also began to make plans to gather additional forces that he could quickly shuttle into X-Ray, should they be needed. With only the 16 Hueys of the original lift capacity available, however, Brown couldn't have sent in more than a company that evening in any event.

Considering overland reinforcement the next best option, Colonel Brown ordered forces to assemble at two nearby landing zones. The 2nd Battalion, 5th Cavalry, was to gather at LZ Victor, less than two miles southeast of X-Ray, while most of the 2nd Battalion, 7th Cavalry, would assemble at LZ Macon, less than three miles north of Moore's battlefield. One company, D, from the 2nd of the 5th would be helicoptered directly to Moore as soon as they could have the cover of darkness.

Water and ammunition in the 7th Cavalry perimeter had begun to run low. There was no water supply available within, or near, Moore's perimeter, and his men were already suffering from thirst. Some even aggravated their dehydration by drinking the salty liquid from their C-ration cans of ham and lima beans. Fortunately, the almost continuous barrage of tube and aerial artillery support prevented the NVA troops from massing for any significant assaults against X-Ray before nightfall.

Indeed, the heavy fire support seemed to sap the energy from the counterattacking enemy soldiers. By 1700, they had withdrawn from the immediate firing zone, and resorted only to sporadic harassing fire against the
air cavalry position. This allowed 120 men of B Company, 2nd of the 7th,
to land safely. These welcome reinforcements, under Captain Myron Diduryk,
were parceled into several weak spots on the existing perimeter, while
most of them went to fully enclose the circle by protecting against attack
from the north.

More Huey sorties brought in the much-needed water, as well as medical supplies, ammunition, and rations. They also carried away the wounded
and KIA, in a series of shuttle flights that lasted much of the night. Overhead, a C-123 flare ship circled throughout the hours of darkness, dropping
a steady stream of illumination so that the landings and takeoffs could continue safely, and without interruption.

The flares also served to illuminate the surrounding forests and clearing. Much of the area was marked by huge anthills or termite mounds,
some of them towering up to eight or ten feet in height, and these added a
dramatic and surreal texture to the tropical locale. The American cavalrymen caught sleep as they could, with at least a third of the men staying alert
at all times. Though almost all of them had experienced intense combat for
the first time in their lives, morale was good—they were proud of the job
they had done, and confident they could see it through to completion.

Many of the men feared a mass night attack, but that did not materialize. Instead, the enemy sent probing patrols, generally fewer than a dozen
men at a time, to try to locate the machine-gun and other heavy weapons
positions in the defensive perimeter. Moore had instructed his men not to
rise to the bait, however, and the probes were driven off with small-arms
fire, occasionally underlined by one or two RPGs. When one probe, against
B Company's portion of the line, showed signs of growing into a major
attack, the Air Force lent a hand: aided by the continuous flare illumination, a group of A-1E Skyraiders pummeled the jungle, deftly avoiding
"friendly" hits against both Moore's perimeter and the small position held
by Sergeant Savage's still-stranded 2nd Platoon, B.

The enemy did make three determined attacks during the night, all of them against the isolated platoon. The surrounded troopers fought back furiously, and were ably assisted by the concentrated fire of a circling gunship, an Air Force AC-47 "Spooky," that poured more than 10,000 rounds into the jungles uphill of Sergeant Savage's precarious position. The sergeant also did not hesitate to call in artillery support from the tubes at LZ Falcon, often bringing the explosive ordnance in to hammer the ground within a short stone's throw of his own position. So effective was this defense that the platoon suffered no further casualties during the night attacks; the battered NVA soldiers surrounding them were so stunned by the explosive bombardment that they didn't even press the attack again once dawn lightened the battlefield.

The rescue of the stranded platoon remained Colonel Moore's top priority as the sun rose on 15 November, and he prepared a new plan, intending to launch the relief effort that he would lead personally shortly after dawn. He planned to launch three almost full-strength companies up the hill, leaving only two to hold the LZ and guard the perimeter. But, as happens often during battle, events developed in such a way that he never got to put this plan into motion.

First, the colonel wanted to make sure that no enemy force had crept close to his position during the night, so he ordered recon patrols out to sweep the area up to about 200 yards from his main line. Shortly before 0700, a patrol on the C Company sector took some small-arms fire, the cavalrymen taking casualties and quickly pulling back to the perimeter. Their return to the line was followed almost immediately by the surprise appearance of several hundred NVA soldiers, disguised by such effective camouflage that they were almost into X-Ray before they were discovered.

A savage firefight along the southern flank of the perimeter quickly merged into furious, hand-to-hand fighting in the C Company foxholes. Captain Edwards, the company CO, feared that his position would be overrun, but Moore remained unconvinced and would not commit the battalion reserve. The captain himself was hurling hand grenades at some of the many enemy soldiers within view when he was wounded by a bullet that left him unable to walk. Moore dispatched the battalion executive officer to take over, but when he was wounded upon arrival at C Company, Captain Edwards had no choice but to continue to exercise command from a seated position.

By this time Moore had given up on the idea of sending an immediate relief force toward Sergeant Savage's platoon, but the colonel was still unwilling to commit his only reserve. He did, however, order a platoon to move from a neighboring company to reinforce Company C's position. It took almost an hour for the 17 men to move a few hundred yards—they lost four casualties in the process—but the survivors took up positions about 15 yards behind Edwards's men. From there, they contributed enough firepower to stabilize the sector.

More attacks continued to develop around the perimeter. By 0745, Captain Diduryk's Company D, 2nd of the 7th, that had arrived the evening before found itself desperately pressed along the north rim of X-Ray. By then some 1,000 NVA regulars were furiously attacking the perimeter from three directions, and had come very near to breaking into the LZ through the juncture of Companies D and C. Small-arms fire slashed throughout the American positions, making many movements dangerous and preventing the landing of any helicopters. Colonel Moore finally committed his reserve to the relief of the D/C connection—where the attack was finally stymied—and called on Colonel Brown for any assistance his brigade commander could provide.

Brown informed Moore that the 2nd Battalion, 5th Cavalry, had been landed at LZ Victor, barely two miles away, and was preparing to move out toward X-Ray by overland trails. Their commander, Colonel Tully, felt confident that his men had not yet been discovered by the enemy. This assumption would prove accurate, and as the three companies of the battalion spread out and marched in battle order through the jungle, they met no enemy resistance on their way to the battlefield.

The timely dispatch of Moore's reserve had, for the moment, stabilized his perimeter, though the North Vietnamese continued to fire into the air cav's position. The colonel took advantage of the stability to order his men to pop smoke grenades around the full ring of the defense. This clearly defined the American perimeter for both the pilots of the air-support elements overhead and the helicopter-mounted artillery spotters. A massive ring of destruction rained from helicopter gunships, strafing aircraft, and the guns at LZ Falcon, taking the wind out of the enemy's sails and significantly slowing down the attack. Shortly after 0800 three Air Force F-100s screamed onto the scene, dumping napalm and high-explosive bombs that exploded within a hundred yards of Moore's front line.

An hour later the situation had calmed enough that a Huey lift could bring in another company of cavalrymen, from the 2nd Battalion, 7th Cavalry, under the command of Captain Joel Sugdinis. His men hastened to the southern edge of the perimeter, the sector most seriously battered in the morning battle. The enemy firing grew more and more desultory as the morning progressed, and the Americans took the opportunity to catch their breath and dig their foxholes a little deeper. Moore judged it still too risky to send some of his small force to the rescue of Sergeant Savage's platoon, but he was relieved to learn that the enemy had ceased to attack the small, surrounded force; the NVA commanders, it seemed, were content to wait on the resolution of the greater battle that still simmered around the landing zone.

It was just a few minutes after noon when Colonel Tully's battalion, which had marched two miles in the shadow of the Chu Pong Massif's foothills without being discovered, marched into the perimeter, significantly expanding the size of Moore's force. Since the colonel of the 1st/7th was the senior officer on the scene, he assumed command of the entire force.

At 1315, a battalion-sized relief force moved out of X-Ray and began to climb toward the stranded platoon. The men advanced under the protection of a moving barrage of artillery and air support, and reached Sergeant Savage and his men about two hours later. The enemy seemed to have withdrawn from the area; the relief force suffered no casualties. They brought back the dead (eight) and the wounded (12) from the previous day. All of the survivors credited their success to the sergeant's steady command presence, and the incredibly close artillery support he had directed through the previous day and night.

The rest of the afternoon and evening passed quietly, at least from an

infantry combat perspective. However, that day marked the first use of
United States Air Force B-52s in a tactical support role: 18 of the massive
Stratofortresses dropped nearly a thousand bombs on the slopes of the
massif above X-Ray. This was the first of the so-called Arc Light raids, and
while the amount of damage it inflicted on the enemy was unknown, the
pyrotechnic pummeling caused by such a massive tonnage of high explosive (HE) bombs was certainly good for American morale.

Colonel Moore took advantage of the lack of enemy pressure, the rescue of Savage's detachment, and the arrival of Tully's battalion to improve
the defenses around X-Ray. He assigned Tully a full third of the defensive
ring, from the southeastern sector to the east and northeast faces, and
pulled two full companies back to his HQ to serve as his reserve. The other
units, all of which had suffered casualties and fatigue through the first two
days of battle, were able to shorten their frontages and dig in to even more
well-defended positions. Flare traps and trip-wire alarms were established
200 or 300 yards outside of the perimeter, providing a good chance to reveal
nocturnal enemy movements. Additional artillery batteries were delivered
to nearby LZs, and the skies over X-Ray swarmed with helicopter gunships
and Air Force fighters and ground-attack aircraft, all ready to pounce on
any target that presented itself.

Those targets appeared starting at about 0400 on 16 November, the
third day of battle at X-Ray. Some of the traps outside the southern perimeter were tripped, igniting flares and revealing the presence of a large
enemy force. Several cavalrymen also heard the shrill whistles used by
NVA officers to organize their units and direct movements and attacks.
Much of the noise originated to the south; but for about 20 minutes nothing seemed to happen.

Suddenly a force of about 300 NVA rushed toward the southern
perimeter of Moore's position, the left flank of an area now held by Captain Diduryk's Company B, 2/7. A barrage of small-arms and machine-
gun fire drove the enemy back momentarily, until another attack surged
against the whole of Company B's front about 10 minutes later. These NVA
were pummeled by a series of lethally accurate artillery barrages that

stopped the attack cold and apparently delivered heavy casualties. Two more attacks on this sector, an hour or two later, also were driven off with relative ease.

A few minutes before 0700, Colonel Moore gave his men free rein to indulge in what he called a "mad minute," a tradition sometimes practiced at Fort Benning by instructors, to teach soldiers the full potency of their automatic firearms. With plenty of ammunition now on hand, the cavalrymen unleashed a searing barrage of small-arms fire into the forests and treetops surrounding LZ X-Ray. No fewer than six enemy snipers who had been concealed in treetop firing positions were killed during this furious burst of fire.

The mad minute had a second effect, bringing on the last serious clash of the battle: a group of NVA soldiers had been carefully approaching the northern rim of the perimeter. Taking advantage of camouflage and every irregularity in the terrain—including the big anthills—they had approached to within about 150 yards without being discovered. The sudden, loud fusillade caused them to launch their attack prematurely, perhaps under the impression that their position had been discovered. Many of them were killed by rifles and machine guns fired by the defending troopers, and more of them perished under the sudden and accurate artillery barrage that chased them from the field.

Gradually, as the morning of 16 November progressed, the Americans got a strong sense that the enemy had departed. By 1000, Colonel Moore had ordered patrols out around the entire perimeter. Pockets of enemy wounded were discovered, and one more cavalryman was lost during these mopping-up operations. The patrols swept through a landscape that had been savaged by artillery and airpower, and was scattered with heaps of brown dirt, bodies, and parts of bodies. But it was clear that the surviving enemy troops had departed—they had apparently withdrawn along the beginning slopes of the Chu Pong Massif, maneuvering back along the Ia Drang Valley toward Cambodia.

The Americans who had survived the battle were weary but triumphant. They had suffered grievous losses: 79 killed and 121 wounded. Many of the companies and platoons that had landed in the early lifts had been reduced to a fraction of their initial strength, and all of the men who had fought here during the three-day struggle for survival would need a period of rest and recovery.

But the survivors and their fallen comrades had won a major victory in the largest American battle of the war to date, and they had proven the soundness of the airmobility doctrine. They had killed a confirmed 650 or so NVA soldiers by body count, and suspected that at least that many, perhaps even a thousand or more, had been killed and carried from the field. General Mân's B3 Front had been badly battered, though it—like so many NVA and VC opponents in this war—would be back in action soon enough. And, as the 1st Cavalry Division would soon discover, the front still had some reserves of fresh soldiers, and all of them were itching for a fight, and for revenge.

All of Moore's battalion, and several other companies that had suffered major losses at X-Ray, were evacuated by evening of the 16th to Camp Holloway, a major base near Pleiku city. That left the better part of a battalion, the 2nd/7th Cav, and Company A from the 1st/5th Cav, at X-Ray, ready to move out for the next phase of the Ia Drang Campaign.

And the fresh units of the B3 Front would be ready and waiting.

AMBUSH AT ALBANY

Two reasonably fresh battalions remained at LZ X-Ray after Colonel Moore's 1st Battalion, 7th Cavalry, had been pulled back for a well-deserved rest at Camp Holloway. Both would receive marching orders on the morning of 17 November. Colonel Tully's 2nd Battalion, 5th Cav, was ordered to LZ Columbus, which lay about three miles to the north and east, while Colonel McDade's 2nd Battalion, 7th Cav, was directed to LZ Albany, a similar distance away to the north. Since some of McDade's men had been pulled back to Camp Holloway because they had been heavily involved in the X-Ray battle, Captain George Forest was ordered to attach his Company A, 1/5, to McDade's battalion.

The two units moved out at 0900, with Tully in the lead. They had been

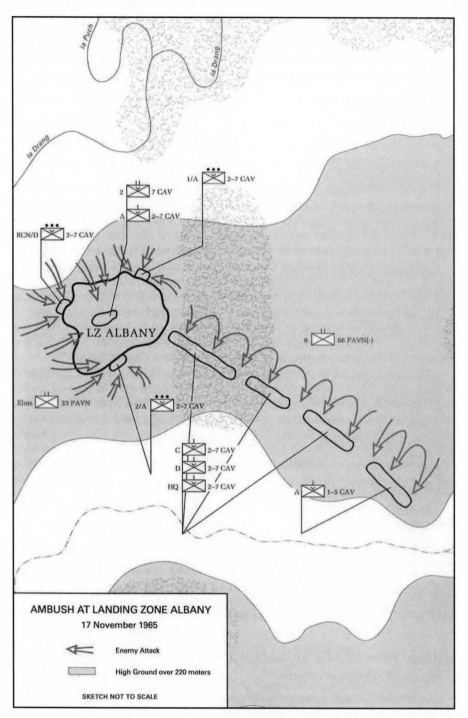

Ambush at LZ Albany

CENTER OF MILITARY HISTORY, UNITED STATES ARMY

told to give wide berth to the area at the base of the Chu Pong Massif, since a large B-52 raid was scheduled to saturate that area with bombs later that day, so the two battalions would march together for the first part of the move. Colonel Tully had arranged for a moving barrage of artillery to pound the terrain in the path of the march, hoping and expecting that the fire would clear out any hidden enemy troops that might be preparing an ambush. After about two hours, the paths diverged, with Tully turning east toward his destination while McDade's battalion was to continue north to Albany. Worried that the rolling barrage would serve only to reveal his position to the enemy, McDade declined the continued artillery support and continued on toward Albany, a little more than a mile away.

Although it was declared a landing zone, and had been scouted from the air, LZ Albany was not yet occupied by American troops. Neither McDade nor his men knew what they would find there, except that it would be a clearing large enough to accept multiple helicopter landings. The colonel had only commanded his battalion for a few weeks, so he was content to let the company dispositions be arranged by the individual captains.

At the head of the column marched the reconnaissance platoon, nominally a part of Company D but attached to Captain Joel Sugdinis's Company A for the march. The captain deployed his two rifle platoons to the left and right in tactical formation, trailing the recon platoon, and put his headquarters unit between the rifle platoons, with the mortar platoon bringing up the rear of A Company.

Company C, under Captain John Fesmire, also began the march with his men dispersed in line. As the day grew hotter, however, and his men began to lose sight of each other in the tall grass and tropical foliage, he allowed them to ease into a much more comfortable column of march. Behind him, Captain Henry Thorpe of D Company also didn't make any special precautions for tactical defense. To the men, it was simply another walk in the woods, toward a mysterious destination. Only at the rear of the column, with Captain Forest's Company A, 1st of the 5th, did tactical precaution again become apparent. Forest's men also spread out with flankers in the woods to either side.

The Americans heard distant explosions as they marched, and realized that the B-52s were dropping their multiple tons of ordnance on the slopes of the massif. The advance was slow, the temperature hot, but the officers knew that the column didn't have far to go. As they approached the first clearing of the Albany LZ, however, the point men of the recon platoon abruptly came upon, and captured, two disheveled NVA deserters. Captain Sugdinis notified Colonel McDade, and the whole column came to a stop for half an hour or more while the colonel made his way to the prisoners and, through an interpreter, conducted an interrogation. The men claimed to be frightened of the B-52s, but said they knew nothing of any enemy presence in the area—they said they were deserters who had fled their units, and had no knowledge of NVA plans.

It was after 1300 by the time the initial elements of the column entered the clearing of LZ Albany. As the recon platoon and the two rifle platoons of Company A moved to explore the perimeter of the large open space, Captain Sugdinis had his mortar platoon set up in a grove of trees that lay in the middle of the LZ, in effect dividing it into two large clearings. In the meantime, Colonel McDade and his HQ team halted as they entered the clearing, with the colonel deciding he wanted to confer with his company commanders before concentrating the battalion at Albany. As a consequence, the entire column halted again while the captains, with their radio teams, made their way toward battalion HQ. Captain Forest, whose Company A was bringing up the rear, had to push forward some 500 yards to reach the colonel.

None of the Americans knew that PAVN scouts had observed their march, and that several powerful units happened to be very near to the landing zone. General Mân's B3 Front had been bloodied, but not destroyed, and the North Vietnamese commander had been looking for an opportunity to strike a return blow as revenge for the damage his front had suffered at X-Ray. He had a fresh battalion, the 8th of the 66th Regiment, reinforced by several additional companies near at hand. They had been bivouacked just to the north of Albany, and with the approach of the American column, their commander, Le Xuan Phoi, had taken care to lay out a lethal ambush.

His men remained hidden as they formed a strong defensive position on the far side of the clearing from the trail where the column had entered. About half of Phoi's men held this position, and would be supported by mortars and emplaced machine guns, while the rest infiltrated their way southward and set up a line just to the right of the American column's line of march. The effect, graphically, was like that of an upside-down L, with the base of the L blocking the path of advance, while the tall side leg ran parallel to the strung-out formation of sweaty, trudging cavalrymen.

McDade's men had no idea that the NVA troops were nearby until the firing began at 1315. The lead elements of the column, including the recon platoon, were within about 50 yards of the enemy when the first shots crackled through the cavalrymen. The firing quickly rose to a roaring fusillade, with Americans diving for whatever cover they could find. Many were killed before they even had a chance to raise their weapons.

Unfortunately for the American column, all of the company commanders with their radios were concentrated at McDade's HQ, at the edge of the clearing. At the first shots, Captain Forest took off for his company, which was farthest from the clearing. His two radiomen ran with him, but both of them were killed before Forest finally sprinted all the way back to his own unit. Company A was already deployed in a tactical formation, and the captain quickly whipped it into a semblance of a perimeter. Taking cover behind whatever natural protection they could find, Forest's men set up a lively return fire.

The men of Companies C and D, in the middle of the column, were tragically unprepared for battle. The enemy soldiers came charging out of the underbrush, and within seconds the battle was a hand-to-hand melee, men fighting in small groups or alone, lacking any sense of where their comrades were, where the enemy was, and what they should do—besides fight for their very survival. Their captains, Fesmire and Thorpe, remained trapped with McDade's HQ; the battle for those two companies would be managed by junior officers and NCOs.

In the clearing, three groups of Americans had formed small pockets of resistance, each employing the makeshift shelter of a huge termite mound. The recon platoon had been the farthest forward unit, but also contained some of the finest soldiers in the column. They wasted no time in returning fire, and made good use of the hill at the north of the clearing to protect themselves from direct enemy attacks. Captain Sugdinis gathered a number of his riflemen around a second hill to the south of the clearing, while the colonel organized a third strongpoint to the east. At the same time, the mortar platoon held off attacks and returned fire from the grove of trees at the center of the clearing.

Soon after the battle began, the brigade commander, Colonel Brown, arrived overhead with his fire control officer in a Huey. They had plenty of artillery on call, but the scene below was so chaotic that they could not ascertain any targets. In fact, they couldn't even make out the desperate fights being waged by the men of Companies C and D in the thick jungle; and even if they had, the NVA and Americans were intermixed so closely there that artillery would have been deadly to both sides.

Finally, battle lines in the clearing became distinguishable, and helicopter gunships gave the first supporting attacks, spitting salvos of rockets into the enemy ranks. Soon thereafter came Air Force ground-attack planes— A-1E Skyraiders based at Pleiku—delivering lethal canisters of napalm that encompassed entire formations of enemy soldiers in searing, oily fire. There is no doubt that some cavalrymen were also killed in these airstrikes, but many of the survivors attested that, without the air support, the entire column would have been overrun.

At the rear of the column, Captain Forest's company held firm, and— perhaps because the enemy soldiers were thin on the ground at the tail of the column—the attackers soon moved off toward the easier targets in the middle of the formation. At 1830, a fast-arriving lift of Hueys delivered an understrength company of reinforcements to the LZ, dropping them off and racing away so quickly that they didn't even take any fire. Brown had also ordered more cavalrymen, including two companies from LZ Columbus, to march to the sound of the guns. The first of these reached Forest, and helped to hold the perimeter of Company A, throughout the night.

The men of Companies C and D spent a hellish night, fighting real enemies and spooked by shadows. They were often very near, but couldn't see or reach, wounded comrades desperate for water and relief. Some of those men made their way to the perimeters at the head and tail of the column; others linked up with fellow cavalrymen and defended the ground that they held; and all too many of them died. Toward morning the combat abated as the surviving North Vietnamese withdrew, bearing away their own wounded, and leaving the 1st Cavalry Division (Airmobile) to assess the costs of this new kind of war.

AFTERMATH

The two bloodiest battles of the Ia Drang campaign, one a solid victory and the other a potential disaster narrowly averted, reinforced the two profound realities that the Marines had grasped during Operation Starlite: helicopters were a great asset for mobility, but they needed safe landing zones to operate effectively. Powerful, continuous, and accurately directed air support was crucial to the success of American operations—and in fact at LZ Albany air support was the only thing that allowed the American force to survive.

General Kinnard would shift his battle-weary brigade back to An Khê and bring fresh troops up to the Pleiku and Ia Drang regions, but the fighting there was over for 1965. Not for the first time, NVA forces that had been damaged but not destroyed were able to cross the border into Cambodia, where American forces were forbidden to pursue. And that, to a greater or lesser extent, was a reality that would continue for the rest of the Vietnam War.

THREE

HAMMER THE AMBUSH

THE BIG RED ONE AT SROK DONG
AND MINH THANH ROAD

This was one of the few times that they did what we wanted them to do rather than us doing what they wanted us to do.

MAJOR GENERAL WILLIAM DUPUY, CO 1ST
INFANTRY DIVISION, AUGUST 1966

Following the conclusion of the Ia Drang campaign in autumn 1965, the North Vietnamese Army, the Viet Cong, and the United States all stood down from large operations and setpiece battles in favor of building up their forces for the campaigns ahead. The North Vietnamese continued to funnel supplies and manpower to the south via the Ho Chi Minh Trail, which was protected from American interdiction for most of its length by the alleged neutrality of Laos and Cambodia. The PAVN developed huge depots in areas of South Vietnam, storing thousands of tons of rice, as well as medical supplies, weapons, printing presses, photography studios, and ammunition, in hidden bunkers throughout the country. As a general rule, they set these bases up in areas of strong Viet Cong control, or at least limited South Vietnamese presence.

In America, meanwhile, a massive effort was under way to collect men and matériel for deployment to Vietnam. By 1 January 1966, the United States had 115,000 Army personnel in country, in addition to a further 41,000 Marines. President Johnson and Defense Secretary McNamara determined that, by the end of 1966, they wanted to deploy just short of 400,000 US troops into the country of South Vietnam. They had further reaffirmed their decision that they would do so without activating the reserves or extending the enlistments of already deployed soldiers and Marines.

This massive commitment of manpower would strain both the Army and the Marine Corps to their limits. It involved scouring far-flung bases around the globe for available soldiers, with a very intense emphasis on the quest for helicopter pilots and flight service personnel. And it would involve the quick deployment of some of America's most legendary and venerable military units.

Chief among those units was the 1st Infantry Division, the "Big Red One." All three of the division's brigades had arrived in Vietnam by the end of 1965, though not without untoward incident as the 2nd Brigade was redirected from its original landing port and found itself ashore at Bien Hoa, just outside of Saigon, without most of its supplies, including rations. By early 1966, however, the entire division was positioned in the key III Corps area northwest of Saigon, and was ready to go into action.

In March 1966, General Westmoreland appointed his MACV chief of operations, Major General William Dupuy, as the new commanding general of the Big Red One. Dupuy had served in the country for some time, and he was an aggressive and skilled officer also known to be intelligent and determined. Westmoreland knew that he could expect the 1st Infantry Division to achieve some results. The division would be posted in the Saigon area and—except for one mission to sweep the banks of the Saigon River downstream from the city—would concentrate on the provinces west and northwest of the capital, which were the main avenues of the enemy's supply and support conduits from Cambodia.

The primary focus of the 1st Division's operations would be the provinces of Binh Long, Phuoc Tuy, and Binh Duong, all of which were adjacent to or encompassed parts of War Zone C. The latter was an area of few towns and roads, known to be a VC stronghold nestled hard against the Cambodian border. This broad area was the operational setting for North Vietnam's B2 Front, and in 1966 was occupied by the crack 9th PLAF Division, the 5th

PLAF Division, as well as the 7th PAVN Division recently arrived from North Vietnam. Another highly trained and motivated unit, the 70th Guard Regiment, was dedicated to the protection of the COSVN headquarters, which was the central, coordinating HQ for all Viet Cong units in the country.

Beginning at the end of March, units of the Big Red One conducted a number of operations, all designed to locate enemy units, bring them to battle, and destroy them. Like the rest of the Army, the division was coming to grips with a new kind of conflict, termed *area warfare*. Most of the battles of America's previous wars had been frontal conflicts, with various terrain objectives sought by two foes, each with its own territory. The victors and losers in those battles were generally determined by who controlled a given piece of ground at the end of fighting.

Area warfare required a whole new kind of approach. It was already obvious that American military forces could take control of virtually any geographical position they chose to capture; but it was also clear that merely holding those positions would not facilitate victory or even hasten bringing about an end to the war. Instead of occupying his physical strongpoints, this enemy must be defeated by locating and destroying his forces in battle.

Under General Dupuy, the 1st Division made a number of attempts to do this. Operation Abilene began on 29 March, and was a sweep through Phuoc Tuy province in an effort to attack elements of the 5th PLAF Division. With the exception of one bloody skirmish, which resulted in 35 American KIA, the operation produced few enemy contacts. From 17 April until 5 May, elements of the division focused their efforts on the Saigon River's length between the capital city and the South China Sea; although some VC depots were captured, contact with enemy troops was quite sporadic and involved only very small units.

Operation Birmingham, commencing in late April, sent two brigades of the division west again, into the huge enemy sanctuary of War Zone C. These activities included an exchange of fire against VC forces in Cambodia—an incursion allowed by the right of "self-defense" outlined in US rules of engagement—and the destruction of an enemy base near the town of Lo Go. For the first two weeks in May, the division continued to probe through War

Zone C, seeking the elusive COSVN headquarters. Finally, with the heavy rains of the monsoon turning the area into a sea of mud, Dupuy pulled his division out of War Zone C and set about looking for a more accessible target.

One significant trouble spot ran just to the east of the war zone. Highway 13 was a north-south commercial route that had been subject to several VC ambushes over the past few months. Military convoys along the highway were routinely formed with significant strength, often including an armored complement. Strategic towns in the contested area adjacent to War Zone C along the road included (from north to south) Loc Ninh, Srok Dong, and An Loc. On 11 June, an all-day battle was waged around two hills near Loc Ninh. Elements of the 1st Division's 3rd Brigade and the 273 PAVN Regiment's 1st Battalion fought for more than ten hours, with both sides suffering heavy casualties—including 33 Americans killed. For the rest of the month Dupuy's men patrolled Highway 13, sweeping for mines and seeking enemy forces in some of the roadless countryside to the east, in Phuoc Long province.

SURPRISE ATTACK AT SROK DONG

It was not until 30 June that a decisive engagement developed between 1st Division and the Viet Cong, but when it happened it proved to be a key battle for both sides. On that morning a convoy of engineers moved north along the highway, planning to install an armored-vehicle-launched bridge (AVLB) or "scissors bridge" across a creek south of Srok Dong. (The original bridge had been damaged too much to carry armored vehicles.) A troop of armored cavalry (B of the 1st Squadron, 4th Cavalry) and an infantry platoon (1st of C Company, 2nd Battalion, 18th Infantry) accompanied the column as it departed from An Loc early in the morning and rolled north on Route 13. Each troop included several M48 Patton tanks. All of the soldiers, cavalrymen and infantry alike, rode in or atop the armored personnel carriers (APCs).

The bridge installation proceeded smoothly, and the span was in place before 0900. The location was labeled Check Point Golden Gate, a name that was also applied to the bridge. The terrain to either side of the highway was a mix of dense jungle, with trees lining both sides of the road, and rice paddies. However, there was a clearing near the bridge that was large enough to provide a helicopter landing zone, should one be required.

As C Troop of the 1st Squadron and the rest of Company C (2/18th) moved up in support, A Company (2/18th) remained on alert in An Loc, ready to respond quickly as a reaction force. Lieutenant Colonel Leonard Lewane, CO of the 1st Squadron, 4th Cavalry, flew over the scene in a light observation helicopter (LOH) as shortly after 0900 the second phase of the operation commenced. This was to be a reconnaissance in force up Route 13, with additional probes investigating short lengths of Highway 17, an east-west road that crossed Highway 13 a mile or so north of Check Point Golden Gate.

The column advanced in two sections, with the original bridge escort component under the command of Troop B's CO, 1st Lieutenant James Flores, in the lead, and the following combined arms element, commanded by Troop C's Captain Stephen Slattery, following closely behind. They quickly reached the intersection with Highway 17, establishing Check Point 1 at that crossroads.

Three mortar carriers and a platoon of infantry established a perimeter at the checkpoint, while Lieutenant Flores's Troop B and one infantry platoon turned east on Highway 17, advancing as far as the first crossing stream—less than half a mile away. The highway crossed the stream at a ford that proved to be a significantly deep obstacle, so Flores elected not to press on eastward. After designating this ford to be Check Point 2, the Americans reversed course, and at Check Point 1 they resumed their northward progress along Highway 13.

At the same time, Captain Slattery's Troop C, with two infantry platoons accompanying, moved west on Highway 17. They proceeded nearly a mile, crossing a bridge over another of the many streams in the area. Here the men dismounted from their APCs and began combing the surrounding jungle, seeking signs of an enemy presence.

And the enemy was indeed in the area, albeit just a little north of Route 17. The 271st VC Regiment had recently been ordered to ambush an American force that dared to travel Highway 13 in the Srok Dong area. The enemy had embraced the opportunity created by this small convoy's expedition to do just that. Most of the Viet Cong troops were concealed in the heavy jungle to the west of the road, where they had further bulwarked their position by arranging piles of logs that both concealed the ambushers and provided them with significant protection against American small-arms fire. This hidden position extended some 2,000 yards, all the way to the hamlet of Srok Dong. There, the cap of the ambush—which was shaped in the classic L-formation—barred further progress up the road. The VC had several recoilless rifles and mortars emplaced at the northwest corner of the ambush, where the two legs of the L met. The VC behind the log barriers were well equipped with machine guns and rocket-propelled grenade (RPG) launchers. In addition to the many VC entrenched to the west of the road, a smaller number of enemy concealed themselves in the forest to the east, a fact that would make it difficult for the Americans, initially, to determine just where the bulk of the Communist forces were.

The lead element of the convoy moving north on Highway 13 was still B Troop, with the 3rd Platoon plus the attached infantry platoon in the lead, followed by Lieutenant Flores's command vehicles, with 2nd and 1st Platoons bringing up the rear. At about 0940, the lead APCs of the 3rd Platoon passed between two rice paddies and approached the few visible structures of Srok Dong. There they quickly came under fire from mortar, small arms, and recoilless rifles. The platoon halted as the volume of fire, pouring in from both the northwest and northeast, quickly increased in intensity.

From his position about 800 yards back in the column, Flores could see the explosions caused by the attack on his lead platoon. He immediately contacted Lieutenant Colonel Lewane. The squadron commander, overhead in his light helicopter, spotted the concentration of enemy heavy weapons and was able to divert an airstrike of fighter-bombers that were already aloft, en route to a different target.

Troop B quickly returned fire, vehicles angling toward the left, from which the Americans soon discerned the bulk of the enemy fire emanated. The tank with the 3rd Platoon was struck repeatedly, but kept up a volume of fire even after its track was disabled, rendering it immobile, while the heavy machine guns on the APCs raked the enemy positions. The northernmost point of the advance of the convoy was designated Check Point 3, and here the APCs and the tank struggled to maintain an all-around defense.

The 2nd Platoon, with two more tanks, plus one detached from the 1st Platoon, raced forward to reinforce, deploying on both sides of the beleaguered 3rd Platoon. This enabled many of the APCs caught in the initial ambush to pull back to Check Point 1, carrying out wounded and seeking to replenish rapidly diminished ammunition supplies.

Within a half hour of the first shots being fired, all four of B Troop's Patton tanks had been knocked out, and it seemed that the unit was in dire danger of annihilation. Once again, airpower provided the margin of survival as, following the initial bombing runs of the diverted Air Force attack planes, several Huey gunships arrived on the scene, adding their rocketry and machine guns to the defense of Troop B. Colonel Lewane also urgently ordered Captain Slattery to bring Troop C back to Check Point 1.

Very quickly the VC attack expanded to include direct fire against the checkpoint at the highway intersection, which prevented medical evacuation, or "Dust Off," helicopters from landing. As a result, the evacuation LZ was designated back at Check Point Golden Gate, with several APCs carrying the wounded the short distance down Route 13 to the location of the freshly emplaced bridge.

Working its way through the traffic jam that had developed around Check Point 1, Slattery's Troop C quickly moved north to surround the battered vehicles and men of Troop B. The column was led by one M48 tank, which was struck in the turret barely 200 yards north of Check Point 1. Both the commander and loader were badly wounded, but they were quickly evacuated and the tank continued to lead the column forward. With visibility choked off by the heavy jungle on both sides of the road, Troop C cavalrymen chucked hand grenades to the right and left, spraying the unseen enemy with shrapnel.

Before the damaged tank was able to reach Troop B's position, it was struck again, this time with an impact that wounded the gunner and disabled the power to the tank turret. The injured man was evacuated, and the driver kept advancing. Three soldiers jumped aboard to help, climbing inside to operate the turret manually, and the Patton rumbled right past the wreckage of Troop B. Once in the clear, the ad hoc crew located the linchpin of the enemy ambush, to their northwest, and fired off every round of the tank's ammunition supply.

The APCs of Troop C, following the tank, split up to advance to either side of their Troop B comrades. The new arrivals added their machine guns to the defense of Check Point 3, allowing the men of Troop B to fall back to the intersection, leaving their mostly disabled APCs and tanks behind. Once they replenished their ammunition, the cavalrymen, advancing on foot, followed Highway 17 to the west of the checkpoint; there, they intended to set up a blocking position to repulse any enemy attempt to retreat in that direction.

From the air, Colonel Lewane directed artillery onto the enemy positions, raining shells on the ambushers to the east of the highway while a steady stream of airstrikes roared in to hammer the enemy forces to the west. In addition to Air Force attack planes and Huey gunships, these strikes were aided by huge, heavily armed CH-47 Chinook helicopters, affectionately known as "Guns-A-Go-Go" to the men on the ground. Aided by this firepower, Troop C formed a solid perimeter at Check Point 3 and was able to hold off all attacks.

As the morning neared noon, forces beyond the battlefield were already moving to take advantage of this clear proof of a VC troop concentration. Company A, 2/18th, raced up the road from An Loc, arriving at the crossroads before 1200, and quickly deployed into the woods to the west, relieving some of the pressure on that key intersection . Two South Vietnamese units were approaching from the north and east, positioned to block any enemy attempt to retreat in those directions.

Under the pressure of the convoy's stout defense, plus the support of air and artillery strikes, the initial attackers apparently had suffered enough; the Viet Cong started to withdraw westward. Soon Company B, 2nd/18th, also reached the battlefield, together with the battalion commander, Lieutenant Colonel Herbert McChrystal. He pushed all three of his companies out from the crossroads until they encountered heavy VC resistance to the southwest of the initial ambush.

McChrystal focused two of his companies against this strongpoint, and by 1615 the enemy had fallen back far enough to break off contact. By this time, General Dupuy had taken note of the engagement, and ordered his 1st Brigade commander, Colonel Sidney Berry, to pursue the retreating VC with all forces at his disposal. On 1 July, the brigade, in concert with units from the ARVN's 5th Division, moved through the battlefield and found no signs of surviving enemy—though they did encounter a number of VC bodies that had been abandoned or buried hastily.

Deducing correctly that the 271st Regiment was in full flight toward the Cambodian border, Colonel Berry pressed three battalions of infantry in hot pursuit. His counterpart, Colonel Cam, brought up his 273rd Regiment to screen the retreat, and the reinforcing VC initiated an attack near sunset on 1 July against a company of Colonel McChrystal's 2/18th Battalion. The battalion commander hastily concentrated his forces and forced the enemy to break off contact after dark.

However, they were back again before 0600 on 2 July, hammering Companies A and C with attacks from multiple directions. These assaults were supported by mortars, but consisted mainly of VC light infantry swarming forward in ground assaults. With inclement weather keeping the air support temporarily grounded, the American infantry hunkered down and held on. When the skies cleared, Air Force planes based out of Bien Hoa immediately commenced attacks with napalm and high explosives, shattering the impetus of the enemy counterattack.

The fight at Srok Dong proved to be an engagement with significance that went far beyond the size of the forces deployed. The initial ambush was well placed, and came as a complete surprise. Yet the 1st Division had reacted swiftly and aggressively, turning a potential disaster into a battlefield victory. General Dupuy would later comment that "US forces nearly lost this battle. Air Superiority proved to be the deciding factor, inflicting severe losses on the enemy."

And the general had a new idea: he would try to use the enemy's penchant for ambush against him, surprising those who would make a surprise attack. His chance to test this idea would come very soon indeed.

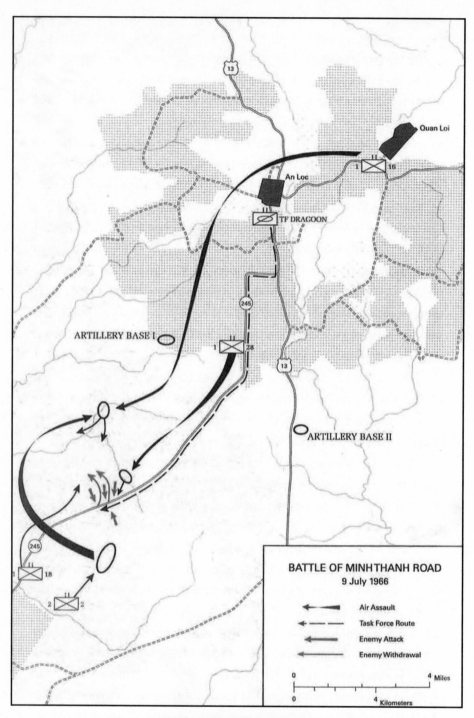

Battle of Minh Thanh Road
CENTER OF MILITARY HISTORY, UNITED STATES ARMY

TURNING THE TABLES AT MINH THANH ROAD

Some have the impression that the Viet Cong was a relatively primitive force, soldiers dressed in sandals and "black pajamas," living more or less off the land (or what they could plunder from farmers and other civilians) and armed mainly with personal weapons such as the ubiquitous and very effective AK-47, the standard rifle of all Communist armies of the era.

While it is true that the VC did not have access to armored vehicles and airpower, they did have considerable resources in tactical weaponry, such as heavy machine guns, mortars, and recoilless rifles—the latter packing enough punch to disable a tank. Furthermore, they had a detailed command-and-control structure, going all the way to an in-country headquarters, and a communication network connecting widely dispersed battalions and regiments to their higher command.

In the Big Red One's area of operation in the summer and fall of 1966, the American infantry primarily faced the VC's 9th Infantry Division; the headquarters controlled the 271st, 272nd, and 273rd Regiments. All of these were battle-tested formations manned by seasoned soldiers, and were maintained at or near full strength by frequent reinforcements brought in from North Vietnam. The 272nd, in particular, was considered an elite unit. Although it had been badly damaged in the earlier battles around Route 13, it had received nearly a thousand men as reinforcements during the first week of July.

While Army intelligence did not have an exact fix on the location of the regiment's headquarters, radio direction finding enabled it to place it generally in an area west of Route 13, near a winding provincial road known as Route 245, or the Minh Thanh Road. General Dupuy latched on to this information in issuing his operational orders to Colonel Berry, his 1st Brigade commander: he directed Berry to set a trap for the VC by luring them into ambushing a convoy that would in fact contain a lot more firepower and durability than the enemy expected. Once the Communists committed to the attack, additional infantry battalions would come in from all directions, attempting to encircle the ambushers and preventing their withdrawal.

Since a number of American troop movements that should have been secret had been intercepted by the enemy, General Dupuy suspected that a VC spy was leaking information from the provincial headquarters in Binh Long. He turned this hunch to his advantage by informing the staff of the nearby ARVN HQ that he would be moving a convoy of bulldozers and supply trucks down Route 245 on July 9, allegedly to make repairs on the airfield at Minh Thanh that had suffered some damage previously. This narrow highway ran generally southwest from An Loc to the town after which the road was named, starting as a branch off of Route 13 and gradually diverging away from that main artery. Dupuy informed his alleged allies that the convoy would be lightly escorted by armored cavalry.

The bait for the trap, naturally enough, would be the men and armored vehicles of the 4th Cavalry—the unit that performed so well in repulsing the ambush at Srok Dong. Instead of a single platoon or troop, however, Task Force Dragoon would include two full troops (B and C) of the 1st of the 4th Cavalry. Company B, 1st Battalion of the 2nd Infantry, would also join the road convoy, with the men riding atop the cavalry's armored personnel carriers and tanks.

Preparations for the 9 July expedition began several days earlier, with 1st Brigade officers running multiple wargames to try to assess the possible enemy response. Based on the proximity of the enemy HQ suggested by signals intelligence (SIGINT) and the terrain traversed by the narrow, curving road, the Americans fixed the most likely spot for the ambush— though the plan would allow operational flexibility to adjust to different battlefield locations as well. Aerial reconnaissance was employed extensively to locate suitable landing zones for the future use of the infantry that would be assigned to close the trap.

Two artillery bases were established, one (Artillery Base II) right off of Highway 13, and another (Artillery Base I) to the west of Route 245. Since AB I would require a significant move into an area with no US troops, a cover operation was set up on 7 July to conceal the real purpose of the move. Some 30 Hueys loudly motored in to an LZ just north of the future base, which was hammered by the usual artillery and airstrikes before the helicopters actually touched down. Shortly after, a massive bombing strike launched by B-52s blanketed the surrounding area, where it was suspected the 273rd VC Regiment was concentrated. Under the screen of this action, batteries of 105-mm, 155-mm, and eight-inch howitzers were deployed to the artillery base, in range to provide supporting fire along the entire length of Minh Thanh Road.

A number of 1st Brigade units were moved into position to support the convoy, should it—as hoped—encounter an enemy ambush. The overall plan was to have the armored cavalry occupy the road, relying on its own vehicles and the ready support of artillery and airstrikes to withstand the initial attack. Additional battalions would move by helicopter, road, and foot march to compress the attackers and hopefully cut off their retreat.

Deception remained the order of the day. In order to mask the American strength gathering to the south of the suspected ambush site, the 2nd Battalion, 2nd Infantry, was helicoptered down to Minh Thanh in small groups, where it reinforced the 1st Battalion, 18th Infantry. A full artillery battery was also positioned there. Another battalion, the 1st of the 16th Infantry, was temporarily attached to the 1st Brigade and stood by for action just a short distance east of An Loc. One day before the convoy set out, the 1st Battalion, 28th Infantry, was helicoptered to Artillery Base I. Battalion commander Lieutenant Colonel Robert Haldane moved them east of that location to set up a blocking position around an abandoned air base in the jungle, north and west of Route 245.

A series of checkpoints were marked in advance along the route of the convoy, to aid in coordinating the movement of reinforcements. These began with Check Point John, at the intersection of Route 13 and Route 245, followed by CPs Gordon, Hank, Dick, and Tom at specific locations along the Minh Thanh Road. The best guess of the mission planners was that the ambush would occur somewhere in the short distance between Check Point Dick and Check Point Tom. The latter was about two and a half miles north of the Minh Thanh rubber plantation; it was presumed that the ambush would occur in the more dense concealment of the jungle, before the vehicles reached the plantation.

Task Force Dragoon was scheduled to set out first thing in the morning of 9 July, but was delayed two hours by a heavy overcast and lingering fog. At 0900, the weather cleared enough for operations, and the column moved down Route 13 from An Loc. After two miles it made the right turn toward the west and southwest, following the narrow track of Route 245 through an area of rubber plantations, and into a region of heavy jungle. As he had done at Srok Dong, Colonel Lewane—commander of the cavalry squadron and designated task force CO for this mission—flew overhead in a light observation helicopter.

Captain Slattery's Troop C of the cavalry led the way, while Captain David Kelly's Troop B rolled after. A rolling artillery barrage pummeled the landscape about 300 yards before the task force and to either side of the road as the convoy trundled on, while helicopter gunships flew just over the horizon, ready for swift intervention. In places that looked especially likely to conceal enemy forces, precautionary airstrikes splattered the ground with napalm, while the turrets of the cavalry's tanks turned to either side and fired canister and high-explosive rounds into the jungle.

A bridge crossed a small stream at Check Point Dick, and Captain Slattery's attached engineering team found that span to be mined. The column paused for a few minutes while the explosives were cleared, and then resumed the advance. At 1050, a forward air controller (FAC) in one of the scouting helicopters spotted a group of VC crossing the road about a quarter of a mile ahead of the column in the vicinity of Check Point Tom. About 20 minutes later, having slowed the pace of the convoy to move at full alert, Lieutenant John Lyons—commander of the 1st Platoon of Troop C—spotted more VC at the checkpoint. Like the first group, they were moving from the north side of the road to the south.

The battle commenced at 1110, when Lieutenant Lyons's lead tank opened fire on the visible VC. Almost immediately the jungle to both sides erupted into fire and lead as all three battalions of the VC 272nd Regiment opened up with small arms, 75-mm recoilless rifles, mortars, and RPG-2 blasts directed against the American armored vehicles. The American vehicles pulled off to face right and left, alternating in a herringbone pattern so that their more stoutly armored frontal sides faced the enemy and the heavy machine guns on the APCs could be easily brought to bear.

The bulk of the VC attacked from north of the road, but the initial volleys were so intense that the cavalry couldn't immediately determine to which side was the strongest enemy presence. As per the original plan, the artillery batteries in the two bases opened up by pounding the ground to the north of the road with massively heavy concentrations of explosives. The airstrikes had initially been slated for the south side of the road, and within the first minutes of the battle the FACs called in dozens of strikes on those targets. At the same time, Colonel Berry ordered Major John Bard, commanding the 1st/18th just north of Minh Thanh, to move toward and take up a position in the jungle off the enemy's right flank. Soon thereafter he ordered Lieutenant Colonel Jack Conn's 2nd/2nd, to take up a reserve position south of Route 245.

After a few minutes, Captain Slattery's men began to realize that the enemy strength lay primarily to the north. From the air, Colonel Lewane ordered Troop B forward, positioning it beside Troop C and doubling the strength of the column at the critical focus of the ambush. Meantime, the air controllers redirected the airstrikes to the north, and Air Force fighter-bombers, assisted by US Navy carrier-based aircraft, relentlessly pounded the attacking VC.

At one point, as many as five waves of attacking aircraft were "stacked up" over the battlefield, each strike waiting for the preceding planes to discharge their ordnance and move out of the way. Helicopter gunships swarmed in at lower levels, adding rockets and gunfire to the air support against the entrenched enemy. At one point during the battle, a big, twin-engine CH-47 Chinook helicopter was disabled, but made a crash landing on Minh Thanh Road south and west of the fighting; the chopper would later be extracted by an even more powerful helicopter, a CH-54 "Flying Crane."

The reinforcing battalions were moving toward the fighting by 1115. Major Bard's battalion found the going very slow as they ran into VC-fortified positions while attempting to push north through the jungle, so Colonel Berry modified the advance, sending the 1/18 along the north side of the road. They moved into the jungle only as they approached Check Point Tom, and thus achieved their goal of applying pressure to the enemy's right flank.

At 1130, Lieutenant Colonel Haldane's 1/28th, sitting tight around the abandoned air base near Artillery Base 1, was ordered to mount up and fly into Landing Zone LD, a small clearing just northeast of the battlefield, hard by the attacker's left flank. By 1210, the battalion was airborne, and 20 minutes later they were set down at the LZ, perfectly positioned to deny the VC withdrawal to the northeast. The battalion was placed under the operational control of Lieutenant Colonel Lewane, and quickly moved to attack. They at first brushed aside some enemy snipers, but by 1330 or 1400 had run into a sizable VC force and settled into a fierce firefight.

For nearly 90 minutes from the initial shots, the action at the ambush site raged furiously. Small groups of VC charged from concealment and attempted to swarm over individual armored vehicles, only to be driven off by the cavalrymen and their accompanying infantry. The tanks blasted round after round of canister into the enemy infantry, while the recoilless rifle and RPG attacks from the VC pounded into the armored vehicles. One tank and four APCs were wrecked in the first hour of the battle, while many other APCs were immobilized by damage to their tracks or engines. But the vehicle armor provided solid protection for the convoy, and despite the damage the column was never in danger of being overrun. By 1230, the firing had started to taper off as the VC, stunned by the firepower delivered against them, were forced to accept the fact that their intended target had turned the tables in this fight.

By 1330, aerial observers could see that the enemy was pulling back, primarily moving to the northwest—which was the only direction not yet blocked by the reinforcing infantry battalions. More than 2,200 rounds of artillery had smashed the VC positions, and prisoners would later admit that some of the VC companies had simply broken and fled under the weight of American ordnance.

Now it was the Big Red One that went over to the attack. Colonel Berry ordered Lieutenant Colonel Rufus Lazzell's 1/16th Battalion to helicopter to an LZ straddling the enemy's line of retreat, while the infantry at the ambush site, as well as the advancing 1/18th Battalion, pressed from the southwest and southeast. Realizing that Lieutenant Colonel Conn's 1/2nd Battalion, posted to block movement to the south of the ambush, was now out of position, Colonel Berry ordered the unit to redeploy by helicopter, using the same LZ where Colonel Lazzell's troops had just landed. The battalion commander himself was soon evacuated after being struck in the chest by a bullet.

Despite all of the converging strength, the dense jungle proved, as it would so many times, to be the enemy's greatest asset. Moving in small groups, many of the survivors of the 272nd Regiment made their way around the American positions, retreating west toward the 9th PLAF Division's stronghold in War Zone C. Nevertheless, they left some 240 dead on the field, with perhaps an equal number killed and carried away by the retreating survivors. Americans killed in the savage fighting numbered 25, with a little more than a hundred wounded.

The plan to reverse the ambush had worked as intended, and inflicted a significant defeat on an excellent VC regiment. Among the lessons of the battle, it was proved that an armored column could stand up to a significant volume of enemy fire and still deliver punishment to the attackers. As usual, the presence of artillery and air support added the firepower that proved crucial to an American victory.

Finally, in official acknowledgment of the unit's accomplishments at both Srok Dong and Minh Thanh Road, the 1st Squadron, 4th Cavalry, was awarded the Presidential Unit Citation.

TURNING DEFEAT INTO VICTORY

OPERATION ATTLEBORO BLOCKS
THE ROAD TO SAIGON

The plan was ludicrous. Command and control of the separate attacks was impossible. There was no linkup plan whatsoever. There was no appreciation of either the terrain or the enemy. I had a rather heated discussion. . . . But since I was a major at that time, and he was a brigadier general, obviously I lost.

MAJOR GENERAL GUY S. "SANDY" MELOY (RET.),
LECTURING ON OPERATION ATTLEBORO
AT SCHOFIELD BARRACKS, HAWAII, IN 1996

Not all victories are recognized at the time they are won. This fact was dramatically illustrated by the battle fought by the 196th Light Infantry Brigade early in the large offensive known as Operation Attleboro. The 196th was a brand-new unit organized in 1965 for service in the Dominican Republic, only to be transferred to Vietnam at the last minute. Under a new commander, with barely a month in country, it launched an operation that would grow into the largest engagement of the war to date, eventually swelling to become the first corps-sized offensive of the Vietnam War.

The 196th suffered heavy losses in the early going, and was handicapped by bad generalship, so when the surviving soldiers were relieved after three days of nonstop battle, they might be forgiven for feeling as though they had blundered into an ambush, and only made it out alive because of dumb luck and the help of some more veteran units that came to their rescue. This perception would hold for many of the 196th men long after they were sent home, were discharged from the Army, and continued on with their lives.

In this case, however, the truth is far different from that perception, and the victory, while unsuspected at the time, was very real indeed.

A NEW FOCUS FROM THE NORTH

The Viet Cong insurgency in South Vietnam was manned by local soldiers for the most part who were in rebellion against the government based in Saigon. But the Communist rebellion was not by any stretch a purely homegrown operation. In fact, it was run out of Hanoi, the capital of North Vietnam, and was organized as a bureaucracy, controlled by the Central Office of South Vietnam (COSVN). The HQ was centered in the thick forests northwest of Saigon, near the Cambodian border, and was responsible for bringing a great deal of war matériel to the south, as well as trained NCOs and replacement soldiers. It also provided a strategic structure and operational orders for the conduct of the war against South Vietnam and its increasingly assertive ally, the United States of America.

In 1966, the leader of that powerful bureau was General Nguyen Chi Thanh, and he was engaged in a bitter disagreement with North Vietnam's defense minister—and highly venerated hero of the war against the French—Vo Nguyen Giap. Giap sharply criticized the tactics that had been employed by the VC since America's entry into the war, arguing that Thanh was too willing to engage in costly firefights that exposed his men unnecessarily to the enemy's artillery and air support. Giap advocated a return to the hit-and-run tactics of a classic guerrilla war.

Thanh vehemently disagreed, and he made his point in front of the North Vietnamese Politburo in July of 1966. Well known for his zealotry—Thanh was a true believer in the Communist doctrine of class warfare—he didn't try to mask his passionate beliefs. At that conference, he made a strong argument that the war would only be won when the American public grew weary of the casualties inflicted by a tenacious foe who seemed to be willing to wage the war as long as necessary to achieve the ultimate goal. He pointed to the still-nascent, but steadily growing antiwar movement in the United States as proof of the validity of his views.

After this eloquent speech, Thanh's views prevailed in the halls of North Vietnam's government. Thanh was authorized to initiate aggressive action against the Americans at his discretion, and he knew exactly where he wanted to attack: the Tây Ninh province, a lightly populated, heavily forested area lying between the South Vietnamese capital of Saigon and the North's most reliable sanctuary, Cambodia. The province, in fact, was right on that border, and far enough from the capital city that governmental control in the area was almost nonexistent. Furthermore, the Saigon River ran through the province, and even amateur strategists could see that the river valley provided a ready avenue for a thrust that could originate in Cambodia but eventually drive all the way to the center of South Vietnam's government and economy.

Already Tây Ninh was a stronghold of VC power, including several massive supply depots, numerous Viet Cong irregular formations, and one of the rebellion's most veteran and effective units: the 9th Viet Cong Division. Thanh ordered the 9th Division commander, Senior Colonel Hoang Cam, to select an American unit for engagement and annihilation. He would have a formidable force with which to complete this task, with the three regiments of his division (the 271st, 272nd, and 273rd Peoples Liberation Armed Force, or PLAF, Regiments) reinforced by a regular regiment of the NVA, the 101st, and a fresh local force battalion, the 70th PLAF.

For a target, Cam would need to look no further than the newest American unit to arrive on the scene, conveniently posted at a base adjacent to Tây Ninh City: the 196th Light Infantry Brigade.

EVERYTHING IS SUBJECT TO CHANGE

The 196th Light Infantry Brigade was formed in September 1965, organized and trained in Massachusetts for nearly a full year, and designed with one express purpose in mind: it was to be stationed in the Dominican Republic as a stabilizing presence for the young government there. It would take over the job currently being performed by elements of the Army's 82nd Airborne

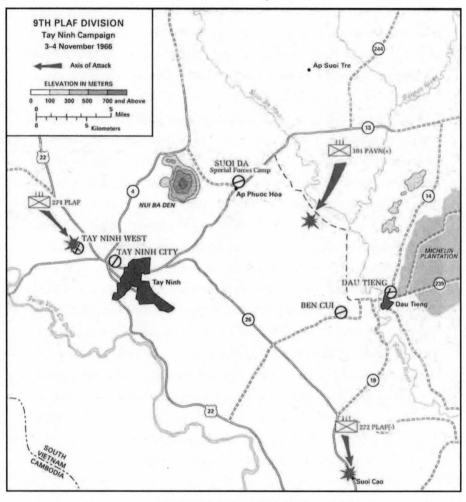

9th VC Division Attack Plan

CENTER OF MILITARY HISTORY, UNITED STATES ARMY

Division, an elite and venerable formation that was needed for service in more significant parts of the world.

Crowded into a small base some 40 miles west of Boston, at Fort Devens, the brigade used larger Army training grounds on Cape Cod and at Camp Drum in New York for its actual training. It was officially activated in time to march in the Armed Forces Day Parade in May of 1966. Plans were made and transport berths assigned for the brigade to embark aboard troopships in Boston, with provisions and weapons—including the old standard rifle, the M14—as defined for the peace-keeping and civil defense mission in the restive Dominican Republic.

Following a relatively peaceful election there in June of 1966, however, the American powers that be decided that the island was not so restive after all, and that the 196th would not be needed. When General Westmoreland, in Saigon, was asked if he could use a fresh and unplanned-for reinforcement, he all but leaped at the opportunity, even requesting that the 196th be sent to Vietnam as quickly as was humanly possible.

That turned out to be very quickly indeed. The brigade was informed on June 24 that it would not be going to the Dominican Republic, but would embark on Navy troopships on July 15 for a journey halfway around the world, to Vietnam. Fortunately, the brigade had trained under a very capable commander, Colonel Francis Conaty. Conaty was popular with his men, and ably guided them through the mission conversion, including the qualifying sessions with the newfangled M16 rifle. Right on time, the unit embarked, arriving in Vietnam after a month-long journey by sea.

General Westmoreland and MACV wasted little time in deciding where they wanted to deploy this fresh unit. Since the 25th Infantry "Tropic Lightning" Division was encountering unexpectedly heavy resistance in the Hau Nghia province, the 196th would be placed in the adjacent Tây Ninh, freeing up the 25th from at least one potentially problematic flank. By August 16th, the 196th had been airlifted to its new home, where it began the construction of a base, to be called the Tây Ninh Combat Base—and later Tây Ninh West—just outside of Tây Ninh City, less than ten miles from the

Cambodian border. It would become an important installation for the rest of the American involvement in Vietnam, and even beyond.

One more detail remained, however. General Westmoreland had a policy requiring that a general officer command every brigade in his command. Colonel Conaty would be allowed to stay on as an adviser, but for command of the green unit Westmoreland selected one of his staff officers, Brigadier General Edward deSaussure. DeSaussure was an experienced officer of artillery dating back to World War II, and lately had been widely acknowledged as not just a good staff officer, but one of the Army's real experts on the use of guided missiles.

But he had never commanded a large infantry formation in his life.

ATTLEBORO PHASE I: THE 196TH BRIGADE TAKES THE FIELD

The brigade had been in country only a month when it was sent into its first action, structured as a series of missions into the rolling, forested terrain around Tây Ninh City. The action would take its name from the Massachusetts city close to the base where the unit had been formed, and be called Operation Attleboro. The initial probes involved one of the brigade's three battalions going into the field and looking for signs of enemy activity, depots, or installations, while the other two battalions stayed behind and finished the construction of the base facilities that were literally rising from the ground around the men.

The was an innovative tactic representing a new approach to the war implemented by MACV, called search and destroy. Since the Viet Cong were proving uncooperative in meeting the US Army and fighting traditional battles—clashes in which geographical objectives were attacked and defended, and ground gained or lost—the Army in Vietnam would adapt by seeking out enemy forces in the field and then trying to inflict massive casualties upon them.

For a month, these searches continued with no productive results. Finally, in the middle of October, elements of the 25th Infantry Division, operating in the adjacent Hau Nghia province, just to the east of Tây Ninh, discovered a surprisingly large supply of rice near the Saigon River, some 20 miles southeast of Tây Ninh City. The 25th Division commander, Major General Frederick Weyand, suggested that deSaussure have his men seek similar depots, and expand the range of their missions farther to the east than they had previously been deployed.

On 19 October, one battalion of the 196th began to search the area around the important district city of Dau Tieng, adjacent to a vast plantation formerly established by the Michelin Corporation for the harvesting of rubber. Dau Tieng was some 15 miles east of Tây Ninh City and an equal distance southwest of Minh Thanh, amid a region of lightly populated countryside patched with areas of thick jungle and generally flat terrain.

For several days the searchers failed to discover anything meaningful, but on 23 October the 196th struck pay dirt: one of the brigade's patrols encountered a camouflaged network of low sheds, all concealed by sheets of black plastic and filled to overflowing with an incredible abundance of rice—rice that had been commandeered from the local farmers to supply the needs of the insurgents. Encouraged by this success, deSaussure pressed on, with his troops finding several more huge caches of VC supplies. He asked for and received permission to move his brigade command post from the base at Tây Ninh to Dau Tieng, and by 30 October, Operation Attleboro was the focus of the full strength of the three battalions of the 196th Light Infantry Brigade.

Altogether some 850 tons of rice had been "liberated," but it proved to be too much for the available transport to carry out. Since it was located in a roadless area, several miles from the Saigon River, it had to be bagged and then hauled out by CH-47 Chinooks—and those big helicopters were very much in demand for other, more urgent needs. After they'd been able to lift out about 150 tons of the rice, the men of the 196th were forced to burn the rest as, by 2 November, the brigade needed to be ready to move against another suspected enemy stronghold.

ATTLEBORO PHASE II: HARD CONTACT

Intelligence reports and aerial scouting had suggested an enemy concentration of forces about four miles north of Dau Tieng, where a stream called Ba Hao merged with the Saigon River. To support his still-green infantrymen, deSaussure was loaned a unit from the 25th Infantry Division. The 1st Battalion of the 27th Infantry "Wolfhounds" would spearhead the search, which initially would include two 196th battalions in addition to the 1/27. The general called his battalion commanders to a council of war on the evening of 2 November to lay out his plan.

The action was to begin the next morning. The area of operation would be a region of tall, triple-canopy forest, broken by "clearings" covered by sharp-edged elephant grass that could grow up to 12 feet high. No roads or even marked trails crossed the region, which lay to the west of the Saigon River. DeSaussure intended to sweep the area with six separate columns, with two of the Wolfhound companies being placed on the opposite flanks, about five miles apart. Each of those companies was to hold a blocking position, while the two battalions of the 196th—six companies in total—were to advance between the two blocking forces in four distinct and separate probes.

The 1/27th was under the command of Major Guy S. Meloy, a veteran infantrymen who had held several levels of command in infantry, mechanized, and airborne units. He had commanded his battalion for a long enough time to be thoroughly familiar with its personnel and capabilities. And Major Meloy was appalled at deSaussure's plan, which would involve units operating near to each other, but beyond direct contact. He made his objections known at the brigade conference, but he was overruled.

Unknown to deSaussure, Meloy, or any other Americans, Senior Colonel Cam of the 9th VC Division was also planning for an operation to commence on 3 November. He had made a plan and positioned his units for a complicated assault against three different objectives. He intended to send the 271st PLAF Regiment, some 1,500 men, against the new base at Tây Ninh. They were to engage and destroy any of the 196th Brigade units that remained in reserve there. The 272nd Regiment, less one battalion, was to strike at an ARVN territorial base at Suoi Cao, some 20 miles south of Tây Ninh City. His most important target, reserved for the 101st North Vietnamese Regiment, reinforced by an extra battalion from the 272nd as well as all of Cam's heavy weapons components, was to attack and destroy a Special Forces camp at Suoi Da. This attack would be made by some 3,000 NVA and PLAF regulars.

The Americans moved out first. On the morning of 3 November, the six companies of Battalions 2/1st and 4/31st Infantry moved northward from the site of the earlier-discovered cache to quickly get swallowed up in the dense jungle. The companies followed four axes of advance, none of which led within sight or easy communication of the others. About 20 minutes later, Company B of the 1/27th came to ground at an LZ on the northeast flank of the operational area, just west of the Saigon River. The designated landing zone was one of the areas of elephant grass, which was too tall for the helicopters to actually reach the ground, so the infantrymen had to leap into the grass and hope they didn't land on anything unpleasant. They were mildly surprised and relieved to find the surface to be covered by a few inches of water, but without mud.

The landing was unopposed, and the company—under the command of Captain Robert Garrett—formed up and began moving due west, toward an eventual, hoped-for rendezvous with their fellow Wolfhounds of Company C. The latter, under the command of Captain Frederick Henderson, also made an unopposed landing in a field of elephant grass on the northwest corner of the operational area, and quickly moved northeast into the heavy jungle.

Almost at once Company C moved into range of a large, fully alerted VC unit, with a hail of bullets slashing into the American infantry from concealed positions and fortified bunkers. The enemy would turn out to be the reconnaissance company of Colonel Cam's 9th VC Division. A dozen Americans were badly wounded or killed in the first volleys of the ferocious, close-range firefight; both the company commander and his first sergeant were among the casualties who would perish before they could be evacuated. The fire was so intense that, for a time, even the Dust Off medevac helicopters could not set down in the LZ.

Major Meloy, flying overhead in a command-and-control Huey, decided that he needed to get down to his isolated company. In what the self-effacing but very capable officer would later describe as one of several "dumb decisions" he made during the battle, he had the aircraft swoop low across the LZ so that he and his command group—which included a sergeant major, artillery fire control officer and three radio operators—could all jump to the ground. The sergeant major was wounded, and the Huey was damaged, though it did manage to fly away.

Reaching his wounded company commander and sergeant, Meloy knew they needed immediate evacuation; but when a pair of brave helicopter pilots tried to bring their chopper into the LZ, it was hit and exploded, crashing in a fiery pile. One crewman was killed, another wounded, while the two pilots somehow managed to throw themselves free of the crash and the pyre. Despite the futile act of heroism, Captain Henderson and the first sergeant both died minutes later. Knowing that he needed reinforcements quickly, Major Meloy ordered his battalion's third, reserve company, to airlift in from the Dau Tieng airstrip. Company A soon joined the fight, and by 1245 was anchoring the right flank of Company C.

Meloy also ordered Captain Garrett's Company B, which had landed several miles to the east, to march overland to strengthen the beleaguered position of Company C, a move that would have concentrated the entire 1st Battalion of the Wolfhounds. General deSaussure canceled that order, however, apparently determined to maintain a blocking force to the east of the battlefield. Instead, the 196th Brigade commander ordered his own unit, Company C, 3/21st, under Captain Russell DeVries, to be flown from the base at Tây Ninh to the fight. It reached the LZ and was able to link up with Meloy and Company C, where it went into line on the right flank, allowing the major to form a rough horseshoe-shaped position, arranged to defend against increasingly aggressive VC attacks from the north.

Although Major Meloy would remain unaware of the fact until they showed up on the battlefield, General deSaussure also ordered two companies of his 2nd Battalion, 1st Infantry to fly to the firefight; they, too, were airlifted into the hot LZ, operating under the command of Major Ed Stevens, the battalion operations officer. Even before they arrived, Meloy had pulled his badly bloodied Company C out of the line and sent his other two companies forward to envelop and finally overrun the VC position. When the two companies under Major Stevens rolled up around 1800, Meloy was able to use them to reinforce his perimeter, and had five companies under his command as the men hunkered down for what turned out to be a relatively quiet night, though there were sporadic small-scale attacks around the perimeter.

On the other side of the battlefield, Company B of the Wolfhounds had returned to its original blocking position, near where it had landed. It was joined by three companies from the 196th Brigade's 4th Battalion, 31st Infantry. Those four companies spent a night free of enemy harassment.

However, the VC were far from idle during the hours of darkness. As a matter of fact, Colonel Cam, commander of the 9th VC Division, had decided to scrap his earlier, rather elaborate plan that had involved three separate regimental-sized attacks. Instead, he would focus his division's efforts on an attempt to wipe out the American infantry that had shown the temerity to venture into the jungle that Cam considered his stronghold. He canceled the attack against the Special Forces camp, ordering the 101st NVA Regiment to move quickly toward Meloy's position. He also reduced the other two attacks to diversions so that he could pull more men into the developing battle.

In the early hours of 4 November, part of the 272nd Regiment made a vigorous "diversionary attack" against the ARVN camp at Suoi Cao—they charged into a hail of small-arms and artillery fire with such ferocity that more than 50 VC were killed in a few minutes. The attack on the base at Tây Ninh was downsized to a mortar bombardment, but that was sufficient to knock out much of the 196th Brigade's communications. Concerned about the damage, General deSaussure flew from Dau Tieng to the brigade's home base shortly after daylight, which unfortunately removed him from the scene of the greatest action of the upcoming day. Before he left, however, he did issue maneuver orders for the engaged companies, dispatching the brigade's assistant operations officer to Meloy at first light with a map detailing the intended movements.

Looking at the hand-drawn map, Meloy could see many potential challenges in communication and possibilities for friendly-fire encounters, as the various companies were to split up and move independently. DeSaussure intended to link the divergent companies back up into their battalion formations, which was a laudable goal, but as with so many battlefield operations, enemy activity would quickly negate the bulk of the plans.

Still, Meloy started out by sending the two 2/1 companies that were currently in his position under the command of Major Stevens eastward. They were to move overland until they swung north to resume the advance they had begun the day before. Since Meloy was to take his companies northeast and try to link with his Company B, he gave Stevens a two-hour start before he moved out, hoping that the two columns wouldn't blunder into each other in the dense forest.

That concern proved moot, since Meloy would soon discover that Colonel Cam had moved a regimental-sized force into prepared, fortified positions, no more than 500 yards north of the position where the Wolfhounds and attached companies had spent the night. The VC maintained careful fire control as the American column advanced through the jungle; when they finally opened up, they hit with a fury of fire louder and more intense than anything Meloy or his men had ever experienced—the major would late compare it to a "Mad Minute" fire spree at Fort Benning.

Dozens of Americans were killed and wounded in the initial attack. The enemy had laid down careful fire lanes through the woods, and all of their bunkers were mutually supporting. The hail of fire immediately drove the Wolfhounds to the ground and pinned them in position. Meloy was able to call in some supporting artillery, but it seemed to have no effect on the enemy. The Americans would later discover a well-fortified camp, which included bunkers formed from poured concrete—a rarity for the enemy— and protected overhead by heavy berms of logs and dirt. These positions would protect the occupants from a major bombardment, since only a direct hit by a large-caliber shell could break through the protective cover. Tunnels connected many of the enemy strongpoints, and dozens of machine guns were emplaced to cover every conceivable angle of approach.

Meloy tried sending one of his companies around each enemy flank, but these probes were effectively pinned down as the enemy position was gradually revealed to be surprisingly large. When the major called for reinforcements, the two companies under Major Stevens were quick to respond, but even though they marched quickly to the fight, they couldn't help to turn the enemy flank.

Three times over the next few hours the VC burst out of their entrenchments and made swift charges right into the American lines. Each time the attackers were driven back, but Meloy's position was becoming increasingly perilous. Additional reinforcements, including companies from the second of the Wolfhound's two battalions, were helicoptered to nearby landing zones, but communications failures prevented them from joining up. Even though smoke grenades proved that the two American positions were only about 100 yards apart, such a concentration of enemy entrenchments lay between them that neither Wolfhound battalion could move. In the shooting, both the advance company's commander and the 2/27th CO, Lieutenant Colonel William Barrott, were killed. Eventually two of the 2/27th companies swung wide enough around the enemy strongpoint to make their way to Meloy's location, but C/2/27th remained pinned down and virtually surrounded a short distance away.

Once again Meloy's ad hoc formation settled in for a tough night, and this time the enemy kept the pressure on. The major ordered the stranded company to maintain strict radio silence and fire discipline, and despite several VC probes, it survived the hours of darkness without sparking a lethal engagement. Meloy's own force, seven companies strong now, again formed a horseshoe perimeter, with an eighth company hunkered down quietly just a hundred yards away.

When the fighting resumed on the morning of 5 November, the CO of B Company of Meloy's battalion, Captain Bob Garrett, decided that he would march to the aid of his fellow Wolfhounds, with or without orders. Along with two companies from the 196th that had bivouacked with him the night before, Garrett started moving toward the sound of the guns. He followed a fortuitous path, since his column came upon the rear of the enemy fortifications. His men were able to knock out some of the bunkers and link up with the stranded C Company.

When these three companies arrived, Major Meloy, a battalion commander who was officially in charge of three companies, now found himself with eleven companies under his direct command! It was after noon when a VIP arrived in the person of Major General Dupuy, commander of the 1st Infantry Division. When he asked Meloy if, as reports indicated, he really had eight companies with him, Meloy told him that the number was now up to eleven. Under the general's sharp questions, he further acknowledged that he hadn't been contacted by General deSaussure for more than forty-eight hours—the last conversation being the heated discussion during which Meloy had objected to the general's orders, only to be overruled.

This conversation marked the start of the next, and final, phase of Operation Attleboro. Anticipating the need, General Dupuy had on the previous day ordered the 3rd Brigade of his division up, intending to deploy it to relieve the battered Wolfhounds and light infantry. Since half of Meloy's force remained in contact with the fortified enemy positions, he was forced to use some creative tactics to extract his men. He hit upon a technique of calling in artillery strikes almost upon his own men, then quickly pulling back while the shells came screaming through the air. In this dramatic, risky fashion, he was able to get his troops back to the landing zones, where they could be helicoptered to Dau Tieng and finally get a chance to rest and recover from their three-day ordeal of battle.

For the 196th Light Infantry Brigade, the battle was over—though it would be a long time before the weary survivors could fully understand the success that their sacrifice had bought.

For the rest of the US Army in the II Corps area, the fight was just getting warmed up.

THE OPERATION EXPANDS

Even before General Dupuy met Major Meloy on the battlefield, the commanding general of the 1st Division had been moving his units in position to take control of the battle. It was clear to him that the 196th Brigade had run into a buzz saw, one that required larger units and more effective

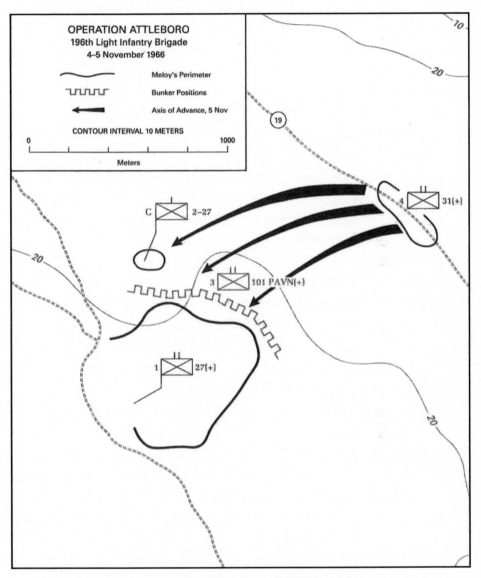

Operation Attleboro—Battle Map

CENTER OF MILITARY HISTORY, UNITED STATES ARMY

maneuver to bring the fight to a successful resolution. On the night of 4 November, he airlifted one of his battalions from the division base camp into Dau Tieng. Two whole brigades, the 2nd and 3rd, also moved to that forward base, though the 3rd continued on to Suoi Da, the Special Forces camp that had originally been on Colonel Cam's list of objectives. By 6 November, both brigades had moved into the field.

In the more than half a year that Dupuy had commanded the 1st Division, he had developed a philosophy of battle that seemed appropriate to the Vietnam War: "Find the enemy with the fewest possible men and destroy him with the maximum amount of firepower." He disdained the kind of "march straight into the jungle" tactics that General deSaussure had employed, on the solid reasoning that such an approach very often resulted in American troops walking right into a preplanned enemy fire zone, inevitably suffering casualties at the very start of an engagement. Instead, Dupuy ordered his troops to employ a tactic he called cloverleafing. This involved one squad moving forward a short distance, perhaps fifty to a hundred yards, and then establishing a firing position while another squad moved out on one flank and circled to approach the area ahead of the unit from the side, rather than head-on. The process would be repeated with another squad advancing, and clearing the other flank. Though the process was slow, it allowed for a thorough search of even heavily forested terrain, and significantly lowered the chance of a deadly ambush.

By evening of 6 November, Dupuy already had three battalions in contact with the enemy, though no major firefights developed during the day. However, one small ambush squad of seven men from Dupuy's 3rd Brigade discovered a VC patrol numbering some 150 men moving along a trail. The Americans unleashed a volley of claymore mines against the rear of the column after it had passed. These mines had already proved themselves to be a powerful tool for American soldiers in Vietnam. The claymore was set up in a fixed position, and could be fired remotely. When discharged, it sent a spray of shrapnel in a precise direction, rather like the blast of a giant shotgun. Claymores were frequently employed to set ambushes, and also for perimeter defense when a unit in the field settled into a night position.

After this initial volley, the American infantrymen called in a concentration of artillery. The next morning, the bodies of 70 enemy KIA were discovered from this short, lethal encounter. Elsewhere in the jungle, airstrikes and artillery pounded suspected enemy locations throughout the night, resulting in the destruction of many fortified positions and killing at least another hundred VC.

General Weyand, acting as the corps-level commander in the area, felt that the contacts made by the 196th LIB and the 1st Infantry Division had provided an opportunity to finally fix and punish the 9th VC Division. He quickly realized that even a divisional command was not large enough to contain the size of the enemy force engaged, and as more and more forces moved toward the fight, the operation fell under the control of the II Field Force, making it the equivalent of a corps-sized battle. The 25th Infantry Division quickly moved in to join the action, as did the 173rd Airborne Brigade, a brigade from the 4th Infantry Division, and several battalions from the South Vietnamese Army. Before it was over, more than 22,000 soldiers would contribute to the massive effort to trap and destroy the 9th VC Division once and for all.

The 25th Division, under the command of Major General George O'Connor, dispatched part of its 2nd Brigade to the Tây Ninh area, where the 196th had originally constructed its base camp. The first moves were accomplished on 7 November, with the rest of the brigade's battalions following shortly thereafter. From there, the "Tropic Lightning" Division would push north on the left flank of the 1st Division.

Several of Dupuy's battalions had ventured northeastward of the camp at Suoi Da without meeting any opposition. The easternmost of these, the 1st Battalion, 28th Infantry, under the command of Lieutenant Colonel Jack Whitted, was ordered to prepare for an airlift to a new location on the morning of 8 November. However, Whitted's men occupying listening posts outside his perimeter heard signs of enemy movement. The colonel pulled the outposts back into the perimeter, and the battalion opened up with mortars and small arms.

Hidden VC immediately returned fire. Just at dawn, a full company of enemy regulars charged the perimeter, but they were decimated by a well-placed volley from claymore mines, with the survivors quickly retreating. Unfortunately, the battalions supporting the artillery batteries were already in the process of moving, so Whitted was left without artillery support for close to a half hour. However, it took that long for the VC to muster a second attack, and when they charged again they were pounded by an artillery barrage and slashed by a second line of claymores.

These enemy troops proved to be NVA regulars from the 101st Division, and they kept up the attacks as the sun rose into the misty air. The enemy units were committed one at a time, instead of in concentration, so each attack was beaten off with heavy enemy casualties. As full daylight brightened the battlefield, tactical airstrikes added to the American arsenal and the enemy's misery—though the growing light of day also gave away the position of Whitted's company commanders, who were betrayed by the radio antennae near each captain. All three of them, and Whitted himself, were wounded, but by 1130 the enemy had been driven off. Later discovery of enemy after-action reports chided the 101st's men for "lack of determination" in these bloody, futile attacks. After the battle, the reason for the NVA's staunch resistance was discovered as Whitted's men unearthed a huge cache of enemy supplies, right where the enemy attack had originated. In addition to the ubiquitous rice, the Americans discovered all kinds of ordnance, including a large number of grenades.

In the following days, Dupuy's 3rd Brigade also joined the operation, bringing eight of the Big Red One's nine battalions into the fight. For several days, both the 1st and 25th Divisions continued their search, but the enemy seemed to be in full retreat. Even as the 25th drove into War Zone C and approached the Cambodian border, no contact was made with significant enemy forces.

The reason for this was not so much that the 9th VC Division was consciously maneuvering to avoid contact, but that its command and control had virtually collapsed. When the battered 101st NVA Regiment was assigned to guard an important ammunition storage depot, the unit broke and ran—and the service troops joined the retreat, leaving no one behind to bring up resupply to the units still in the fight!

Two of the enemy regiments, the 271st and 272nd, managed to muster enough strength to make nighttime mortar bombardments of two American bases, but they made no direct attacks, and withdrew before US patrols could engage them. Mechanized infantry from the 25th Division continued to press north, and made several successful attacks against small enemy positions, including an antiaircraft company that—with help from the 271st Regiment—managed to hold up the US brigade for half a day. But lack of coordination between the two enemy formations prevented the battle from turning into more than a momentary stumbling block.

One more significant firefight happened during Operation Attleboro, as the 1st Division's 3rd Brigade airlifted into a forested area northwest of an old French fort at the edge of War Zone C. When the Hueys flying away from the LZ took heavy ground fire—three were shot down, though their crews survived—the brigade commander, Colonel Edwin Marks, used Dupuy's cloverleaf tactic to locate the enemy strongpoint, which was well hidden and thoroughly fortified. The resulting airstrikes were so punishing that they actually cleared away a lot of the jungle, as well as wiping out most of the enemy troops; when the Americans advanced into the position after the airstrikes, they found a very large, and thoroughly destroyed, VC base.

Sporadic searches continued until 25 November, when the operation was finally concluded. It had grown from a single brigade's search and destroy mission to the largest US military action since the Korean War. The 9th VC Division had been badly damaged, and forced back into Cambodia to lick its wounds. Any potential threat of an imminent offensive against Saigon had been destroyed, and huge caches of VC food and weaponry—including 2,400 tons of rice, 24,000 grenades, and 2,000 pounds of explosives—had been discovered and destroyed.

As usual, air support by bombardment and napalm were key to the American success. Also, Air Force cargo planes had flown more than 3,000 sorties in support of the operation, including bringing 11,500 troops into position to join the battle. At one point, while Dupuy was concentrating his men at the Dau Tieng base, the C-123s were coming in at seven-minute intervals. In addition, tactical support aircraft dropped some 12,000 tons of ordnance on enemy positions.

As for the 196th LIB, General Westmoreland reluctantly acknowledged that it had been a mistake to give it to General deSaussure, a general with limited experience in infantry tactics. Many men of that brigade finished their tours in Vietnam thinking that they had been badly surprised, and nearly defeated, by a veteran enemy force during Operation Attleboro. It wasn't until decades later that the records of the former enemy revealed that the brigade had dished out far more punishment than it had received, and that the courage and sacrifice of the green soldiers during the three days of terrible battle had been the initial tipping point in the operation that had wrecked Colonel Cam's plans, and would soon send his powerful division reeling from the field of battle.

FIVE

COOLING OFF AN INSURGENT HOTBED

OPERATION CEDAR FALLS AND THE IRON TRIANGLE

> You go in there, leave the same day, and the VC are back that night. . . . We're going to clean out the place completely. . . . The purpose here is to deprive the VC of this area for good.
>
> MAJOR ALLEN DIXON, BRIEFING REPORTERS ABOUT OPERATION CEDAR FALLS, 7 JANUARY 1967

A region of dense forests, few roads, and only a couple of population centers, the area named the Iron Triangle had been a nest of the Viet Cong insurgency since long before the American military buildup in Vietnam. In fact, this narrow zone had been a focal point of Vietnamese resistance to the French colonizers since the 1880s. A relatively small area of about 120 square miles, it was located on the Saigon River, only 20 miles or so northwest of the capital city. With the major river marking the southwestern angle of the triangle, a smaller tributary stream—the Thi Tinh River—formed the eastern boundary, while the flat northern extent of the area was a densely wooded swath of the Thanh Dien Forest Preserve.

One major community, Ben Suc, stood very near the western edge of the triangle, right on the Saigon River. The town had been a base for the ARVN during the early years after Vietnam's division into two countries, but in 1964 the Viet Cong had captured the town and driven out the ARVN battalion-strength garrison. After executing Ben Suc's political leaders, the VC had barricaded the roads leading into and through the area and begun indoctrinating the people into the Communist National Liberation Front (NLF) doctrines, including a heavy dose of anti-American propaganda when the United States began to make its presence felt in the war. The VC taxed the population for rice or money, and many recruits for the insurgency came from the young men of the town of Ben Suc and the few surrounding hamlets and villages nearby.

Though the ARVN had made attempts to enter and garrison the triangle, those efforts had all been repulsed. A few months after the initial elements of the 1st Infantry Division arrived in country, a battalion of soldiers from the Big Red One had made a sweep into the Iron Triangle during October 1965, and had been repulsed by an ambush of small-arms and mortar fire that had killed six men and left more than 40 wounded. With plenty of other insurgent targets near enough to Saigon to present significant danger, the Americans left the triangle alone for the next 15 months. Still, it was too close to the capital, and too dense of an enemy stronghold, to be ignored for any longer.

Following the successful conclusion of Operation Attleboro (see Chapter Four), General Dupuy, commanding general of the 1st Infantry Division, was eager to launch another large operation against a VC "main unit" force, such as the 9th VC Division that had been so badly mauled by Attleboro. General Westmoreland was generally supportive of the idea, and the two commanding officers were looking forward to clearing VC-infested areas in War Zone C, near the Cambodian border. However, Westmoreland's chief of intelligence, Major General Joseph McChristian, raised a cautionary objection.

For almost a year, McChristian had overseen Project Rendezvous, which had been a massive intelligence-gathering operation targeting enemy activity in and around Saigon. Using extensive signals intelligence (SIGINT) to monitor VC radio activity, including frequency of broadcasts and the location of transmissions, as well as code-breaking efforts, the project also involved detailed logs of observation by US and ARVN officers. For example, intelligence specialists counted the number of sampans moving up and down the Saigon River, plotted the location of every small

VC attack or ambush, and tracked these locations on a map to make educated guesses regarding enemy headquarters and strongholds. This comprehensive gathering and scrutinizing of data was termed "pattern activity analysis," and had allowed McChristian to locate specific targets in the Iron Triangle, even though it was ground that had been essentially off-limits to American and ARVN forces during most of 1966.

The intelligence chief was convinced that the triangle presented a threat to Saigon itself, and argued that it would be foolish to ignore this location in favor of the big battle that Dupuy was proposing in War Zone C. Three attacks near the end of 1966 added support to this idea: on 4 December, a VC battalion attacked the huge air base at Tan Son Nhut, just west of the capital city, damaging or destroying more than a dozen aircraft. That same evening a bomb exploded inside an American compound in Saigon. Then, on 9 December, a VC force attacked and attempted to blow up the Binh Loi Bridge over the Saigon River, one of the key arteries connecting the capital to the regions north and west.

Just before the end of the year, American division, field-force, and MACV generals held a conference to determine the next course of action. The location was the headquarters of Lieutenant General Jonathan Seaman, commander of the II Field Force, which included all of the American units in the III Corps area—the zone of South Vietnam that included Saigon, its surroundings, and the area up to the Cambodian border including War Zones C and D. Two division commanders, General Dupuy of the 1st Infantry "Big Red One" Division, and Major General Fred Weyand, commanding the 25th Infantry "Tropic Lightning" Division, held divergent views regarding the next operation. Dupuy, desiring to destroy large enemy units or at least drive them into Cambodia, continued to advocate an attack into War Zone C, while Weyand wanted to follow McChristian's suggestion and root out the enemy presence in the smaller Iron Triangle first. General Westmoreland, who was also present, sided with his intelligence chief and General Weyand. Though the MACV commander indicated that he still intended to unleash strong American forces into War Zone C, this would have to wait until the triangle had been cleared.

The resulting operation would be called Cedar Falls, named after the hometown of Robert John Hibbs, a 1st Division infantryman who had post-humously been awarded the Medal of Honor for his actions in March 1966. Seaman proposed sealing off the triangle by at least six full brigades, creat-ing an "anvil" on the south bank of the Saigon River with two brigades under control of the 25th Division, and sending four brigades to hammer through the area and crush any enemy forces between the two. Unlike Attle-boro and later operations against large enemy formations, Cedar Falls was not expected to trap any main-force enemy units; rather, it was intended to discover and destroy many key VC infrastructure elements, and sweep the insurgents from a key stronghold menacingly close to the capital city.

Unlike War Zone C and areas farther out in the countryside, the Iron Triangle included a significant civilian presence; and those civilians were known to have been subjected to fierce indoctrination by the Viet Cong for several years prior to the operation. Seaman's plan also included the forcible removal of all civilians from the triangle, which would then be declared a free fire zone—meaning that anyone discovered there after the operation would be assumed to be an enemy combatant, subject to attack or capture. The civilians thus displaced were to be resettled by the South Vietnamese government, with help from the American government's USAID program.

Although several South Vietnamese Army units would be given roles in Operation Cedar Falls, General Seaman was convinced that the VC had penetrated the staffs of many of the ARVN units in the Saigon area. Since he was determined to achieve tactical surprise, he ordered that secu-rity requirements prevail over operational planning. Thus the South Viet-namese Army units that would participate would not receive their orders until the operation was already under way.

Preliminary moves to position forces for Cedar Falls commenced on 5 January 1967. The 272nd PLAF Regiment was known to be operating about 15 miles to the north of the target area, and the Americans wanted that potentially disruptive formation moved out of the way. General Seaman ordered the launch of a steady stream of airstrikes against the unit; these attacks had the intended effect of driving the VC regiment north to avoid the bombardment, which also removed it from the area of the upcoming operation. At the same time, elements of the 25th Infantry Division moved into a location just to the south of the anvil position, on the Saigon River. The once-green 196th Light Infantry Brigade, having been bloodied and seasoned during Operation Attleboro, was now attached to the 25th Division for the operation. The LIB prepared to move into the northern sector of the blocking position on the west bank of the river. In the process, it swept through the Ho Bo woods with four battalions, without encountering enemy resistance.

The beginning date, or D-Day, for Cedar Falls was set for 8 January. One day earlier, the central army intelligence office provided all of the attacking units with a printout listing the names and probable map coordinates of specific VC headquarters, installations, and facilities within the zone of the operation. These sites, based on General McChristian's pattern activity analysis, included hundreds of suspected insurgent centers, each precisely located. Although no large enemy forces were expected, three local force battalions and an equal number of independent companies were suspected to be operating in the triangle. Some American casualties were anticipated.

The largest community in the operational zone, Ben Suc, was expected to hold the greatest concentration of potential adversaries. The approaches to the village, with its population of about 3,500, were known to be heavily mined and defended with fortified strongpoints. Assuming that the enemy would defend the town against ground approach, General Seaman decided to concentrate most of his helicopter mobility on securing the village with an air assault in the opening hour of the operation.

D-DAY FOR CEDAR FALLS

The initial attack was made by a battalion from the 1st Division, the 1/26 Infantry (the "Blue Spaders") under the command of Lieutenant Colonel Alexander Haig. The unit had been moved to the Dau Tieng Air Base prior to Cedar Falls, from which, for deception purposes, it seemed to be preparing to move north into War Zone C. Sixty Hueys would transport 500 men in the first lift, the air armada being supported by 10 helicopter gunships.

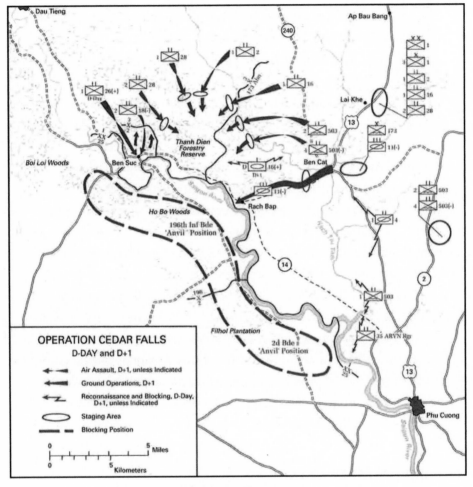

Operation Cedar Falls

CENTER OF MILITARY HISTORY, UNITED STATES ARMY

As the choppers swarmed in for the initial lift just after dawn on D-Day, often with less than a hundred feet between machines, a delicate aerial dance took place with the aircraft landing, loading, and hovering as they waited for the rest of the battalion to get into the air. With precise timing, Haig's infantrymen smoothly boarded their transport choppers so that, by 0725, all of them were aloft.

The pilots, following a precisely timed plan, took another 20 minutes to align the 60 choppers into two huge V-formations, each consisting of three strings of 10 Hueys. By 0745, they were 2,500 feet in the air, and departed from Dau Tieng on a bearing due south, a course taking them somewhat away from Ben Suc, until they reached a position about eight miles west of the target. At that point, the large formation of Hueys descended in unison to treetop height and made a beeline for the village at nearly 100 mph, arriving over the place at precisely 0800. Operation Cedar Falls was officially under way.

Four landing zones squared off a grid right around the village periphery. In keeping with the intended surprise, there had been no artillery or airstrike preparation of the LZs, so when the 60 loud helicopters roared into the space above Ben Suc, the villagers—not to mention the many Viet Cong present—were completely surprised. The first lift dropped most of Haig's battalion into three of the four LZs, those to the east, north, and west of the village. The infantrymen debarked in less than two minutes, and the helicopters flew back to Dau Tieng for the next lift as the first wave of soldiers spread out to secure the immediate area of the landing zones.

Now artillery began to fall, not on the village but pounding the woods to the north of Ben Suc. The purpose of the bombardment was to deter the flight of both villagers and Viet Cong into the jungle, and it worked as intended. That forest was also raked by rocket and machine-gun fire from the gunships that had accompanied the transport machines and continued to chatter back and forth through the noisy, smoky air.

As the troops deployed to surround the village on three sides, a lone Huey circled overhead. It was equipped with a loudspeaker, and an ARVN soldier addressed the people of Ben Suc at maximum volume, sternly ordering the villagers to stay in their homes. Anyone caught moving around would be considered to be Viet Cong, and therefore a target. By 0830, another lift of Hueys brought a company to garrison the LZ to the south of the village, and Ben Suc was completely surrounded.

Over the next two hours the Americans secured the town's outskirts, dealing with minefields and a few enemy snipers who were quickly killed. In all, about 40 VC died in these skirmishes, while a small number of US soldiers suffered wounds. After this interval, a second announcement broadcast from the airborne speaker ordered the villagers to congregate at the school, and about a thousand people complied right away. Helicopter-dropped propaganda leaflets showered Ben Suc, informing the villagers that if they were loyal to the government they were not in danger, that the Viet Cong had been deceiving them, and so forth. Sheaves of safe-conduct passes were included, offering any insurgent who wanted to do so the chance to defect, or, as it was termed, "rally" to the South Vietnamese side. Around 1030, another airlift brought in an ARVN battalion—not coincidentally the same unit that had been driven from Ben Suc some two years earlier—and several platoons of South Vietnamese rural police.

The latter organized the villagers into groups, segregating men between 15 and 45 years of age for further questioning, while the ARVN battalion commenced a search of the buildings and facilities of the village. By a little after noon, the assembled crowd of villagers had grown to about 3,500. A field kitchen was established to feed the sullen, but not violent residents of Ben Suc, and a medical station also offered care to anyone who needed assistance from a doctor.

The plan for Operation Cedar Falls called for the South Vietnamese government to provide a flotilla of river craft that would arrive at Ben Suc in the afternoon to carry the noncombatants to an assembly camp, also managed by the Saigon regime, in the river town and provincial capital of Phu Cuong, just to the southeast of the Iron Triangle. This part of the operation, however, completely failed to go according to plan. No transport boats of any shape or size showed up near the town on the afternoon of D-Day.

There were several explanations for this failure, which certainly undermined the efforts to convince Ben Suc's citizens that the government would welcome them back. Part of the fault lies with General Seaman's focus on security: here, that lack of communication prior to the operation got in the way of actual accomplishment. The South Vietnamese who were ordered to collect the boats for the evacuation were notified too late to act on 8 January and, apparently, they were also annoyed by the peremptory behavior of some of their American contacts. Nor were many preparations made in Phu Cuong to handle the eventual influx of refugees that would arrive one way or another in the next few days.

As the afternoon waned and it became clear there would be no transport during January 8, the citizens were told to return to their homes and await further orders. It would take two days before the transport, mainly trucks and landing craft drawn from 1st Infantry depots by an irate General Dupuy, would arrive to carry the people of Ben Suc—and their livestock, including numerous water buffalo—down to the assembly camp at the provincial capital. Many soldiers thus found themselves diverted from action. The mood of the citizenry would remain resentful but nonviolent. At one point even the unhappy villagers were forced to laugh when a squad of American soldiers were trying unsuccessfully to coax a very large, and very belligerent buffalo into a landing craft. Only when the 11-year-old boy from the family who owned the animal came along to direct the buffalo did the creature saunter placidly aboard.

The Army did use Chinook helicopters on the afternoon of D-Day to transport the assembled male population to Phu Cuong, where they were subjected to further questioning. About a hundred of these men were detained, including 28 who were determined to be Viet Cong. One of these turned out to be a platoon leader, while another—a mathematics professor trained in Peking—was apprehended as he tried to sneak out of the village through a rice paddy.

The rest of the operation proceeded much as planned. The "anvil" force included two brigades on the southwest bank of the Saigon River. The 196th Light Infantry Brigade, now under the command of General Richard Knowles, occupied the left, northernmost position, beginning just north of (and across the river from) Ben Suc, continuing down the river-bank through the Ho Bo woods, to the midpoint of the blocking position near the Filhol Rubber Plantation. Reinforced by two mechanized battalions, the 196th moved into its position with little resistance, and soon had established a front along the entire bank of the river in their sector.

The 2nd Brigade, 25th Infantry Division, covered the rest of the anvil position, occupying the rubber plantation and continuing down the river-bank just south of the Saigon River's junction with the Thi Tinh River, which flowed from north to south into the larger river. Several battalions of the 2nd Brigade used helicopter airlift to move into positions, and one of these encountered a full battalion of VC right on their intended LZ. This resulted in several prolonged firefights in which the Americans gave better than they got; by the end of the day, the VC melted away, leaving 100 dead behind. Six men of the 2nd Brigade were killed in these encounters, while some three dozen more were wounded.

On the eastern edge of the operational area, the 11th Armored Cavalry "Blackhorse" Regiment was attached to the Big Red One for this operation. It had remained in its base in the Saigon area before the operation in order to maintain the element of surprise, but first thing on D-Day it swept up Highway 13, covering some 60 miles in the first few hours of the operation. These troopers then advanced to form a cordon along the Thi Tinh, which sealed off the second of the three sides of the Iron Triangle, the north-south boundary on the east. They ended D-Day in position to attack into the triangle the following day.

Operations along the northern, heavily forested leg of the triangle also proceeded smoothly on 8 January. Although General Dupuy had initially intended his 2nd Brigade to handle this search, the amount of enemy personnel and matériel discovered at Ben Suc caused him to revise his plan, and he ordered his 3rd Brigade and intended reserve to move into the forest on D-Day+1. On 9 January, the 3rd Brigade, 1st Division, and the 173rd Airborne Brigade—like the 11th ACR, attached to the 1st Division for the operation—flew by air transport into several LZs that had been cleared in the Thanh Dien Forest.

These landings were carefully staged to utilize the available helicopter transport efficiently and effectively. Following a series of B-52 bombing raids that initially pummeled the landing zones, more than a dozen batteries of artillery combined their firepower to bombard the first of the seven potential LZs that had been selected. After half an hour, the big guns started targeting the second LZ while a 60-helicopter flight lifted an entire battalion onto the initial landing zone. Helicopter gunships accompanied the lift, raking the surrounding jungle with guns and rockets. The landing was so successful that the same procedure was repeated for six more LZs during the day, so that seven battalions had been dropped into forward positions in the triangle before nightfall. Only in the last LZ was trouble encountered, when the clearing turned out to be mined; as a result, that battalion set down in Ben Suc and would move overland to its location on 10 January.

At the same time as the 1st Division battalions were reaching their landing zones, the eastern leg of the triangle came under attack by the American units lined up along the Thi Thanh River. The punch here was thrown by Task Force Deane, named for Brigadier General John Deane, commander of the 173rd Airborne Brigade. His brigade was reinforced by two squadrons from the 11th ACR. The task force moved west first thing in the morning on 9 January, using two bridges to cross the Thi Tinh and then charging down an overgrown dirt road toward the center of the triangle and a small hamlet known as Rach Bap. The column detached squads along the way so that they could form a blocking screen to prevent VC movement toward the south, where several ARVN units were moving up to enter the triangle on the following day.

INTO THE WOODS

By the end of D-Day+1, the north and east sides of the Iron Triangle were blocked by powerful units. From west to east and using the face of a clock for reference, the units aligned with the 3rd Brigade covering from the Saigon River at 10 o'clock around to a juncture with the 173rd at about 1 o'clock; the 1–3 o'clock sector belonged to the airborne troops, while the Blackhorse Regiment completed the seal to the east, from around 3 to 5 o'clock. All three units pushed their companies and battalions south and westward from their landing zones, encountering little active resistance but finding lots of signs of recent VC activity. The cavalry column was followed by a procession of massive bulldozers operated by engineers. These actions included the initial use of the Rome plow, a huge, armored bulldozer with a blade sharp enough to cut off large trees at the base. Their initial task was to make sure the road was passable, but they quickly set out to widen it.

Once the task force's leading elements reached Rach Bap, which they did by midmorning, a helicopter announcement similar to the one used at Ben Suc was used to order the residents to stay in their homes and await further orders. It was intended that they would be collected and organized for transport, but for an unknown reason some American soldiers set several houses on fire. This triggered a general panic, and most of the hamlet's residents fled into the forest, leaving their possessions and animals behind.

With the search of Ben Suc proceeding relatively peacefully, the anvil forces had assumed their stations and were fully posted along the Saigon River. There they had occasional opportunities to capture or kill VC trying to cross to their bank of the waterway—at one point a raft carrying 15 VC drifted toward a position occupied by a 25th Division company. The Americans used a 90-mm gun loaded with canister to destroy the raft and kill the exposed enemy soldiers.

By plan and practicality, the main action on D-Day+1 and beyond would involve the clearing of the Thanh Dien Forest and the other jungle-covered regions of the triangle. The 196th Brigade and the 2nd Brigade, 25th Infantry Division, would continue to comb the forests along the south and west bank of the Saigon River. More engineers and bulldozers moved in to start clearing paths to the river and along its environs.

CIVILIAN SNAFU

General Dupuy seemed to be showing up everywhere in his division's area of operations. At Ben Suc, he watched the refugees loading their animals aboard transport, and when he saw a panicked sow running around, desperately seeking her brood of piglets, he barked an order demanding that the porcine family be reunited without delay. Naturally, it happened. When he came upon a collection of the civilians who had fled Rach Bap and made their way across the Thi Tinh River to an impromptu collection and holding area with only the clothes on their backs, he directed that they be returned to their village so that they could gather their possessions—though they, like the rest of the civilians in the Iron Triangle, were still to be relocated.

Dupuy's most dramatic confrontation occurred when he visited the large holding camp at Phu Cuong, where the refugees were to be mustered before being moved to their new homes. The general had suggested even before the operation began that the 1st Division be given responsibility for feeding, transporting, and housing these civilians, but he had been over-ruled. The task had been assigned to the South Vietnamese, to be coordi-nated by an American civilian adviser—John Vann, the head of the US Agency for International Development (USAID) in Vietnam. Vann was a conscientious official, a former colonel in the Army Rangers, and a man possessing great familiarity with Vietnamese culture. He was a good man for the job, but he was hamstrung by his position between the US Army and the South Vietnamese government.

The South Vietnamese not only failed to transport the evacuees, but were very slow to react to the growing number of refugees arriving at Phu Cuong. This was probably due to a combination of factors: resentment of American high-handedness; shortness of notice (because of mission secu-rity) to make the necessary preparations for such a move; and an institu-tional reluctance to waste any effort or resources on a population that the government deemed to be enemies of the people.

On 11 January, while the movement of the refugees was in full swing, General Dupuy visited the large relocation camp in Phu Cuong. He quickly decided that the conditions in the camp were terrible as they related to hygiene, shelter, food, and medical care. He told General Seaman that his division should take over the refugee situation, and rebuked Vann in forceful terms when the latter called him on the telephone to try to work out the situation. In any event, Seaman wanted the Vietnamese government to handle the issue, and denied Dupuy's request.

Nevertheless, the Big Red One did furnish truckloads of tents, clothing, food, and water for the camp's residents, while Vann's efforts finally persuaded his South Vietnamese counterparts to put more effort into the relocation project. John Vann would continue to direct these efforts long after Operation Cedar Falls was concluded. By summer, about 6,000 people who had been living in the Iron Triangle had been relocated to an area south of Saigon, and were living in concrete block buildings with about the same level of support and comfort as the families of ARVN soldiers. Nobody claimed to be entirely happy about the whole procedure, and the refugees' own wishes were never consulted, but the process was handled with at least a minimal level of humanity and care.

AN UNDERGROUND VILLAGE

Meanwhile, the searching and sniping through the triangle continued. South Vietnamese forces combing through Ben Suc found that the community, which looked like a typical village on the surface, in fact concealed a complete network of underground facilities. Some of these tunnel and compartment complexes extended three levels deep, and included storage facilities, medical treatment areas, headquarters rooms containing bountiful reams of documents, maps, and lists, as well as rooms for the manufacturing of materials including explosives, and other chambers devoted to large sewing shops where VC uniforms could be produced. An incredibly complex network of tunnels connected all of these locations, clearly representing the work of decades.

The tunnel network was literally too big to be thoroughly searched. By 13 January, the last of the village's residents had been removed, and the destruction began in earnest. The Rome plows now rolled in to destroy every building in Ben Suc. As these massive excavators scraped away the ground, it was not uncommon for additional tunnel entrances to be revealed—sometimes with VC popping right up from the ground in the wake of a bulldozer's passage.

The destruction of the village took a full five days. When the ARVN troops departed, after mining every bit of intelligence data they could find, the engineers dug a wide hole some 30 feet deep, right in the center of the underground complex. They filled this pit with many of the explosives that had been captured in the village and throughout the Iron Triangle, then scraped a thick layer of dirt on top of the explosives to channel as much of the blast underground as possible. Finally, the engineers set a fuse timed to burn for more than two hours, and then got the heck out of there. The explosion shook the ground just after sunset on 17 January, reducing what had once been a thriving village to the status of a smoldering crater.

All through the Iron Triangle enemy underground emplacements were being discovered. Some proved to be intelligence gold, including the signal and coding center for the VC's Military Region 4—the headquarters responsible for activities just outside of Saigon. A crucial find was a list naming South Vietnamese officials who had proven helpful to the insurgents, and others describing a complicated black market in which American goods, weapons, and supplies were being stolen and sold for use by the enemy. In another location, an underground hospital with more than a hundred beds turned up. In that case, the presiding doctor and his staff put up a savage fight, killing several Americans before they finally escaped during the hours of darkness.

A new trend in the Vietnam War presented itself in this latter stage of Operation Cedar Falls, as for the first time the Americans and ARVN were taking as many enemy prisoners as they were killing enemy soldiers in action. Vigorous efforts to persuade former VC to return to the government's side were beginning to pay off, as nearly 500 such "ralliers" were convinced to come over. Some of these wrote eloquent pleas to their former comrades, calling them out by name, informing them that they were being well treated, that their families had been fed and sheltered, and urging the VC to turn against the Communist cause and side with the South Vietnamese government again.

RESULTS

By the time Cedar Falls terminated on 26 January, the former enemy sanctuary of the Iron Triangle bore only a passing resemblance to the place it had been. Roads had been plowed back and forth through the jungle, ensuring that access would be much easier for any allied units that might be compelled to return here. All of the settlements had been razed, and all the inhabitants moved out, so those VC who did move through the area found no local population base to support them with food or information. And since the area had been designated as a free fire zone, anyone attempting to cross the triangle needed to do so very carefully or face the real chance of a sudden and fiery death from the sky.

Furthermore, General McChristian's pattern activity analysis of intelligence gathering was vindicated in a big way. To give one example, the units of the 11th ACR had been given information on 177 possible enemy positions based on pattern activity analysis. During the operation, the cavalrymen located 158 locations corresponding to the information, with many of them within a couple of a hundred yards of the coordinates McChristian's men had identified on the maps.

Finally, nearly a half-million documents had been recovered from various VC facilities, with about 10 percent of them being deemed useful enough for examination and translation in the Combined Document Exploitation Center located in the capital. Included in the mass of data were the names of several VC secret agents working in Saigon and its environs, as well as crucial details about the organization and structure of the Viet Cong throughout the country.

Though the fixed battles had been limited, at least 700 VC had been confirmed as killed in action during Operation Cedar Falls. American fatalities numbered 72, with another 11 ARVN soldiers losing their lives. Very many concrete, heavily fortified bunkers were left behind to be targeted by B-52 raids. The tactics employed by II Field Force were also proved effective to a great extent. The security precautions prior to the operation hampered coordination with the South Vietnamese, but did ensure that the initial entry into the Iron Triangle achieved complete surprise. General Knowles wrote enthusiastically about the use of mechanized forces in support of search and destroy operations, even when few roads were available.

General Seaman, too, was satisfied with the operation. He cited five areas in which Cedar Falls had greatly degraded enemy operational capabilities: (1) the loss of a base area the VC had taken 20 years to develop; (2) the vast amounts of rice and supplies that had been denied to enemy forces; (3) the depopulating of the area, which would prevent the VC from reestablishing any kind of significant activity there; (4) the intelligence haul that compromised a number of VC operations; and (5) the impact that the operation's success would have on the morale and planning of North Vietnam, the COSVN hierarchy, and VC sympathizers in South Vietnam.

General Dupuy, for his part, concluded that Operation Cedar Falls was "the most significant operation thus far conducted by the 1st Infantry Division." He lauded the efforts of the engineers, in particular, for clearing so much of the jungle, allowing for ready access to the triangle in the future, should it become necessary. He went so far as to call the operation a "turning point" in what he readily admitted he expected to be a long war.

Cedar Falls was, indeed, a significant victory. It was the first big battle of 1967, but it most certainly would not be the last. And unlike what happened in Cedar Falls, when II Field Force soon ventured into War Zone C in force, they would find an enemy waiting there that was more than willing to meet the Americans in open battle.

SIX

PLAYING HORSESHOES WITH CHARLIE

OPERATION JUNCTION CITY
HITS WAR ZONE C

They're all over my track! Dust me with canister!
COMMANDER, TRACK 10, TROOP A, 3RD SQUADRON,
5TH CAVALRY, 20 MARCH 1967

Although he was quite satisfied with the clearing of the Iron Triangle, General Westmoreland wasn't about to let his subordinate commanders rest on their laurels. The bigger aim of clearing War Zone C remained very much on his front burner. The commanding generals of his divisions in the Saigon area supported this concept enthusiastically. The planning for the next big operation, already in early detailed stages, had only been put on hold for a month or so to allow Operation Cedar Falls to run its course.

The next offensive would be called Operation Junction City, named for a community near the 1st Infantry Division's home base in Kansas. The core units of the operation would be the same as those that performed so well in the triangle: the 25th Infantry Division, under General Weyand, and the Big Red One—now with a new commander, Major General John Hay.

This transfer of command reflected one significant way in which the United States' war in Vietnam differed from earlier conflicts such as World War II: as with the soldiers in the ranks, officers of both low and high rank were routinely transferred in and out of their positions. For enlisted men, notably draftees, this was good for morale because it seemed more fair to the men than would an unlimited term of deployment. For officers, the motivation was to expose as many of them as possible to actual wartime operations.

The bold plan for Junction City involved blocking forces quickly taking positions around a large part of War Zone C, in the shape of an inverted horseshoe, with a two-brigade mobile force sweeping into the horseshoe from the south. Soldiers familiar with the overall plan quickly applied a name to the offensive: "playing horseshoes with Charlie." ("Charlie," of course, was the widely used slang term for the enemy, both a singular soldier and any and all sizes of units.) The western boundary of the area was based generally on a north-south road, Highway 22. The northern rim, extending practically to the Cambodian border, was demarked by a path called Road 246, which was in fact little more than a track for carts and foot traffic that meandered through the scrub and forest just on the South Vietnamese side of the border; while the eastern boundary was another fairly narrow road called Route 4.

An extra brigade, the 3rd of the newly arriving 4th Infantry Division, was attached to the 25th for Junction City, and as was the case during Cedar Falls, the division would also control the 196th Light Infantry Brigade. The division's first assignment was to block the western flank of the horseshoe, generally following the line of Highway 22 from the start line up to the Cambodian border, including the very northwestern corner of the top of the arch.

The top of the horseshoe, in the center and eastern edges, would get covered by the 1st Brigade of the 1st Division, reinforced by two small ARVN units, a ranger battalion, and a troop of armored cavalry that was designated Task Force Wallace. The 173rd Airborne Brigade, under 1st Division command, would place three battalions around the northeastern curve of the horseshoe. Third Brigade, 1st Division, would place four battalions in blocking positions along Route 4, on the eastern boundary.

The mobile force at the open, southern end of the horseshoe would also operate under 25th Division control, and consisted of the 2nd Brigade (25th Division) on the left, with three infantry battalions, and the 11th Armored Cavalry Regiment, with two cavalry squadrons and an attached mechanized

infantry battalion to the right. These brought the total strength of the attacking forces to 22 battalions. Two ARVN Marine battalions would also support the attack, while the 1st Brigade, 9th Division, would be available near
Saigon if needed as a reserve. Seventeen artillery battalions would occupy a
series of firebases around the rim of the battle zone, and of course massive
air support would be available to hit preplanned targets and to support the
ground forces on an on-call basis.

The horseshoe did not encompass the whole of War Zone C, leaving out
a narrow strip to the west of Highway 22, extending up to the Cambodian
border, including a sizable bulge of South Vietnamese territory called the
Elephant's Ear (because of its appearance on the map) to the north and west
of the arch. The second part of Zone C not included was larger, and included
some of the territory that had seen earlier fighting during Operation Attleboro and the battle on Minh Thanh Road; the sector fell mainly between the
north-south highways of Route 4 and Route (or Highway) 13.

The targets of Operation Junction City were deemed to be worthy of
this massive effort. Most significantly, Westmoreland and the II Field Force
commander, Lieutenant General Jonathan Seaman, hoped to capture or destroy the main headquarters of the COSVN as well as to locate Senior General Nguyen Chi Thanh; they also hoped to disrupt several subordinate
headquarters and a number of depots and other enemy installations. It was
also hoped that several old familiar foes, the 9th VC Division and the 101st
NVA Regiment, could be cornered and brought to battle, though MACV
had no reliable intelligence that these units were present in the horseshoe in
significant numbers. Still, the area had been under Viet Cong control since
the country had been divided in 1954, and the American high command
felt confident that the operation could create a significant disruption in
enemy operations and logistics.

For the first time during the war, II Field Force established an advance
HQ near the intended scene of fighting, choosing to establish this at Dau
Tieng. As he had done during Cedar Falls, for security reasons General
Seaman declined to inform the South Vietnamese high command of the
operation prior to D-Day. Unlike the move into the Iron Triangle, however,

the target area of Operation Junction City was almost unpopulated, so it would be assumed that anyone encountered there was hostile.

PITCHING THE HORSESHOE

Operation Junction City's D-Day was set for 22 February 1967. Deception was again the order of the day, so most of the units were positioned well back from the horseshoe. The exception was the 25th Division, which had previously conducted Operation Gadsden along the Cambodian border. This preliminary action served to disrupt several key border crossings known to be logistically important to the Viet Cong, and also left the 3rd Brigade, 4th Division (attached to the 25th), in ready position to move onto Route 22 and assume its blocking position on the western flank of the horseshoe.

As for the rest of the blocking forces, surprise was of the essence—and the means to achieving that surprise was speed. To that end, all of the forces around the northern rim of the horseshoe would move in by air. This vertical insertion entailed two significant components: first, the only battalion-sized parachute landing of the Vietnam War; and second, the unprecedented number of more than 250 helicopters transferring a total of eight battalions to landing zones along the northern rim of the intended battle zone.

The day began with a series of B-52 Arc Light bombing raids against locations suspected to hold enemy headquarters or troop concentrations. Helicopter and tactical airstrikes began against the first landing zone to be occupied, a meadow only about a mile south of the Cambodian border, and some six miles northwest of the town of Katum, which marked the crossroads where the track of "Road" 246 met the northern terminus of Route 4. Even as these strikes pounded the meadow, the 1st Battalion, 28th Infantry, boarded 70 Hueys at the Minh Thanh airstrip. The battalion was landed without opposition by 0730, with the helicopters returning to the airstrip to pick up two more battalions to be landed, successively, at LZs about three and eight miles west of the position of the 1/28. Troops quickly spread out along the path of Road 246, securing the northeastern rim of the horseshoe.

At the same time, more helicopters lifted a battalion of troops of the 196th

LIB from their home base at Tây Ninh, depositing them in an LZ very near the intersection of Route 22 and Road 246, about two-thirds of the way up the western leg of the horseshoe. The other two battalions of the 196th moved north from Tây Ninh by truck in order to lessen the time needed for the Hueys to fly back and forth; the wave of choppers returning from the first insertion met the truck convoy, loaded up a second battalion, and transported it to the second LZ, then repeated the process with the 3rd Battalion, completing the placements just a little after noon. None of either brigade's helicopter assaults encountered more resistance than a little bit of enemy sniping from the woods.

The parachute drop, to be made by the 2nd Battalion, 503rd Infantry—a component of the 173rd Airborne Brigade—would turn out to be at least a little controversial. General Deane, commander of the 173rd, would jump with his men, and the attack had the blessing of General Westmoreland himself, who had also spent time as an airborne officer—and in fact had commanded the only airborne regiment to fight in the Korean War.

There were good reasons to make the airborne attack. Certainly a parachute drop was a means to put a lot of men on the ground in a hurry, which would increase the chance of surprise, and it would free up a lot of helicopters to be used for other insertions. Still, there were some who thought that it was more of a "glory" exercise than a true tactical necessity. There were inherent dangers to making a parachute landing in enemy-controlled territory, since no soldier is more vulnerable to enemy small-arms fire than a paratrooper slowly drifting downward out of a clear, sunlit sky. Accidents and injuries upon landing were also to be expected, but in the end these risks were deemed to be operationally acceptable by the man who really mattered: the commanding general of MACV.

Airlift for the 845 men who would make the parachute attack was provided by a mere 13 huge C-130 "Hercules" transport planes, each making a single sortie with the flight originating from the large air base at Bien Hoa, near Saigon. The target landing zone was a relatively broad stretch of savannah just north of Katum, which, like the other LZs, had been punished severely by tactical airstrikes and helicopter gunships before the drop. The 13 massive transport planes flew over the landing zone in formation, each disgorging two "sticks" of 15 men on the first pass. Wheeling around grace-fully, the planes crossed over again, each dropping another 30 paratroop-ers. For several minutes the skies were filled with a bouquet of blossoming chutes as the airborne soldiers drifted down. (One of those troopers, Chief Warrant Officer Howard Melvin, was a grizzled veteran of airborne opera-tions, having jumped into North Africa, Sicily, Italy, and Normandy during World War II.)

A very few VC snipers took shots from concealed positions below, resulting in one paratrooper wounded, while 11 others suffered relatively minor injuries, mostly from awkward landings. All in all, however, the jump was remarkably successful. Just in case it had gone otherwise, how-ever, a battalion of the 173rd had been standing by with 70 helicopters to reinforce the landing; given the smooth landing, that battalion was heli-coptered into another LZ in the vicinity of Katum.

With the paratroops on the ground and organized around unit com-mand posts before 0930, the flights of C-130s resumed overhead, this time to make supply drops. Though some of these loads suffered damage, every-thing from rations to radios to vehicles and even medium artillery pieces was soon unpacked and ready for use by the paratroopers.

One glitch in the plan resulted in a minor disappointment, though not any injury. General Deane had maintained considerable secrecy about the target of the landing, even to the point of designating another LZ some 20 miles away, and only making the change to the actual target the day before the landing. General Westmoreland was planning to observe the launch from his own air-craft, but he didn't get word of the revised location. As a result, he was watching the dummy LZ as the actual parachute drop began, and was only able to fly over and witness the last of the airborne soldiers reaching the ground.

On the ground, the 3rd Brigade, 1st Division, began a northward drive along Route 4, with an armored cavalry squadron (the well-experienced 1/4th) in the lead. They lost some vehicles, fewer than a dozen in total, to enemy mines, and the engineers needed to install three AVLBs at stream crossings, but the column was able to join up with the 173rd Airborne by 1500, sealing the eastern leg of the horseshoe. Engineering elements of the brigade would be busy through the next days, improving the road and clearing the approaches to either side. At the same time, the 3rd Brigade, 4th Division—already nearly in place due to Operation Gadsden—advanced slightly east from Route 22 to secure a blocking position on the western leg of the horseshoe.

Finally, the 2nd Brigade, 25th Infantry Division, moved up to the western extent of Route 247, which marked the open base of the horseshoe, while the 11th Armored Cavalry advanced to the same start line on the 2nd Brigade's right flank. All of the blocking forces were in place, and the two mobile units were ready to commence their maneuvers on D-Day+1. Total American casualties of the first day included four men killed, and another two dozen wounded. Some small-arms fire had been given and taken, but it was not known if any VC had been hit.

CLEARING THE HORSESHOE

On 23 February, D-Day+1, the 2nd Brigade of the Tropic Lightning Division and the "Blackhorse" 11th Armored Cavalry Regiment pushed northward from their starting positions along Route 247 at the base of the horseshoe. Although the more or less flat terrain was not the most tangled the Americans had entered in Vietnam, it presented enough challenges that the going was slow, as water obstacles had to be bypassed, thickets penetrated, and gullies and ravines traversed—though no enemy resistance was encountered.

Still, by the end of the day, every unit except one squadron of the Blackhorse Regiment was behind schedule. To balance out the rest of the advance, General Weyand shifted the operational boundaries between the infantry brigade and the more mobile armored cavalry so that the 11th ACR would advance to the top of the horseshoe and then wheel left, filling in some of the space that had originally been marked for the attention of the 2nd Brigade. The general also ordered Task Force Alpha, two battalions of ARVN Marines, to be airlifted into the 196th LIB sector on 24 February. They would join the armored cavalry in sweeping the interior of the horseshoe.

As the mobile forces swept forward, the units poised around the rim of the horseshoe continued to fortify their positions and to carry out search and destroy missions into the surrounding countryside. One unit of the Big Red One discovered a large base camp that included shower facilities, and also contained a stash of thousands of pieces of footwear made from worn-out truck tires—the so-called Ho Chi Minh sandals commonly worn by the VC. But aside from a few very small-scale encounters, no enemy troops were revealed.

The same pattern continued on D-Day+2 and beyond, with many enemy installations turning up, but few to no actual VC. As day after day of the advance passed without a significant encounter with enemy troops, General Weyand became increasingly frustrated. Engineers were well on their way to finishing a new airstrip at Katum and were clearing the flanks of Route 4 out to 75 yards from the roadway. But where were the Viet Cong?

On the northern edge of the horseshoe, the 1st Brigade of the Big Red One fought its way against light opposition into what proved to be a complex of camps associated with the military affairs headquarters of COSVN. Though the Americans encountered some resistance here, engaging in small-scale firefights, the complex was not seriously defended, even though it proved to contain large mess halls, supply depots, classrooms, and a trove of supplies— including three dozen high-quality Japanese transistor radios with thousands of batteries for the same. They also found recreation halls complete with Ping-Pong tables, and a kitchen containing living livestock and partially prepared food. A calendar posted on the wall of the kitchen was turned to 23 February—the day before the 1st Division men had entered the complex.

By the end of the third day of Junction City, the search of the horseshoe was well advanced, and had yielded many locations and matériels, but little combat. Total losses at this point were 42 confirmed enemy KIA and a few prisoners/deserters, while American units had suffered 14 killed, with nearly a hundred wounded, almost all from sniper attacks and mines.

On 26 February, one company of the 4th Division, operating on the western side of the horseshoe along Route 22, came upon a battalion of the VC 271st Regiment in a large encampment west of the road—and thus outside the boundary of the original horseshoe. The outnumbered Americans came under heavy fire for a short time as the VC swarmed around both flanks to surround them. Only the arrival of reinforcements allowed the unit to extricate itself. Five Americans died, with 19 wounded, while 11 VC were confirmed KIA.

On 28 February, a company of the 173rd Brigade made a significant intelligence find in the forest north and east of Katum. In what appeared to be an office of media and propaganda for a COSVN public affairs team, US soldiers discovered more than a hundred reels of movie film, and many more color and black-and-white photographs. In future weeks, intelligence analysts would pore over the films and pictures, identifying several influential South Vietnamese who were thought to be loyal to the government, but in fact turned out to be working with the Viet Cong. They also identified high-ranking North Vietnamese, both military and civilian, photographed in local settings yet who had not been known to have visited South Vietnam. The haul also included numerous pictures, and several busts, of Communist leaders.

At that same time, the most furious firefight of Junction City to date erupted in the eastern edge of the operational area, also outside of the horseshoe. Company B of the 1st Battalion, 16th Infantry, began to move eastward from the battalion's bivouac along Route 4 at 0800, advancing toward a stream known as Prek Klok. That same name had been applied to a firebase right off of Route 4, just a few miles north of the 1/16's position. A 105-mm howitzer battery of the 2nd Battalion, 33rd Artillery, had already been installed at the firebase, and as was customary during 1st Infantry Division operations, the guns were dropping a steady barrage of marching fire in front of the company as it moved eastward on its search and destroy mission.

The company was under the command of Captain Donald Ulm. While moving through an area of dense jungle, littered by huge deadfalls, he posted his 3rd Platoon in the lead, with the other two platoons trailing slightly behind and positioned to the right and left. While advancing, Company B employed the cloverleaf search tactic that General Dupuy had previously instituted. Small-arms fire, quickly joined by at least three machine guns, broke out against the front of 3rd Platoon at 1030 as the company entered a more open area of ground, terrain broken by patches of underbrush and some of those big, downed trees.

The firing quickly spread from the front to the right front of the lead platoon, and Captain Ulm requested that the artillery shift to cover the new enemy position. A command-and-control Huey was soon overhead, and a forward air controller arrived shortly thereafter. The first airstrikes would come in with loads of cluster bomb units (CBUs). These were deadly antipersonnel weapons that exploded at treetop height and sprayed the ground underneath with a blanket of shrapnel; with a blast radius limited to about 30 yards, they could be dropped close to friendly units.

Despite the pressure of frequent airstrikes, the Communist ambushers pressed home the attacks, and by 1050 had cut off the 3rd Platoon from the rest of the company. For two hours the Americans fought to link their units together, which they did just before 1300—at which time another enemy maneuver completed an encirclement, leaving the entire company surrounded. For the next three hours, the fight raged continuously, Ulm's men using smoke grenades to direct airstrikes almost on top of their own positions. After 54 tactical airstrikes, and hours of artillery, the enemy attacks slackened off, and by the time the brigade commander had pushed another two companies into the area, the battle was over.

Inspection of the dead revealed that the company had been attacked by a battalion of the 101st NVA Regiment, one of the units that had been an original target of the operation. In the bloody battle the Americans suffered heavily, with 25 US soldiers killed in the fight and an equal number wounded. The retreating NVA regiment left 167 bodies on the field.

As noted, this attack took place just outside the edge of the horseshoe, to the east of the operation's original perimeter, and was more significant than any combat that had occurred in the target zone. By 1 March, General Seaman, still frustrated by the lack of enemy combat units within the original area of attack, had resolved to expand Junction City's scope. Though the Americans had discovered plenty of VC bases, and even some HQs, there had been very little contact with enemy soldiers—they seemed to have gotten away just in the nick of time. One possible explanation for this emerged some forty years after the war, as author Dinh Thi Van published a book in Hanoi strongly suggesting that a spy in Saigon had tipped off COSVN about the intended target of the initial attack.

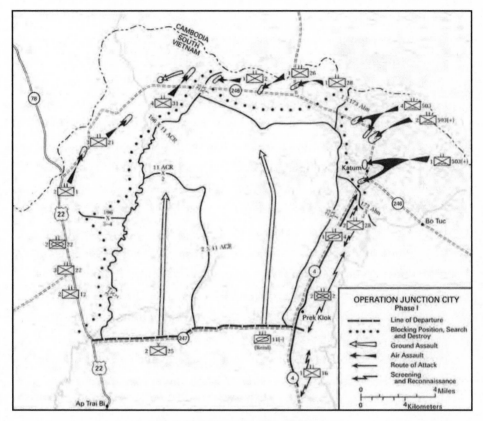

Operation Junction City Phase 1

CENTER OF MILITARY HISTORY, UNITED STATES ARMY

JUNCTION CITY PHASE I FINALE

On the first day of March, the 1st and 25th Infantry Divisions were ordered to break from the confines of the original horseshoe perimeter. The 25th, starting on the northwest corner of the arch, was directed to turn westward and sweep very close to the Cambodian border, continuing a search and destroy operation through the area termed the Elephant's Ear.

General Weyand pulled his 2nd Brigade, and the 196th LIB, back to their home bases at Cu Chi and Tây Ninh, respectively, while he used the 3rd Brigade, 4th Division, to hold a blocking position along Highway 22. The 11th ACR was to strike north to the border, then wheel left and follow that national boundary down to the 3rd Brigade. Any enemy forces encountered—most likely the 271st VC Regiment—would either be trapped by the maneuver or forced to withdraw into Cambodia.

The cavalry began the maneuver on 7 March, and a few days later came upon another huge base camp that had only recently been abandoned. On the 11th, advancing American units encountered a second camp, and in this one a strong contingent of VC put up a furious defense. The leading troop of armored cavalry was rocked by volleys of RPGs and recoilless rifles as well as small arms. A full company of VC occupied well-fortified bunkers and trenches, and showed no inclination to leave as the cavalry spread out and increased the pressure. The position was barely more than 200 yards from the river separating Cambodia from South Vietnam, and in order to keep the enemy from pulling across the border, helicopter gunships flew up and down the waterway, strafing any Communist soldiers they spotted. At night, a continuous series of flares illuminated the scene, even as a steady rain of artillery and air attacks pounded the enemy strongpoint.

However, by morning it was determined that the enemy survivors had managed to slip through the net, though they left behind the bodies of 28 comrades killed in the action. An investigation of the site yielded an unusual find: two massive, electronic printing presses that had been manufactured two years earlier in China. Each weighed nearly a ton, and was capable of printing tabloid-sized papers and pamphlets. Somehow, the

Viet Cong had transported the huge presses, and the generators needed to power them, deep into the jungle to this remote hideaway.

This was the last significant action for the 11th ACR during Phase I of Junction City as, on 15 March, it was posted back to its original bases east of Saigon. On that same day the 3rd Brigade, 4th Division, was pulled back to Dau Tieng.

The units of General Hay's 1st Division, meanwhile, were also expanding their search beyond the original horseshoe, focusing on areas to the east of Route 4. General Deane's 173rd Airborne Brigade remained attached to the Big Red One for this part of the operation, and on the afternoon of 3 March, a company of the 173rd was hit hard by an ambush. The attackers proved to be a battalion of the 70th Guard Regiment, the unit that was reputedly responsible for the security of the COSVN headquarters. In an intense, furious 30-minute battle, 20 Americans became casualties; 39 VC bodies were discovered after the enemy withdrew under the cover of darkness. That same day other elements of the 173rd about 10 miles to the south fought and killed a half-dozen VC that were subsequently identified as belonging to the 272nd Regiment. This confirmed the presence of yet another enemy main-force unit in the expanded operations zone.

General Hay maintained his 3rd Brigade along the length of Route 4, where three firebases had been established and were in the process of being improved. They ranged from Suoi Da in the south to Prek Klok—where a new Special Forces camp was under construction—about halfway up the eastern side of the horseshoe, and to Katum in the north. These camps were less than 10 miles apart, in ready range to offer supporting artillery fire to their neighbors.

The most robust of the three firebases was Prek Klok, which was garrisoned by some 900 men, including a combat engineer battalion, most of a mechanized infantry battalion (2nd of the 2nd Infantry), and two batteries of artillery, all under the command of Lieutenant Colonel Edward Collins. The camp was very near the site of a COSVN military affairs headquarters, and it was later learned that when the senior officers of that enemy HQ desired to make an escape, they decided that a diversionary attack against the Prek

Klok firebase was necessary. On 2 March, they had ordered the 272nd Regiment to make this attack, and over the following days the VC tactical units began to move into position.

By 7 March, Collins's men had encountered enough small groups of VC in the vicinity to suspect that something was up. That night the camp's defenses were improved by posting a ring of APCs in a "wagon train" circle around the perimeter, with the boxy armored M-113s posted at 50-yard intervals. The guns of Batteries B and C, 2nd Battalion, 33rd Artillery, were placed in the middle of the circle, which also included a small airstrip; twin 40-mm "Duster" light antiaircraft vehicles as well as quad .50-caliber self-propelled guns, were posted at key points around the ring. Foxholes were excavated in the spaces between each of the APCs; in the event of battle they would be manned by infantrymen, combat engineers, and whatever artillerymen were not needed to operate the guns. By the night of 10 March, the enemy was ready to attack—and thanks to the vigilance of intense patrols and alert listening posts, the Americans were ready to defend.

The attack began at about 2200 with a punishing barrage of mortar rounds, some 150 in total. The American heavy mortar platoons quickly opened up a return fire, and would launch 435 projectiles before the battle was over. The enemy bombardment included some massive 120-mm rounds, which had never been encountered in the III Corps area before; the attackers also fired well-aimed rounds from a 75-mm recoilless rifle, hitting several of the "tracks," as the APCs were often called. As soon as the shelling let up, the VC launched a company at the southwestern edge of Collins's perimeter, and almost immediately followed up by hurling an entire battalion at the eastern edge of the ring. At the same time, the VC lobbed a few shells into the firebases at Katum and Suoi Da, hoping to prevent them from supporting Prek Klok.

The diversions proved unsuccessful, and the full firepower of the camp met the human waves of the main attack, which included two full battalions. Artillerymen at both nearby firebases shrugged off the annoying local attacks and pounded the approaches to Prek Klok with a relentless bombardment while waves of tactical aircraft quickly joined in with close bombing runs.

Medevac Hueys came in with landing lights on, carrying out the wounded even as they took small-arms and automatic weapons fire. The attack was shattered in less than an hour. Though three American soldiers lost their lives, battlefield inspections the next morning turned up more than 200 VC dead—the enemy had sacrificed half a battalion for almost no gain.

One more action marked the end of Junction City's Phase I, during which a company of the 101st NVA Regiment made a halfhearted attempt to break up a battalion of the 173rd Airborne. The enemy quickly determined he had bitten off more than he could chew, withdrawing from the fight after an hour. The paratroopers had a reputation as being always ready to fight, and they proved it in this case: despite the enemy flight, the airborne solders were not finished with them, and continued the pursuit of the enemy for three days. Eventually more than 50 NVA were killed, against the cost of 14 Americans wounded.

This battle was the final action for the 173rd in Junction City. As General Seaman moved his forces into position to begin Phase II of the battle, the 173rd was released from control by the 1st Infantry Division and returned to the roster of II Field Force units.

OPERATION JUNCTION CITY PHASE II

Though Junction City would technically entail three phases, for all significant purposes it would reach climactic intensity and resolution during Phase II, which commenced on March 18. Before the second week of April, three of the most savage firefights of the Vietnam War—each instigated by a VC attack—raged around American landing zones or firebases in War Zone C. Many lives would be lost on both sides, but when these three fights were over, the Viet Cong would be forced to acknowledge that it would never be able to stand up in a toe-to-toe slugfest with the US Army and walk away with a victory.

Most of the activity in this part of Junction City would occur to the east of the original horseshoe. Whether they had been forewarned or not, the VC had mostly been able to evacuate the target zone, but the sharp engagements at the end of Phase I convinced General Seaman that General Thanh was willing to commit his forces to battle, if pressed hard enough. And Seaman intended to press hard enough.

To this end, the 196th LIB moved to Highway 4, the eastern rim of the horseshoe. The 1st Brigade, 1st Division, slid eastward as well, still in the northern part of the operational area. The brigade immediately commenced operations along Road 246, the east-west dirt road marking the northern boundary of operations. During the first week of March the 1st Brigade, 9th Division, was placed under control of General Hay's Big Red One. It immediately began to patrol the old familiar ambush route of Highway 13 so that supply convoys and a very important engineer deployment could move into the northern part of War Zone C without fear of ambush.

One of several command transfers also occurred between phases as General Weyand turned command of the Tropic Lightning (25th) Division over to Major General John Tillson. Tillson's division would manage operations in the west, and would retain control over the 3rd Brigade, 4th Division, while the Big Red One operated in the east. General Seaman planned to give the division commanders more control over their individual operations than he had previously; to this end, he dismantled the forward headquarters at Dau Tieng and returned to the II Field Force main base at Long Binh, just outside of Saigon. Before Phase II of Junction City concluded, Seaman, too, would be replaced by a new Field Force II commander as Lieutenant General Bruce Palmer Jr. rotated into the position.

The most important preliminary work for Phase II would involve engineering projects, not combat. The 1st Engineers, escorted by two 1st Division brigades, moved north on Route 13 to An Loc, and commenced work on improving Road 246, installing a Bailey Bridge over the Saigon River where that road crossed the water, and building an airstrip just to the west of the river, adjacent to the road. The bridge, which was a prefabricated series of trussed spans and would eventually be 210 feet long, required a concrete pier in the middle of the river. Nevertheless, construction began on 8 March, and by midday on the 12th, traffic was already crossing there.

Phase II of the operation began at one minute after midnight, 0001, on 18 March. Already, however, reorganization and maneuver had proceeded through the previous two weeks to bring units into position for the next part of Junction City. The two primary division headquarters, 1st and 25th Infantry, would continue to control the operation, but some shuffling of subordinate units was implemented as units completed their roles in Phase I. On 17 March, the 2nd Brigade, 1st Division—which had been detached during the early part of Junction City—was brought up to join its parent headquarters as the 3rd Brigade, 1st Division, moved back to its normal base area. Also, the 173rd Airborne Regiment, detached only a few days earlier, was attached back to the division on 20 March. The 11th ACR Blackhorses would further augment the Big Red One from 1 April through the 15th.

BATTLE OF BAU BANG

One of the 1st Division assignments in Phase II of Junction City was to patrol Highway 13 so that engineering and supply convoys had freedom to move up and down that key artery. By the kickoff of Phase II, on 18 March, the engineers had made a lot of progress on improving Road 246 leading west from An Loc into War Zone Z, including completing the impressive Bailey Bridge across the Saigon River. However, the need to keep Route 13 open for safe truck travel remained imperative.

The units assigned to this road security mission included the 1st Brigade, 9th Division, and the 9th Division's cavalry arm, the 3rd Squadron, 5th Cav (both attached to the 1st Division for this part of Junction City). A number of small firebases were established adjacent to the highway to support this activity. Every morning the patrols rolled out from the firebases to clear their stretches of Highway 13, with the infantry and cavalry returning to their laagers at night. During the hours of darkness the road was closed to friendly traffic.

One of these bases was designated Firebase 14 and was located just to the west of Highway 13 near the hamlet of Bau Bang. An abandoned railway ran parallel to Highway 13, just to the east of the roadway, along this

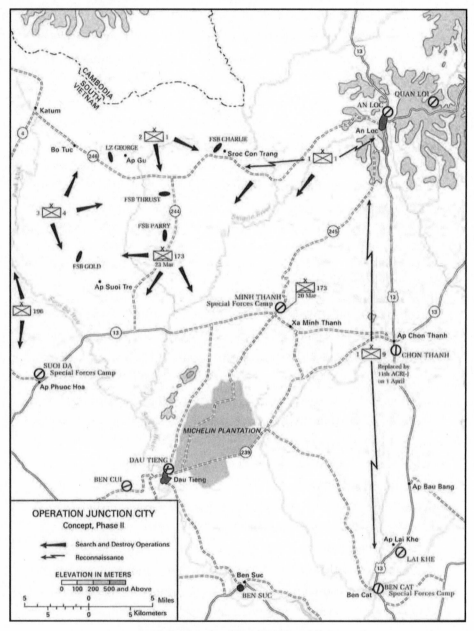

Operation Junction City Phase 2

CENTER OF MILITARY HISTORY, UNITED STATES ARMY

section. As Phase II commenced, Firebase 14 was garrisoned by the six 105-mm towed howitzers of Battery B, 7th Battalion, 9th Artillery, and two platoons of Troop A, 3/5th Cavalry, which included 20 APCs, six tanks, and three mortar carriers manned by 129 troopers. The vehicles were formed into a "wagon train" ring around the position, with about 50 yards between each vehicle. The third cavalry platoon was deployed a mile or so to the north, in an ambush position along a major trail that ran east to west, perpendicular to the axis of Route 13.

At about 2300 on the night of 19 March, which happened to be Palm Sunday, Sergeant Michael Rorie was watching the road to the north of the firebase from his APC, waiting to be relieved, when he was startled by the approach of a herd of about 15 cattle. The cattle were wearing bells, which rang audibly as they ambled across the road from west to east. A short time later, a heavy machine gun opened up from due east of the perimeter. A tank-mounted searchlight quickly identified the weapon as mounted on a wheeled cart that had been pushed down the rails of the abandoned railroad. The machine gun from Rorie's APC, together with the main gun of one of the squadron's tanks, quickly destroyed the unusual weapon, but left everyone feeling jumpy, as if something strange were going to happen this night.

Around midnight, some of the tankers conducted "reconnaissance by fire"; that is, they sprayed an area to suppress or reveal potential VC lurking there. They directed these salvos against the woods beyond the railroad track, to the east of the highway and the firebase. Captain Raoul Alcala, 3rd Squadron CO, reported shortly before midnight that the firing had stopped, and his men were using infrared detection equipment to scan the surrounding area for signs of enemy movement.

No movement or threat was discovered, but the troopers and artillerymen remained restless, a little unnerved by the spooky bovine probe followed by the railroad-deployed machine gun. The men of the detached 2nd Platoon, a mile or so north of the base in its ambush position, had learned of the probes, and they, too, remained in a state of heightened awareness.

At about 0300 on 20 March, the Americans heard the *crump* of heavy mortars launching projectiles, and moments later the explosive projectiles began to impact the firebase. The mortars seemed to be located a mile or so west of the American position, and enemy accuracy proved to be very good. One of the first rounds scored a direct hit on the APC of the CO of 1st Platoon, Lieutenant Roger Festa. Festa's sergeant was wounded and his track damaged. His platoon, with responsibility for the western half of the firebase's perimeter, now began to see enemy infantry closing in along the whole length of their line. The attackers were disciplined, and followed a moving barrage of mortar rounds as they moved toward the camp.

But the VC weren't just coming from the west; other attackers swarmed out of the darkness to the north and south. All of the Viet Cong wore the dark-colored fatigues that Americans commonly referred to as "black pajamas," and they charged the cavalry armored vehicles with reckless abandon. Searchlights illuminated the approaches to the perimeter, and tank guns, APC machine guns, and handheld small arms all barked out an angry reply. In that illumination, it quickly became clear that this was a very large attack, probably several battalions strong.

Another M-113 was quickly struck and disabled by an RPG, while a third took three hits from recoilless rifle rounds. That vehicle burst into flames, and the badly wounded crew had to be evacuated, opening a gap in the perimeter formed by the circled "wagon train" of APCs. In addition, two tanks were struck by recoilless rifle rounds, but the damage was insignificant enough that the big Pattons could still fire and, if necessary, maneuver.

In the meantime, Captain Alcala had called for artillery support from neighboring firebases, and a forward observer's aircraft quickly arrived in the dark sky over the firebase. The keen eyes of that observer, coupled with radar from one of the nearby artillery units, allowed the enemy mortar position to be located in a small, abandoned enemy hamlet—as the cavalrymen had suspected, a little more than a mile to the west. That area soon became the target of many American big guns, but the mortars kept firing.

One of the cavalry's mortar carriers launched flares from a large bore, 4.2-inch mortar, and in the sudden brightness it looked like the whole landscape swarmed with vengeful Vietnamese in their characteristic black garb. More VC crossed the highway, moving west, into position to support the attacks to the north and south of the perimeter.

By this time, two tracks had been disabled, and the attackers pressed aggressively into the camp. Several VC leaped on top of Track 10, which was "buttoned up" to provide momentary protection to the crew, but also meant that the Americans in the APC could not directly fight back against the enemy soldiers who were right above them. "They're swarming all over my track!" the APC commander radioed. "Dust me with canister!" After some brief hesitation—caused by worry about injuring their fellow troopers—the crew of a nearby tank complied, firing blasts of antipersonnel ammunition that killed the VC atop the M-113 while only rocking the eardrums and the nerves of the men inside. That was a tactic that had to be repeated several times during this intense firefight, as most of the cavalrymen were sheltering in armored vehicles, fighting lightly equipped infantry attacking furiously from several directions.

A little after 0100, with the perimeter under intense pressure, the 3rd Platoon under 2nd Lieutenant Hiram Wolfe IV, pulled back from the original front line to reestablish a position about 25 yards closer to the center of the circle. At the same time, Captain Alcala had contacted his squadron commander, Lieutenant Colonel Sidney Haszard, who was based at the squadron HQ a few miles to the south. Alcala indicated he thought he could hold his position, though he asked permission to recall his 2nd Platoon from its ambush position. Haszard granted that request, and also ordered another platoon, 1st of Troop B, located a half-dozen miles to the north, to race along Highway 13 to the firefight in case they were needed.

The 2nd Platoon of Troop A, being the closest, was the first to arrive. The VC had set up an ambush along the highway, but with a Patton tank in the lead the platoon crashed right through the barrier, suffering no casualties even as they blasted the enemy troops positioned to the right and the left. Soon thereafter the 1st Platoon of Troop B rolled down the road, with the lead tank spraying canister to the right and left as the VC again tried to delay the armored vehicles. By then, a flight of attack helicopters, augmented by a big

AC-47 "Spooky" gunship, had moved into the sky overhead, adding flares and firepower to the American defense.

Colonel Haszard also decided to ride with his own vehicle and a second command track toward the action. He arrived near Bau Bang at about 0200, smashing through a machine-gun ambush just south of the perimeter. As he attempted to drive into the position, however, his track was hit by two rounds from a concealed RPG-2 launcher, killing the gunner, wounding the rest of the crew, and disabling the track. As another track moved into towing position, the squadron commander himself dropped to the ground, ignoring a hail of enemy small-arms fire to hook up the cable so that his track—loaded with valuable communication equipment—could be pulled into the perimeter.

By shortly after 0200, the perimeter included five armored cavalry platoons as well as the artillery battery. Captain Alcala employed a brisk, aggressive counterattack to expand his perimeter enough to accommodate the extra vehicles, and the fighting slackened considerably. The Americans allowed themselves to hope that the enemy had given up the fight.

At 0300, the VC charged forward again, mainly from the south. They carried hooks, ropes, and wires, and to the troop commander it looked as though their main purpose was to recover bodies. Certainly they snagged many of the fallen VC and dragged them from the field, though that didn't stop some of the enemy from charging to within 15 yards of the perimeter. Airstrikes and artillery support continued to do lethal work during this attack as the enemy withdrew once again.

At about 0500, the enemy made one final attempt to storm the camp. The floating flares continued to render night into day, and this time the attackers were met in the open by airstrikes including cluster bombs and napalm. Those survivors that drew close to the perimeter were driven off by small arms and the fire from the few machine guns that still had ammunition—for the supply of rounds for all types of American weapons in the perimeter had grown perilously short.

But the VC had shot their bolt, and by 0530 a full withdrawal was under way. After a firefight lasting nearly six hours, the troopers slowly and carefully emerged from the base to scour the battlefield. They found 227 enemy dead, and knew that an unknown number of additional KIA had been carried from the field; they took prisoner three wounded enemy soldiers. A total of 29 airstrikes had pounded the attackers, and they had been showered by nearly 3,000 rounds of artillery from the nearby firebases. Three Americans had died in the battle, but more than 60 had been wounded; many of the injured had elected to stay at their positions, even though Dust Off flights had been made continually during the later hours of the battle. The attackers were identified through documents and interrogation as almost the entire 273rd Regiment of the 9th VC Division. That regiment had been in War Zone D during most of Junction City, but it had moved west to Highway 13 so that the men could fight, and many of them die, along that crucial artery.

And, as it turned out, the battle at Bau Bang was only one of two savage firefights that occurred, practically simultaneously, during this climactic phase of Operation Junction City.

SUOI TRE: BATTLE AT FIREBASE GOLD

The first movement of Phase II, Operation Junction City, began early in the morning of 18 March, when Colonel Marshall Garth, CO of the 3rd Brigade, 4th Division (temporarily attached to the 25th Division), dispatched a battalion to occupy a clearing roughly in the middle of War Zone C, some 20 miles north of Dau Tieng. The open space was to be called Landing Zone Silver, and after an overland column of mechanized infantry took control there, Garth intended to airlift two infantry and an artillery battalion to create a powerful fire support base within range of Routes 4, 246, and 13.

The mechanized column, the 2nd/22nd Infantry, commanded by Lieutenant Colonel Ralph Julian, moved out on time and for a while made good progress moving cross-country toward its destination. After a few hours, it began to encounter enemy mines, with several of the tracks suffering damage. Harassing fire by VC detachments armed with RPGs further delayed the battalion's progress. Late in the day, it ran into a stream with steep, high banks to either side, a very effective blockade to mechanized movement. Julian's APCs began following the course of the small waterway, but it was clear they would not reach LZ Silver until, at earliest, sometime during 19 March.

Unwilling to let his entire plan become unhinged by the terrain obstacles encountered by his mechanized battalion, Colonel Garth selected a new landing zone to be taken first thing in the morning on 19 March. This LZ was a clearing that would be designated Firebase Gold, like Silver more or less right in the middle of War Zone C and just a couple of miles northwest of where the 1/28th Wolfhounds and 196th LIB had smashed the 272nd VC Regiment during Operation Attleboro. The slightly oblong clearing would be occupied by a heliborne assault force without having the benefit of the mechanized troops clearing the area ahead of time. Instead, a half hour of artillery bombardment was used to hopefully neutralize any potential enemy threat. As a further security measure, the scrubby forest around the LZ was soaked down with a defoliant.

Two battalions, the 3/22 Infantry and the 2/77 Artillery, would be moved to the landing zone in three lifts of helicopters. The first landings went off smoothly, but chaos erupted as the second wave of choppers was bringing in the remaining infantry. Five massive explosions ripped through the clearing as Viet Cong observers triggered prepared charges at several places in the clearing. Nine helicopters were damaged by the blasts, with three of them crashing. Even worse, 17 Americans, including seven helicopter crewmen, were killed by the blasts, and another 28 were wounded.

Clearly, the VC were not surprised by the Americans' selection of an LZ. Still, with more than half of his initial force already on the ground, and his number of available helicopters depleted, Colonel Garth felt he had no choice but to reinforce the men already on the ground. Those troops were quickly spreading out to clear the area around the landing zone, and they discovered another 20 or so shells prepared for remote detonation. Those were slowly and carefully disabled while the rest of the infantry prepared a defense perimeter and the artillerymen readied their 12 towed 105-mm and six self-propelled 155-mm guns for action.

Late in the day, another battalion, the 2/12 Infantry, was lifted into the

LZ; that unit headed into the bush to the northwest. The mechanized column remained isolated some distance to the west of the infantry and artillery LZ, and still sought a way to cross the troublesome stream. The APCs of that unit, the 2/22nd commanded by Lieutenant Colonel Julian, had been reinforced by a detachment of tanks provided by the 2nd Battalion, 34th Armored of the II Field Force reserve.

In total, some 450 men occupied the landing zone, which, during the daylight hours of 20 March, became operational as Fire Support Base Gold. The commander of the 3/22, Lieutenant Colonel John Bender, was responsible for the defense of the base, while the 18 pieces of artillery and their crews were commanded by Lieutenant Colonel John Vessey, and would be available for action throughout the area of operation for Phase II of Junction City. As night fell, the infantry made plans for intense patrolling to the north of Gold, searching an area where the brigade commander, Colonel Garth, had seen from his command helicopter a large number of hostile forces late in the day of the 20th.

Bender's men established listening posts around the perimeter as dark fell, and the colonel also sent several patrols out into the surrounding brush. At about 0430 on 21 March, one of these patrols reported hearing enemy troops moving around. Word went back to the perimeter, and the patrols hunkered down to wait tensely, expecting an attack at any moment before the sun came up.

However, daylight broke with no further disturbance. Since the VC generally refrained from daylight attacks against strong positions, the Americans relaxed. The night patrol started back toward the perimeter, which was just a short distance away when, at 0630, a sudden barrage of mortar shells erupted from the scrubland around Gold. A wave of VC erupted from concealment on several sides of the patrol, quickly overwhelming it, killing or wounding every American in the listening party.

At the same time, 60-mm and 82-mm mortar rounds showered the firebase, with some of the first explosions rocking a company command post and battalion headquarters with very near misses. Shortly thereafter, a stunningly large number of VC broke from cover and rushed toward the perimeter, AK-47s blazing, while recoilless rifles, RPGs, and machine guns raked the American position. The enemy forces, which turned out to number two full battalions of the 272nd Regiment, charged the base from all sides, with the heaviest attacks directed against the northeastern and southeastern portions of the roughly circular perimeter.

The artillerymen raised their tubes to nearly vertical heights as they lobbed shells toward the positions where the enemy mortars seemed to be located. Batteries from FSB Barry and other locations quickly started to lay down a barrage on the fringes of Gold, trying to suppress the VC who were swiftly moving forward over the relatively open and previously defoliated terrain, trying to charge right into the American lines. By 0655, Colonel Garth was ordering his two other battalions to make for Gold with all possible speed. The 2/12, encamped a couple of miles to the northwest, moved out immediately, striking directly overland instead of taking the more circuitous routes offered by existing trails. The 2/22nd mechanized infantry battalion, still reinforced by tanks attached from the 34th Armored, redoubled its efforts to find a way to cross the water barrier that had vexed it for two days.

The pressure against the southeast rim of the base was strong enough that Company B, 3/22, was partially overrun, with the survivors fighting for their lives in hand-to-hand foxhole combat. A reaction force of artillerymen had been standing by for such an emergency, and they raced into the position, providing enough extra firepower to hold the line, at least for the present. The howitzers of the artillery batteries now lowered their aim to fire high-explosive (HE) rounds directly into the ranks of the attacking VC.

By 0714, a small observation plane, a Cessna O-1E Bird Dog with an Air Force fire control officer aboard, reached Gold. As the craft circled overhead, the officer directed the first strike of F-5 Freedom Fighters to pummel the VC attackers, killing a number of them, while additional planes were soon bombing and strafing the edge of the woods, where the enemy troops were advancing from cover.

Artillery rounds continued to crater the landscape around the camp, and bombs and napalm delivered from the air maintained its killing rain, but the Viet Cong pressed forward with amazing tenacity. By 0711, the Company B commander reported that his first platoon had been overwhelmed by the enemy's "human wave" charges. Before another round of airstrikes could come in for close support, the enemy directed enough heavy machine-gun fire against the low-flying fire control aircraft to shoot it down, killing both the pilot and observer and leaving no one to direct the airstrikes onto important targets.

By 0750, Company B was in dire straits, running low on ammunition, with the perimeter completely breached in the area of the 1st Platoon. The 105-mm howitzers of the 2/77 Artillery were all that stood before the VC and a complete overrunning of the camp. Colonel Vessey ordered the guns lowered to direct fire levels, and had his crews load rounds of antipersonnel "beehive" shot. These were canisters, each of which contained 8,000 fléchette darts; the canister rounds burst as they blasted out of the barrels of the guns, allowing the darts to spread out like a spray of shotgun pellets. The stunning impact of this rarely used, but incredibly lethal, fire mowed down the VC that had been charging through the Company B position. At the same time, Lieutenant Colonel Bender sent a load of ammunition and 20 men from Company A to reinforce the breached sector, where the line was restored—albeit somewhat tenuously—shortly after 0800.

But one crisis forestalled was quickly overshadowed by a new potential disaster, as another intense wave of VC broke through the perimeter at the northeastern edge of the circle. At the same time, a small group of Company A men, who had spent the night in the bush on ambush patrol, managed to make its way around the thronging attackers to run into the American base and take up positions to aid the defense. Once again hand-to-hand combat raged through the American foxholes, with soldiers wielding any implement within reach—including knives, entrenching tools, and even chain saws—until the infantrymen were forced from their holes. The perimeter had been broken along more than a third of its front, from the northeast to the south, and the retreating soldiers pulled back to make a final stand right in front of the guns.

Despite the massive amount of manpower pressing against, and breaking through, the eastern edge of the perimeter, the VC had also managed to maintain intense attacks against the rest of the base. Creeping forward to within hand-grenade range, the enemy lobbed the explosives at the battalion command post and aid stations. The Americans maintained a withering return fire, however, and the enemy lacked the numbers to surge forward in human wave attacks against these sectors of the lines.

As the survivors of Companies A and B formed up before the guns, VC attackers surrounded one of the lethal quad .50-caliber machine guns. A grenade killed or wounded the crew, and the attackers climbed aboard, quickly starting to swing the mount around so that they could bring the four powerful machine guns to enfilade the American defense. Very fortunately, the crew of one of the 105-mm howitzers saw what was happening; they loaded a high-explosive round and wheeled their own gun around just a little faster than the VC. That single round struck the quad dead-on, obliterating with only seconds to spare a threat that might have clinched an enemy victory.

At about this same time, two more Bird Dog air controller aircraft flew into the sky above Gold, and they brought with them the welcome addition of a flight of F-100 Super Sabres armed with napalm. Even as the VC were threatening to swarm through the firebase from two directions, the well-aimed, infernal firebombs wiped out hundreds of them—some within just a few yards of the hard-pressed American defenders. The searing shock of the fireballs, coupled with the lethal antipersonnel fire from the howitzers and the staunch defense of Bender's infantry, finally broke the momentum of the attack. Flights of F-4 Phantoms also arrived and dumped their bomb loads on the attackers. Also, an AC-47 "Dragon Ship" flew onto the scene, pouring lethal blasts from its Gatling guns onto the battlefield.

At just before 0900, as nearly a hundred ground-attack aircraft swirled and circled overhead, the first company of the 2/12, which had hacked its way straight through nearly a mile of bamboo thickets while under fire from VC mortars and snipers, burst from the forest to the northwest of the camp. Bender quickly added them to his perimeter, allowing him to shift some of his own battle-weary troops to strengthen the hard-hit sectors of Companies

A and B. The additional strength allowed the battalion to reclaim its original perimeter, but the battle continued as the VC launched yet another attack.

The strain of the fight was visible on the enemy as well as the weary defenders, as many of the Viet Cong had visible, recently bandaged wounds. Some were too disabled to walk, but charged into the fight while being carried piggyback by comrades, with both the able fighter and the wounded rider firing automatic weapons as they once again pressed close to Gold's perimeter.

Ever since the first call for assistance, the scouts of the mechanized column had been frantically probing for a way to cross the stream. A little before 0900, they found a place where the water seemed to sink under the ground, offering a muddy patch that might prove possible to ford. The column of vehicles took the chance and, tracks churning and Chrysler V-8 engines roaring, pushed through the makeshift crossing and charged toward the sound of the guns, with APCs breaking trail by the simple expedient of crushing any bushes and small trees that stood in their path. The M-113s rumbled forward in a staggered column, widening the path to the right and left so that the larger, slower Patton tanks could follow.

At 0912, in a true life "Here comes the cavalry!" moment, the tanks and APCs burst from the scrub to the southwest of Firebase Gold and immediately rolled into the attack. The tanks fired canister rounds from their massive 90-mm guns while the APCs sprayed the VC with a tremendous volume of heavy machine-gun fire. Some of the VC were literally crushed by the tracks of the armored behemoths as they rolled around the perimeter, bringing the attack to an abrupt end. By 1000, the LZ had been cleared so that helicopters could land and pick up the wounded, while other choppers brought in badly needed supplies—since both infantry and artillery had nearly expended all of their ammunition during the savage, four-hour battle.

The harrowing fight had been one of the most intense of the war to date, and had cost the Americans dearly, with 31 killed and 109 wounded just during this fighting—the casualty count does not include those other brave airmen and soldiers who had been killed by the booby traps during the initial landing. Still, the fight had been far more devastating for the 272nd Regiment. As the infantrymen cautiously moved out to inspect the battlefield, they turned up 647 bodies and took seven prisoners. They recovered 65 heavy weapons, including 50 RPG-2s with 600 rounds for those launchers, and nearly 2,000 hand-thrown grenades.

The battle would be named after Suoi Tre, an abandoned hamlet that was not far away, but some Americans simply remember it as the Fight at Firebase Gold. It had been a harrowing, close-run affair, which had turned into a solid American victory. The 3/22 and 2/22 Infantry Battalions, along with the 2/77 Artillery and 2/34 Armored, were all awarded the Presidential Unit Citations for their valor and success in this fight, described by II Field Force commander General Seaman as "the most decisive defeat the Viet Cong have suffered in the III Corps Tactical Zone in my 18 months in Vietnam."

FINAL FURY: THE BATTLE AT AP GU

One more significant battle loomed in the future as part of Junction City, though the frustrated division and field-force commanders were beginning to wonder if they would ever be able to bring any more significant enemy forces to battle. On 24 March, Lieutenant General Bruce Palmer replaced General Seaman as commander of II Field Force, and he was prepared to abandon much of the search effort in War Zone C. Almost immediately, however, he received intelligence suggesting that a strong VC force, the 271st Regiment, was located in the region around Katum.

The 196th Light Infantry Brigade received orders to conduct a search, but by the time they reached the area the enemy formation had already moved out. Though the Americans didn't know it yet, the 271st had joined forces with two badly mauled regiments of the PAVN 9th Division, the 101st NVA Regiment, and the broken remnants of the 272nd Division.

On 26 March, the 1st Battalion of the 26th Infantry was directed to conduct an offensive operation deep into War Zone C, almost as far north as the Cambodian border. By 30 March, the battalion, still under the command of Lieutenant Colonel Alexander Haig, was ready for a helicopter insertion into LZ George, a large, dry marsh located north of Road 246, about five miles east of Katum and nearly 15 miles west of An Loc. It was within ready supporting distance of two major firebases, Charlie and Thrust. After Haig's battalion secured the LZ, a follow-up landing would bring in another battalion, the 1/2nd. Both units were expected to make sweeps through the surrounding terrain with the hopes of finding the 271st Regiment, or another appropriately large target.

Both battalions were to be landed on the 30th, but bad weather delayed the preparatory airstrikes, so only the 1/26th was able to arrive on the scheduled day. Haig's men landed shortly after noon, and immediately swept through the large clearing, which was covered with tall grass and surrounded by the looming darkness of dense jungle, in the typical clover-leaf patrol pattern. By nightfall they had dug into a fortified perimeter, even to the point of constructing "Dupuy bunkers": entrenchments very low to the ground, with log barriers on top of the foxholes and firing embrasures that ensured every bunker could support its flanking positions, and that every approach route was covered by multiple avenues of fire. They were not molested by the enemy during the night of 30/31 March.

The next morning, the 1/2nd, under the command of Lieutenant Colonel William Simpson, arrived at LZ George and landed with still no sign of enemy opposition. Simpson's men quickly marched toward the southwest, where they would set up a base position a little more than a mile from the LZ. Companies A and C of Haig's battalion, meanwhile, started to sweep the area around George, while B Company remained on the landing zone as a reserve and reaction force. There, the men of the battalion's reconnaissance platoon discovered several warning signs to the northwest of the perimeter. They were printed in English and nailed to trees, sternly warning Americans to avoid the area under the pain of death. Clearly, the landings had not been a complete surprise to the VC.

Disregarding the signs, the recon platoon continued to the north, knowing they were only about three miles south of the Cambodian border. Shortly after 1300, small-arms fire snapped from the jungle growth and the point man went down, badly wounded. First Lieutenant Richard

Hill, the platoon commander, advanced to check on the wounded man, and was himself badly wounded; he would perish before he could be evacuated. Small arms, machine guns, and grenades assailed the men of the recon patrol.

Hill's radioman reported the unit's difficult situation to Lieutenant Colonel Haig, who quickly called in airstrikes and artillery to support the beleaguered platoon. It turned out that B Company was just approaching the perimeter after finishing its own search, and upon hearing the firefight, the company captain didn't wait for orders—he immediately marched his men toward the sound of the guns. While his courage was laudable, the fact that he had moved off without informing his battalion commander complicated the artillery support, since the friendly column was in danger of moving into a lethal target zone.

Haig took to the air in his command helicopter, learning that B Company had become fully enmeshed with a large enemy unit as it had come to the aid of the recon patrol—which may well have been overrun without the immediate reinforcement. In any event, the company captain reported that he was engaged and pinned down by a heavily armed VC force of at least battalion size, and that both the company and the patrol were perilously low on ammunition.

The colonel ordered A Company to move up in support and landed near the fight, from where he advanced on foot to join his men. In the meantime, he sent his fire control officer back up in the helicopter, and the artillery direction improved dramatically, soon bringing a rain of explosives down on the hidden VC. Reaching the battle, Haig discovered that Lieutenant Hill had died from his wounds, and that the B Company captain had been injured. Soon, however, A Company arrived on the scene, bringing fresh ammunition for the depleted magazines of their harried fellow infantrymen.

The renewed volume of fire allowed the Americans to pull back toward LZ George. When the VC emerged from their fortifications in pursuit, they suffered significant punishment from the artillery and finally withdrew. By a little after 1700, the fighting was over for the day. By that time, General

Hay—commanding general of the Big Red One—had dispatched significant reinforcements to Haig's position: most of the 1/16th battalion had already landed, and assumed a position northwest of the 1/26th. The 1/16th, under Lieutenant Colonel Rufus Lazzell, was a veteran of several battles in War Zone C, and together with Haig's men established entrenched positions in mutually supporting perimeters only a few hundred yards apart.

American casualties from the day's action, all from Haig's battalion, numbered seven killed and another 38 wounded. Their comrades, more than 450 strong, spent the night confident and angry, ready to avenge the fallen men as soon as they had the chance. Lazzell's men, entrenched and prepared as thoroughly as Haig's, were also ready for the worst the enemy could throw at them. In the early morning hours listening posts around both perimeters reported sounds of enemy contact to three sides, but for a long time no hostile move was made.

Just before 0500 the enemy lobbed a solitary mortar round that exploded near Lieutenant Colonel Haig's perimeter. Suspecting that to be a precursor of an attack—and, in fact, it seemed to be a trial shot to register the aim of the VC mortars—the Americans quickly went to full alert, every soldier moving to his battle position and carrying a loaded weapon at the ready. Without even waiting for the next move, Haig called in artillery onto the jungle just east of his position.

Within a few minutes, a steady shower of enemy mortar rounds poured onto both American units, with hundreds of shells of 60-mm, 82-mm, and even the big 120-mm coming so fast and from such a close range that some of the infantrymen thought that the mortar batteries sounded like machine guns. Fortunately, the Dupuy bunkers made sure that casualties from this bombardment were limited, and Lieutenant Colonels Haig and Lazzell wasted no time in calling for artillery support from Firebases Charlie and Thrush against the mortar batteries.

At the same time as they started the bombardment, the VC tried a new tactic inspired by the lessons learned about the power of US Army artillery support. The enemy had moved a number of mortars into position to strike Firebase Charlie, and these tubes opened up a bombardment

perfectly timed to coincide with the attacks against the infantry battalions. While the men and guns at George were well dug in and suffered
only a few casualties from this diversionary bombardment, the VC tactic
did interfere with the intensity and accuracy of the support from Charlie.
However, apparently the Viet Cong had not discovered the presence of
Firebase Thrush, and the batteries there compensated magnificently for
the impaired efficiency of the guns at FB Charlie.

The 15-minute bombardment did inflict a few casualties on the two
battalions of infantry, but it also allowed the Americans to get illumination flares, assault helicopters, and several forward air controllers into the
skies over LZ George. At about 0520, the VC burst in great numbers from
the jungles to the northeast of the landing zone, striking hard at the
perimeters of both of the well-entrenched battalions. The attackers gained
a measure of surprise by creeping up after the American soldiers who had
manned the listening posts and had been recalled to the bunkers as the
barrage began. They struck B and C Companies of the 1/26th with stunning
quickness, and were soon through the line of the initial bunkers, even
charging into and capturing three of them. A breach of about a hundred
yards wide had been forced through Haig's defensive perimeter.

Throughout the attack the defenders maintained a savage inferno of
return fire, killing many of the enemy at short range; but this seemed to be
one of those cases where a man would shoot one foe only to have two charge
forward to take his place. The Company C commander, Captain Brian Cundiff, ran fearlessly from bunker to bunker along his hard-pressed position,
rallying a stern defense against the right flank of the VC penetration. Killing
multiple VC personally in hand-to-hand combat, suffering three wounds
without accepting medical aid, he set a standard of leadership that inspired
his men to hold on to their positions without yielding another inch.

Daylight was beginning to brighten the battlefield as, at 0630, Lieutenant
Colonel Haig sent his reserve force forward to bolster the strained positions
of his B and C Companies. After pressing their breach some 30 or 40 yards
into the battalion's position, the attackers reached the limit of their capabilities, halting and then slowly, grudgingly yielding the ground they had gained

at such a bloody cost. Airstrikes picked up in frequency and intensity, with planes dropping cluster bombs and napalm every few minutes. Some of the ordnance struck within 30 yards of the American bunkers. When the VC tried another trick learned from previous experience—they released green smoke, which usually designated American positions, over their own units—Haig told his air control officer about the deception. The next flight of fighter-bombers was directed right onto the green smoke target, obliterating the enemy position and seeming to bring about an end to the attack.

Immediately after that airstrike, and despite his several wounds, Captain Cundiff urged many men of his own company, and a platoon from B Company as well, into a sharp, violent counterattack. The reeling VC fell back toward the jungle, and into the target sites of continuing air and artillery bombardment. Many of the enemy threw down their weapons as they fled toward imagined safety. By 0800, the three-hour battle at Landing Zone George was over. Haig's battalion having borne the brunt of the attack, Simpson's 1/2nd and Lazzell's 1/16th moved out in pursuit of the fleeing enemy, but were not able to catch up with more than a few of them.

And it turned out that a great many of the attackers had simply never left the battlefield. After-action patrols and scouts counted a staggering number of VC dead: the bodies of 491 Viet Cong lay where they had fallen, just outside and within the perimeters of the 1/26th and, in smaller numbers, the 1/16th. Further patrolling brought the number of confirmed enemy KIA to over 600. American losses numbered 17 killed, and just over 100 wounded. As usual, Army and Air Force firepower had made all the difference, with more than 15,000 rounds of artillery fired onto the battlefield, and aircraft making more than a hundred sorties, and dropping about a hundred tons of bombs and napalm onto the enemy.

The fight over LZ George would enter the history books as the Battle of Ap Gu, named for a tiny hamlet just a mile or so from the landing zone. This clash was the last of the big battles of Operation Junction City, which would enter its final phase around the middle of April. That segment of the mission consisted of some small-scale searches that basically confirmed that the enemy had been badly punished by the Phase II firefights, with the survivors going into hiding or pulling back to their Cambodian sanctuaries to lick their wounds.

Lieutenant Colonel Haig, who of course would go on to much greater heights in the Army, eventually becoming commander in chief of NATO, then chief of staff to Presidents Nixon and Ford, and finally President Reagan's secretary of state, summed up the lesson that the Americans, and the Viet Cong, would take from the bloody battles of Junction City when he wrote about the Battle of Ap Gu: "When you get belly to belly with a large VC force, they are not sufficiently flexible to react intelligently. They are going to react like most soldiers, and that is to attack. In this case, we were right on their doorstep. We found them by aggressive reconnaissance, the order was called, and the battle was started."

The rest, one might say, is history.

SEVEN

MAKING A STATEMENT

THE USMC STAKES A CLAIM
TO THE QUE SON VALLEY

My options were two: let the enemy initiate action . . .
and then react, or assume the initiative and strike him first.
I chose the latter option.

COLONEL EMIL J. RADICS, CO, 1ST MARINES,
RECALLING OPERATION UNION, APRIL 1967

For more than 20 years, the Viet Cong and the North Vietnamese comfort-ably and contentedly controlled and exploited the populous and fertile rice-growing region of the Que Son Valley in the northern portion of South Vietnam. Occasionally the ARVN would make a sally into the region, but the South Vietnamese never presented much of a threat to Communist control, and any units that dared to enter the valley would inevitably get roughly handled and leave a little later, much the worse for wear. With many small but rugged mountains, and large rice paddies interspersed by rocky hills and patches of tall forest, the valley, sometimes called the Que Son Basin, was a challenging mix of populous villages in the lowlands and rough, readily defensible places of rocky higher elevations.

The valley occupied the southern sector of the I Corps Tactical Zone, just south of the boundary between Quang Nam and Quang Tin prov-inces. The Americans had assigned the I Corps area to the US Marine Corps, but prior to the spring of 1967 the Marines in I Corps focused on their three main base areas of Phu Bai, Da Nang, and Chu Lai—with a side presence, for a while, protecting the port of Qui Nhon in the II Corps area to the south. The Demilitarized Zone (DMZ) dividing North and South Vietnam at the 17th Parallel also demanded attention from the Marines, and thus for the first year and a half of its involvement, the Corps lacked the personnel to project significant power into the Que Son Valley.

With the buildup of American forces that occurred during 1966, however, the number of troops available to the Corps' overarching headquarters in Vietnam, the III MAF grew substantially, and by the start of 1967 the commander of the 1st Marine Division, Major General Herman Nickerson, decided that the Que Son Valley was important enough to demand some kind of presence. There were two good reasons for this: one, the valley was a tremendously fertile source of rice, and much of that rice was being co-opted by the Viet Cong for use by its insurgent forces; and two, the large population of the area had been fairly thoroughly indoctrinated by the enemy, and the numerous hamlets and villages there had become a productive recruiting ground for new enemy soldiers. It was hoped that an American presence would make both of these assets less advantageous to the Viet Cong and their North Vietnamese allies.

By the summer of 1966 the valley had become the domain of the 2nd North Vietnamese Army Division headquarters, which oversaw the operations of the Viet Cong regular and irregular activities in the area. By early 1967, the 3rd and 21st NVA Regiments had arrived on the scene, and in the coming months the 3rd VC Regiment would move north from Quang Ngai province to add its strength to the division's order of battle.

The valley, like most of the I Corps area south of the borderlands around the DMZ and Quang Tri province, fell under the command responsibility of the 1st Marine Division. The first tentative step in the Marines' entry into the valley happened in the middle of January 1967. Company F, 2nd Battalion, 1st Marines was ordered to relieve an ARVN unit that had been occupying a lonely mountaintop observation post called Nui Loc Son (Loc Son Mountain). This height offered a commanding view of much of the basin from its southern rim, and the slopes were rugged enough to deter anything but a very strong force from disturbing the outpost at its summit. The transfer to the Marine company went smoothly, and at first the enemy seemed to take very little notice of the American presence. Company F, for its part, limited itself to observing the basin and making local sweeps on and around the mountain, while beginning to earn the trust of the nearby civilian population.

The latter included some significant successes as the Marines took part in civic projects with the surrounding villages and built relationships with locals that significantly improved the Americans' ability to gain intelligence about enemy strength, operations, and plans. Furthermore, the USMC commanders knew that such activities could not go unchallenged if the NVA was to retain its influence and prestige in the area. As Colonel Emil Radics, CO of the 1st Marine Regiment put it, this community outreach by Company F represented "the planned and premeditated use of a Marine rifle company to create a situation."

Company F, or "Foxtrot," under the command of Captain Gene Deegan, did have some extra punch beyond the unit's own rifle and heavy weapons platoons. Also positioned atop the mountain were an 81-mm mortar section and a 106-mm recoilless rifle, both from the 2nd Battalion organization, and a 4.2-inch mortar battery on loan (or "chopped") from the 1st Battalion, 11th Marines. And by early April, it began to look like the "situation" sought by Colonel Radics was ready to take concrete form.

In fact, the North Vietnamese had become increasingly irked by the Marines' efforts to befriend the population, resenting those attempts to convince the people that the Communists were not necessarily the guaranteed victors in this war. Such an attitude could not be allowed to thrive and expand, or it could seriously impact the enemy's sources of food, concealment, and recruits from this fertile stronghold that for so long had remained free of South Vietnamese influence and interference.

Colonel Radics had been making a point of visiting his Marines on their isolated hilltop at least twice every week. On one of these visits early in the month of April, Captain Deegan informed his commander that the enemy had been moving troops into the hills west and south of the basin, and that these movements and the gathering enemy strength formed a potential threat to Loc Son Mountain. On 15 April, the Marines observed small units infiltrating positions on the valley floor that lay to the *east* of the mountain. These movements increased over the next two days, and on 18 April, the captain informed the regimental CO that he estimated the enemy strength in the immediate vicinity of F Company's outpost to be two full regiments.

This was just the information Radics had been waiting for. While the western enemy outposts were in terrain as rugged and readily defensible as Nui Loc Son itself, the eastern deployments put the NVA units into terrain where the Marines might be able to employ helicopter insertion to surround and trap a sizable enemy force where it could be engaged and destroyed. Working through the night of 18/19 April, the regimental staff pieced together a plan that would bring about the clash the colonel was determined to force.

OPERATION UNION (I)

The basic idea of what would be called Operation Union—later Union I, after Union II occurred—was that Deegan would march his company down from the summit, toward the village of Binh Son, a collection of hamlets that was known to be a Communist stronghold. The regimental HQ would fly to the mountaintop outpost and conduct the battle from that splendid overlook. If the enemy took the bait offered by Deegan's company, as many as three USMC battalions would be helicoptered in from Da Nang and Chu Lai, enveloping the NVA units and hopefully achieving a decisive victory.

The plan and the units involved were ready by early morning on 19 April, but while the 1st Marine Division's General Nickerson was ready to authorize Operation Union, he ordered it to be pushed back two days to avoid conflicts over resources, particularly helicopters, that were already planned for the 19th. Consequently, Operation Union became a "go" for the morning of 21 April 1967.

On that day, Deegan's men moved out at 0700, following one of the

rocky ridgelines that snaked downward from the summit. Almost immediately the Marines began taking fire from small NVA skirmish parties,
but the Americans were able to brush these harassments aside. More significantly, they observed a sizable force of NVA moving into positions in
Binh Son, which lay about 2.5 miles northeast of the summit. This gathering of North Vietnamese strength, of course, was exactly what Colonel
Radics had been hoping for.

Foxtrot Company made its way to the bottom of the mountain by
about 0900, and began to advance on the village complex. At 0930, the
Marines were met by an intense fusillade of enemy fire and Deegan pulled
his men back to a tree line for cover, at the same time ordering air and
artillery support to zero in on the NVA positions. Ninety minutes later,
the captain sent two of his platoons forward to attack the village, holding
his 1st Platoon back to provide covering fire and to serve as a reserve.

The advancing Marines crossed the open ground with little difficulty,
but as soon as they entered the fringes of Binh Son, they came under intense
small-arms and machine-gun fire. Pinned down so thoroughly that they
couldn't retreat, the forward platoons requested assistance. Deegan sent his
1st Platoon against the enemy flank, but it, too, quickly took to the ground in
the face of a hailstorm of enemy bullets. Additional artillery and airstrikes
pummeled Binh Son, but the enemy was clearly well entrenched, as the
explosive fire support did little to diminish the fire coming Foxtrot's way.

Sensing a crisis and an opportunity, Colonel Radic sent in his first
reinforcement from Da Nang, two companies (I and M) of the 3rd Battalion, 1st Marines, led by the battalion commander, Lieutenant Colonel
Hillmer Deatley. The helicopters brought them in a little more than half a
mile to the southeast of the village, making successful, if hurried, landings
as small-arms fire crackled all around them. The fresh battalion advanced
through a flurry of fire, aided by the screening of near-constant bombardment against what turned out to be the entrenched 3rd NVA Regiment, to
reach the position of Foxtrot Company. Now three companies strong, the
Marines continued to return the enemy fire, and dug in so that they could
resist a counterattack, if one came.

Upon arriving at Foxtrot, Deatley discovered that Captain Deegan had been badly wounded, but had remained in active command until the reinforcements arrived; at that point, the injured company commander finally allowed himself to be evacuated. At the same time, the next wave of reinforcements, from Chu Lai, arrived by helicopter, this time landing a few miles away from the battle, to the east, where they could block the most likely route of enemy withdrawal. This was the 3rd Battalion, 5th Marines, under Lieutenant Colonel Dean Esslinger. With the fight still raging, and the NVA regiment showing no sign of pulling out, Esslinger's Marines advanced toward Binh Son. The fire had begun to slacken as the new battalion linked up with the three companies who had been so heavily engaged. Also, a three-battalion force of South Vietnamese Army Rangers commenced a move southwest from Thang Binh, near the eastern terminus of the valley. The ARVN Rangers would move inland from their base near the coast and maneuver to cut off possible routes of NVA retreat.

As night fell, a third USMC battalion, the 1/1st, arrived from Da Nang. Commanded by Lieutenant Colonel Van Bell, these men debarked from their helicopters atop Nui Loc Son in full darkness, and immediately started marching down the rugged trail toward the battlefield. Several artillery batteries redeployed during the night, including a US Army battery of massive 175-mm self-propelled guns that rumbled from Chu Lai to Tam Ky, south of the battlefield, and a Marine battery of howitzers that was delivered by air to the village of Que Son, to the north of the Ly Ly River that ran through the valley. All the guns of both batteries were within range of the entire operational area.

As the sun started to rise on 22 April, all four of the Marine battalions pressed the attack against the NVA regiment that had fought so stubbornly to hold Binh Son. The pressure proved too much for the Communist troops, and the enemy began to pull out of the complex during the day. For a time the North Vietnamese soldiers had to move out in the open, and they suffered terrible punishment from American artillery and airpower. The battalions of Lieutenant Colonels Esslinger and Bell pursued aggressively, moving through the village, while Foxtrot Company and Deatley's men, who had taken the brunt of the casualties on the first day, were allowed to recover. Deatley's partial battalion moved to the east of Binh Son, while Foxtrot made ready to return to the mountaintop outpost it had garrisoned since January.

Yet somehow, and despite the aggressive pursuit and the encircling positions of the attackers, the enemy troops managed to extricate themselves from the battlefield and, for all intents and purposes, seemed to disappear. On 23 and 24 April, the pursuing battalions kept up the pressure, but they could not find more than a few stragglers from the NVA regiment that had been driven from Binh Son. On the 25th, the division shuffled some forces to and from the battlefield, with all of the 1st Marines (except Foxtrot Company in its lofty aerie) returning to Da Nang, while the 1st Battalion, 5th Marines, including the regimental command post, moved up from Chu Lai to join the 3rd Battalion, already on scene.

The search focus shifted to the rugged country to the south and west of Loc Son Mountain, where previous NVA activity had been observed, but the only enemy presence encountered was a lethal mine, where a large number of linked explosions tore through a landing zone, leaving one Marine killed and 35 wounded badly enough that they required evacuation. An additional reinforcement arrived on 28 April, in the form of Special Landing Force (SLF) Alpha, under Colonel James Gallo, which helicoptered into an LZ near Nui Loc Son.

Despite thorough and intense searches, the Marines could discover no significant enemy presence, even though intelligence reports suggested that the enemy remained in the area in strength. With the basin floor and the southern heights pretty well scoured, on 1 May, Colonel Kenneth Houghton, commander of the 5th Marine Regiment, deployed his 1st Battalion by helicopter right into the rugged heights lining the northern boundary of the Que Son Valley. Operating north of the town of Que Son, the 1/5th Marines, under Lieutenant Colonel Peter Hilgartner, began to search this new sector, and ran into increasingly determined enemy resistance.

On 5 May, one of Hilgartner's companies discovered an NVA regimental storage site, containing ammunition, clothing, medical supplies, and maps. Sensing he was getting closer to pay dirt, the colonel pressed his companies to climb higher into the mountains. His regimental CO, Colonel Houghton—who was a seasoned combat veteran of two previous wars—agreed with this assessment, and ordered the 3/5th Marines to be moved up on Hilgartner's left in support. Soon thereafter, Lieutenant Colonel Peter Wickwire's 1/3rd Marines, which was the battalion landing team (BLT)—the infantry element of the Special Landing Force—was inserted by helicopter into the area around the town of Que Son. It moved through the valley floor for a short distance before also starting to climb into the high country to the north.

It wasn't until 10 May that the Marines made a significant enemy contact, but the encounter would quickly turn into a hard and bloody fight. As Company C of the 1/5 worked its way up an elevation about three miles northwest of Que Son known as Hill 110 (for its height in meters as marked on the map), it began to take fire from a full NVA battalion occupying fortified positions on the neighboring mountain, a broad and rocky massif known as Nui Nong Ham (Nong Ham Mountain). The company pressed on to the summit of Hill 110, but found that to be an exposed position as they continued to be targeted from the neighboring, higher mountain, and had also been spotted, and fired on, by significant NVA forces in a cane field below them. The company captain, Russell Caswell, sent out a message asking for assistance.

Hilgartner's other companies were some distance away, but two companies, B and C, of Wickwire's BLT happened to be in the area just to the north of Hill 110. Colonel Houghton authorized those companies to be temporarily attached to Hilgartner's command, and he directed them to climb to Caswell's assistance. Before they could link up, however, they, too, ran into strong and entrenched enemy positions on the north face of Nong Ham Mountain and were forced to halt.

Artillery from several batteries was quickly directed onto the mountain, but it seemed to have no effect on the enemy firing positions. The broad summit of Nong Ham was clearly revealed as an enemy position of strength, and another company—A of the 1/3rd—was transported in by helicopter. The choppers tried to make a landing east of the current fighting, but they came under such fierce fire dropping off the first platoon that further landings were deemed too risky. In addition, one of the UH-34s was shot down, crashing directly onto the small clearing that had been selected as the LZ.

Yet another reinforcement, Company A of Hilgartner's battalion, was a little more than a mile to the east, but quickly commenced a cross-country march, moving uphill toward the crackling sound of the firefight. When the unit ran into another enemy position, the company captain, Gerald McKay, decided that his men could push through the position and continue the mission with the help of some air support. Tragically, the forward air controller missed as he fired rockets to mark the target with smoke, striking the Marine company instead of the NVA position. Four USMC F-4 Phantoms duly executed their strafing runs, tearing into the advancing men of Company A with eight rockets armed with high-explosive warheads. The misguided air attack left five dead and 24 wounded, and completely broke the momentum of McKay's intended attack.

With four companies having taken significant casualties, all of them remaining pinned down and still under enemy fire, it seemed like everything that could go wrong had gone wrong. It was right about then, just before 1500, that the 1/5th command group, including Colonel Hilgartner, the heavy weapons section, and Company D of the same battalion, reached the summit of Hill 185. From this significant elevation, they could overlook not just the trapped Marines, but most of the NVA firing positions. The mortar men wasted no time in setting up their tubes and, with the impacts on the enemy troops in the cane field clearly visible, quickly zeroed in with an intense, accurate bombardment. They fired as quickly as they could, at such a rate that the barrels of the mortars became "just about red hot."

Within a half hour, Company M, 3/5th Marines, had been helicoptered to Hilgartner's location, and he was able to send Company D down to assist Captain Caswell—whose C Company had triggered the whole, chaotic fight—near the summit of Hill 110. Both of those companies quickly moved into position to provide covering fire for the other Marines, lower down on the slopes. Within another hour all of the companies were on the move, with the BLT pushing the NVA out of the cane field while the rest of Hilgartner's men pushed the enemy down from the northern slope of Nong Ham Mountain.

By evening, the North Vietnamese had broken into full-fledged flight, retreating to the northeast in an attempt to escape the vengeful Marines. Intense bombardment from the big guns and Marine aircraft followed the fleeing enemy troops, killing quite a few before the survivors, their unit integrity broken, finally got away. The Americans had shed considerable blood on this day, with 33 Marines killed and 135 wounded (including the casualties inflicted by the friendly-fire strafing). However, the enemy had been driven ignominiously from the field, and left behind more than a hundred bodies as proof of the punishment he had taken.

On the 12th, the companies of Lieutenant Colonel Wickwire's BLT were airlifted back to their ships, while Lieutenant Colonel Bell's 1/1st Marines returned to action. Working operationally with Esslinger's and Hilgartner's 5th Marine battalions, the Americans maintained constant pressure against all the NVA remnants, mostly at the company and platoon level, that they could find in the Que Son Valley. Late in the day on the 13th, Esslinger's men brought an enemy battalion to bay about three miles east of Que Son itself. A mix of small arms, artillery, and airstrikes killed 122 North Vietnamese in this short, sharp engagement, during which the artillery support had laid down a barrier of fire that effectively blocked the enemy's retreat.

A day later, another Marine company came upon 68 NVA bodies, and deduced that every one of them had been killed by the force of one massive bombardment. The final firefight of Operation Union occurred on 15 May, when two companies of the 5th Marines took on a network of heavily defended enemy bunkers. After a thorough softening up by aircraft and howitzer firepower, the Marines cleared the position and found 22 bodies in the ruined bunkers.

Operation Union had run over the course of four weeks, and had taken a savage toll on both sides. The Marines lost 110 men killed, and had nearly 500 wounded. But the USMC had clearly won a significant victory. Not only had the enemy left nearly 900 bodies on the battlefield (including almost

500 who were confirmed as members of the 2nd NVA Division) but the Americans had forced the enemy to retreat from every position he had attempted to defend. The regimental and division commanders were convinced that the prestige of the Communists in the valley had been significantly degraded, and two permanent bases would establish an American presence in the Que Son Basin that would be clear proof of the USMC victory.

And it was a victory, but like so many such outcomes in Vietnam, it was not permanent. In fact, elements of the 3rd and 21st NVA Regiments would soon move back into the area their division had so precipitously abandoned. But once they were there, the Marines would be ready to go after them again.

OPERATION UNION II

As intelligence sources confirmed that significant enemy forces were again infiltrating the Que Son Valley only a few weeks after the conclusion of Operation Union, Colonel Houghton once again advocated for an offensive to try to destroy these NVA main-force units while they were close enough to be attacked. General Nickerson agreed, and so Operation Union II began, very quickly, to take shape.

This offensive plan would also rely on the South Vietnamese Army for assistance, with the 1st ARVN Rangers and the 6th ARVN Regiment being positioned to move into the interior of the valley from the northeast and southeast, respectively. Colonel Houghton's 5th Marines would provide the main punch on the American side. The operation would attempt to close in on NVA units operating right in the middle of the Que Son Basin, in the area that had been presumably cleared by the intensive sweeps of Union I, just a month or so before.

Operation Union II kicked off on 26 May, with a surprise helicopter insertion of the 3rd Battalion, 5th Marines at Landing Zone Eagle. This LZ was right in the middle of the valley, only about five or six miles southeast of the town of Que Son, and three miles east of the summit of Lon Son Mountain. The first company, L, arrived in two waves during the midmorning, and was challenged only by a few intermittent rifle shots, but as

Company M and the battalion headquarters landed in the third wave they were met by a barrage of mortar and automatic weapons fire. Shortly before noon, a series of lethal hits knocked a big, twin-engine CH-46 helicopter out of the air, causing it to crash right beside the LZ.

Still the choppers kept coming, bringing in Company I "hot"—that is, to a landing zone that was taking enemy fire. The two companies already on the ground moved immediately toward the north to attack the entrenched enemy and relieve some of the pressure on their sister unit as it, too, landed. Aided by a punishing bombardment from artillery and aircraft, all three companies spread out to envelop the North Vietnamese position, which was only about a half mile from the landing zone. By 1630, the enemy had been cleaned out and pushed back, leaving 118 dead behind. Marine casualties in this sharp clash amounted to 38 killed and nearly a hundred wounded. The battalion commander, Lieutenant Colonel Esslinger, was evacuated after being shot in the face and partially blinded.

As the 3rd Battalion pushed the enemy into retreat, three other strong allied formations took positions to surround the NVA and attempt to cut off its withdrawal. The Marine 1/5th Battalion under Lieutenant Colonel Hilgartner moved in to block the route to the northwest, in the rugged mountainous landscape a few miles northeast of Que Son town—on the slopes below Hill 110 and Nong Ham Mountain, from which they had helped to expel the enemy forces less than three weeks earlier. Several battalions of ARVN Rangers occupied another blocking position to the northeast of the battlefield, while a force of South Vietnamese Army infantry battalions advanced from the southeast.

The Communist unit, which turned out to be the 3rd NVA Regiment, should have been trapped between these four strong forces, but once again the enemy somehow managed to slip past the blocking positions. For three days the two Marine and two ARVN forces combed the valley floor with only very minimal enemy contact. They were finally forced to conclude that the North Vietnamese had escaped from the Que Son Valley.

At least, the officers of the South Vietnamese Army were convinced the enemy had departed. As a result, the two ARVN forces concluded their part in Operation Union II and moved back to their bases closer to the coast. Colonel Houghton, however, was not so sure, and resolved to keep the pressure on until he knew for certain that the NVA regiment had been driven off.

Operating on a hunch based on all available intelligence, plus an analysis of the limited maneuver options available to his foe, he ordered his two battalions to move by air into the hills along the southern rim of the Que Son Valley, commencing the search some seven or eight miles southeast of the Marine post atop Loc Son Mountain. The airlift occurred on 30 May, with the 1/5th coming to ground at LZ Robin while the 3/5th—now under the command of Lieutenant Colonel Charles Webster—was inserted very nearby, just to the north of Robin at LZ Blue Jay. Both battalions moved eastward, sweeping through the rugged terrain side by side, but for two days the only enemy resistance encountered turned out to be sporadic sniper fire.

By the first of June, the searching vector turned toward the north, and by evening of that day both battalions of the 5th Marines had moved down from the heights and were again camped on the floor of the Que Son Valley. Houghton ordered them to move out early the next morning in a generally northwesterly direction, which would take them on a path toward LZ Eagle, where Operation Union II had kicked off. Aside from that initial sharp battle on the first day, no significant enemy contacts had been made.

That was about to change, however. On the morning of 2 June, both 5th Marines battalions advanced side by side, with the 3rd on the left and the 1st on the right. Their target was designated as objective Foxtrot, in a complex of hamlets known as Vinh Huy Village. At 0930 that morning, while the Marines were still more than half a mile from their destination, an entrenched force of some 200 NVA soldiers opened fire on the leading companies of the 3rd Battalion.

Once again artillery and airstrikes fell upon the enemy positions, but the Communists kept up a spirited defense that lasted for some three and a half hours before the position was taken by Colonel Webster's advancing Marines. Shortly after the fighting ended and casualties were prepared for evacuation, a Marine helicopter was shot down by a well-placed 57-mm recoilless rifle round.

Even as the 3rd Battalion slowly made progress in its firefight, the 1st Battalion was moving forward to engage a different foe. Moving abreast, Companies F and D (to the left and right, respectively) encountered a long, arcing hedgerow shaped roughly like a horseshoe, with the open end facing the Marines. The only approach to that obstacle was across a flat, dry paddy that was more than a half mile wide. A cautious approach under cover being impossible, the Marines spread out and moved toward the thick band of vegetation.

As the line moved across the clearing, a Vietnamese "Kit Carson" scout—a soldier who had defected from the enemy and elected to assist the Marines—suddenly fired into one of quite a few mats of hay lying on the flat, dry ground. His shots killed an enemy soldier hidden there, and the rest of the Marines immediately opened fire on the other mats, which were concealing Communist riflemen who would otherwise have popped up behind the Americans after they had passed. More than 30 NVA soldiers were killed in these volleys.

While the two companies were in the middle of the field, a strong force of NVA, well concealed in the hedge, opened fire, driving the Marines to the ground. On the left flank, the 2nd Platoon of Company F was hit particularly hard, being caught in a cross fire from guns before and off to one flank. The company reserve platoon tried to ease the pressure on the flank, but it, too, was forced to halt under the hail of intense machine-gun bursts. The Marines of Companies D and F could do little but try to keep their heads down and survive the storm while artillery and aerial munitions pounded the hedgerow.

Captain James Graham, CO of F Company, recognized that his advance platoon was in serious trouble, trapped as it was by the crisscrossing fire of two NVA machine guns. The company commander led a few Marines from his command group through the 2nd Platoon's position, into an attack against one of those emplaced weapons. Whether it was by force of arms, or because the North Vietnamese were shaken by Graham's stunning audacity, they abandoned one of their guns, which allowed the 2nd Platoon, mostly out of ammunition by now, to move back to safer positions. The Marines brought their wounded with them as they retreated, except for one man who was too badly injured to risk moving.

During an attempt to neutralize the second machine gun, however, Captain Graham was himself wounded and was unable to silence the gun. He went to ground beside the badly wounded man to offer such protection as he could, shortly thereafter radioing that he was under attack by 25 enemy soldiers. He was killed in that field; later he would be posthumously awarded the Congressional Medal of Honor for his gallantry, courage, and sacrifice.

Shortly thereafter, the 1st Battalion command post was targeted by an intense volley of enemy heavy weapons, including RPGs, recoilless rifles, and large-bore mortars. When even continuing bombardment from the air, and numerous salvos from the supporting artillery, didn't seem to affect the enemy fire, Lieutenant Colonel Hilgartner was forced to call for reinforcements. Colonel Houghton, CO of the 5th Marines, had no other troops available, so he requested the assistance of the 1st Marine Division's reserve, the 2nd Battalion, 5th Marines. General Nickerson had been recently promoted, and his replacement, Major General Donn Robertson, quickly agreed to the request.

Helicopters were hastily mustered to transport the fresh reserve battalion, which consisted of Companies E and D, 1/7th, and E 2/7th, all operating under the command of Lieutenant Colonel Mallet Jackson Jr. Colonel Houghton ordered an extensive bombardment of the reserve's hastily assigned landing zone, which lay to the northeast of the battlefield. The bulk of the battalion's forces, two companies and the command group, made it onto the ground by 1500, meeting no opposition at the LZ. Although the third company had not joined the reserve as the day merged into night, since the situation of the 1st Battalion remained critical Colonel Houghton authorized Lieutenant Colonel Jackson to advance with the force he had at the time.

Jackson detached a platoon to protect the LZ, which would be needed by the late-arriving company, and moved toward the battle. Almost immediately the Marines encountered NVA soldiers attempting to retreat. A few sharp volleys of fire quickly scattered that foe, but not before the 2/5th suffered a significant number of casualties. In the darkness, a big CH-53 Sea Stallion helicopter landed to collect the wounded, and was nearly struck by a mortar round that impacted just as it was preparing to lift off. Machine guns strafed the chopper as it lurched into the air with the wounded aboard. Inspection back at the Sea Stallion's base in Da Nang would reveal more than 50 bullet holes in the helicopter!

Finally, the approach of Jackson's two companies on the well-entrenched enemy position had its desired effect. The Communists pulled out of their trenches and foxholes and ran toward the southwest, where they became prey to the volleys of both artillery and air support. Two Marine Phantom pilots invented a unique tactic for hunting enemy infantry in an exposed location at night: one aircraft, loaded with napalm bombs, flew with all lights blacked out and trailed the lead aircraft that, in contrast, illuminated both landing and running lights. The first F4 drew lively volleys of fire from the NVA soldiers on the ground. When the muzzle flashes of the enemy guns revealed their positions, the trailing aircraft doused them with the incendiary bombs.

With the enemy having fled the field, the 5th Marines spent a weary night resting, recovering casualties, and evacuating wounded. The battle on 2 June had been a bloody affair, costing 71 Marines their lives and leaving about twice that number wounded. Enemy bodies discovered the next day totaled 476, and revealed that the hedgerow had been a highly developed fortification, with overhead cover and tunnels linking one firing position to the next. When Colonel Hilgartner was asked by one of his company commander if the Marines should fire at NVA work parties who were moving out to collect their dead, the colonel said no, and the Americans took advantage of an unusual day of truce as soldiers from both sides ignored each other while they went about the grim business of bringing in the bodies of their fallen comrades.

By 4 June, the Marines were ready to pursue, but by then the enemy had once more made good his escape from the field. Operation Union II had resulted in a significant victory, and helped secure the Que Son Valley for the rest of the year, as the South Vietnamese government was able to regain control over this fertile and populous area. Subsequent small attempts were made by the North Vietnamese to reassert their presence in the basin, but the Marines now maintained several bases in the area, and each enemy intrusion was quickly repulsed.

As a result of their steadfast abilities and accomplishments during both Union operations, the 5th Marine Regiment and the units that had been attached for these actions were awarded the Presidential Unit Citation.

EIGHT

A HARD AND BLOODY GROUND

THE USMC AND THE
FIRST BATTLES OF KHE SANH

[Battery commander] Captain Golden found me in the
fog by walking artillery rounds to me. . . . [He] put a ring
of steel around my defensive position that was so tight we
were taking dirt from the impact. . . . No doubt it saved
our lives.

CAPTAIN MICHAEL SAYERS, CO COMPANY B, 9TH MARINES,
RECALLING 26 APRIL 1967

Located in the far northwestern corner of the country of South Vietnam, Khe Sanh was a location about as out of the way as could be found in that long, narrow country. It occupies a plateau in a rugged and beautiful area of thick tropical forests, steep hills, and sharp, rocky summits. There are few people living in the area, and most of them are not ethnically Vietnamese, but tribesmen such as the Bru, one of the Humong groups. Khe Sanh occupied a plateau that was not important strategically in its own right: what made it significant was that it held a commanding position over a road.

Route 9, to be precise, which was the most northern of South Vietnam's east-west roads. Here, where the country is at its narrowest point, this short road, in 1967, was really just a rutted cart track that crossed Quang Tri province and linked the Laotian border, just four miles to the west, to Dong Ha, an important depot town on Highway 1, near the coast of the South China Sea. Since the late 1950s, Route 9 had been virtually devoid of traffic, running as it did within 10 or a dozen miles of the Demilitarized Zone (DMZ) on the 17th Parallel that separated the two Vietnams. The landscape around the road, especially west of Dong Ha, had long been an area where Communist formations could operate with considerable freedom.

In addition to the road coming into the country from Laos, Khe Sanh also lay in the path of two infiltration routes from North Vietnam. Both of these paths were well protected from aerial observation. The NVA could cross the DMZ and follow either a lowland trail through forests and dense bamboo groves, or a pathway that followed hillcrests and a ridge, all of which were covered by tropical trees with a canopy some 60 feet or more above the ground. Although Khe Sanh on its plateau lay above the level of Route 9, the base was overlooked by four hillcrests of considerably greater altitude. The highest of these was a solitary mountain about two and a half miles directly north of the camp, while the other three were parts of a large, rocky, and rugged massif extending some three to five miles northwest of Khe Sanh.

Established in the early 1960s as a remote Special Forces camp on the footprint of an old French fort, Khe Sanh had pretty much been a backwater part of the war during the first year of major American involvement in Vietnam. By 1966, it was one of a series of camps and bases that marked the path of Route 9. From west to east, they included the Lang Vei Special Forces Camp, which was right on the road, about three miles east of the border and equal distance west of the village of Khe Sanh. The Khe Sanh Combat Base, on its plateau, was about a mile and a half north of Route 9 and the village of Khe Sanh, on a narrow tributary track, Route 608.

Continuing east on Route 9 was another village, Ca Lu, six miles or so down the road; at that hamlet, Route 9 swings north for about four miles before curving back to the east again. Just northwest of that curve, and about seven miles as the crow flies due northeast of Khe Sanh, the Marines had established Fire Support Base Elliot, forever to be known as the Rockpile since it occupied the summit of a steep, craggy outcropping of karst. It would be a key support base during the fighting around Khe Sanh; it was small in area, but since the summit could only be easily reached by helicopter, it made for an exceptionally strong defensive position.

From below the Rockpile's aerie, Route 9 extended east through increasingly flat terrain about another 12 miles to the important cross-roads town, and Marine supply depot, at Dong Ha, where Route 9 terminated in a junction with South Vietnam's main north-south road, Highway 1. Midway between these key locations was the village of Cam Lo, right on the road. The III MAF had established another fire support base, Camp Carroll, just south of the road and very near to Cam Lo.

FIRST LOOK

Since its construction in 1962, Khe Sanh had included a small airstrip, which was used mainly to support the Special Forces camp. The only attention the base had received from the Marines before September of 1966 had been an expedition by three rifle companies of the 1st Battalion, 1st Marine Regiment in mid-April of that year. They had helicoptered into LZs north and east of the base and spent three days searching the area for signs of an enemy presence. When they turned up absolutely nothing, the battalion commander, Lieutenant Colonel Van Bell, decided to march his men out overland, for the symbolic effect of demonstrating that Route 9 could be used by American troops.

Before embarking on this trek, Bell and his 3rd Marine Division commanders established a fire support base at Ca Lu, about 12 miles east of Khe Sanh. The division also posted another battalion to Dong Ha to make sure reinforcements were readily available should they be needed. Bell's column advanced cautiously, with flanking patrols scouting for ambushes, but again found no sign of the enemy during the five days they spent slowly moving eastward. Once at Ca Lu, they were picked up by a convoy of trucks and rode the rest of the way to Dong Ha, where they were greeted by the III MAF commander, General Walt, and General Westmoreland himself.

For the time, at least, it looked like Khe Sanh occupied a very quiet sector indeed, but by late summer of 1966 intelligence sources were suggesting a significant buildup of NVA forces just north of the DMZ. Several sharp battles in Quang Tri province between the North Vietnamese Army

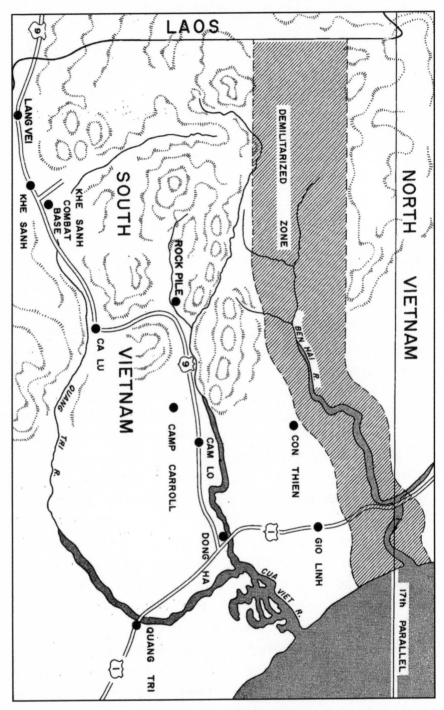

Northern Quang Tri Province

HISTORY AND MUSEUMS DIVISION, UNITED STATES MARINE CORPS

and the United States Marines convinced General Westmoreland that that northernmost province was in dire danger of enemy invasion. The MACV commander in chief urged General Walt to put a Marine garrison at Khe Sanh to guard against enemy infiltration in that remote border region, but Walt and the other USMC command officers demurred. The feeling in the Marines was that Khe Sanh was so far from anything else that it had no inherent value by itself. Too, the Marines were committed to continued pacification and civic developments in the coastal regions of I Corps, while the MACV commander was worried about incursions into South Vietnam in the remote and mostly undefended border regions.

For a while Westmoreland didn't push the issue, but on 26 September American intelligence located with almost complete certainty a North Vietnamese Army base camp just north of the DMZ, and only about 10 miles from Khe Sanh. Seeing the writing on the wall, General Walt made the decision before MACV gave him a direct order, airlifting the 1/3 battalion out of Da Nang on C-130 transports and landing the Marines at Khe Sanh. The Marines quickly established patrols in the vicinity of the base, but they only occasionally encountered signs of enemy soldiers and didn't engage in combat there for the rest of the year.

By this time, however, Khe Sanh had been recognized as the westernmost strongpoint of the Marine line along Route 9. More and more reports were suggesting a major NVA buildup in the vicinity of the DMZ, some analysts even speculating that a three-division force would be invading Quang Tri province from the north in the very near future. In response, General Walt ordered a shift northward of Marine troop strength and organizational positioning. The 3rd Marine Division headquarters was transferred from Da Nang to Phu Bai, while the 1st Marine Division was given increased responsibility in the central and southern I Corps provinces, where, fortunately, the US Army was also able to help out. In the north, 3rd Marine Division commander Major General Wood Kyle ordered one of his high-ranking staff officers, Brigadier General Lowell English, to establish a 3rd Marine Division forward command post at Dong Ha. For a time English had six battalions at his disposal, but as no further contact could be established by the end of 1966, the USMC strength in the far north was reduced to a single regiment, the 3rd Marines, and its four battalions.

As 1967 began, the Marines of the III MAF numbered some 70,000 men in two divisions and their supporting air and logistical elements. While the 1st Marine Division concentrated on pacification efforts in the southern part of the I Corps Zone, the 3rd Marine Division would find itself facing something very much like a conventional war. Brigadier General Michael Ryan took over command of the forward division headquarters from General English at Dong Ha, and the area south of the DMZ was once again reinforced to a strength of six battalions. A United States Army battery of huge 175-mm guns was established at Camp Carroll, while additional batteries of Marine howitzers were established atop the Rockpile, and at Khe Sanh itself.

To support the Marines stationed at the Khe Sanh Combat Base (KSCB) six helicopters, including two each of CH-46 twin-engine Sea Knights, UH-1E Hueys, and older UH-34 Seahorses, were permanently assigned to the base. During January and mid-February, including the period of the traditional Tet Truce, the NVA became increasingly active along the DMZ. General Ryan asked for permission to use his artillery against this part of the country that the enemy had previously used as a sanctuary. The request went all the way to the White House, and was approved on 25 February. Ryan had his batteries immediately commence an aggressive and continuous bombardment.

The NVA retaliated by attacking Marine positions northeast of Dong Ha, and trying to move south between Camp Carroll and the Rockpile. Several companies of the 3rd Marines turned them back after a sharp firefight, with significant casualties on both sides. When several NVA formations were spotted retreating to the north, they were subjected to fierce air attacks that killed more than 200 enemy soldiers. While this fighting was going on, engineers of the 11th Battalion had been working diligently to clear Route 9 of mines and to widen and grade it sufficiently to support truck traffic. On 19 March, the road was opened as far as Khe Sanh, which finally meant that the remote combat base would no longer have to be supplied solely through the air.

INCREASING CONTACTS

By mid-March, the base at Khe Sanh was garrisoned by two companies, B of the 1st Battalion, 9th Marines (Captain Michael Sayers commanding); and the recently arrived Company E of the 2/9, under Captain William Terrill. They were supported by Battery I, 12th Marines, reinforced with two 155-mm guns and two 4.2-inch mortars, and were within range of additional artillery support from the Rockpile and Camp Carroll. The reason for the reinforcement was simple: despite a lot of rain and fog during February, Sayers's men on patrols had forced a half-dozen encounters with the NVA around the base; something more than a dozen NVA had been killed, while one Marine lost his life during these clashes. More significantly, the Americans were finding proof of the enemy's presence virtually every time they ventured out of the base, so on 7 March, Terrill's company was dispatched to double the garrison's infantry strength.

On 16 March, just a few days before the landmark accomplishment of Route 9's completion, combat around Khe Sanh started to heat up. After a quiet overnight ambush mission on Hill 861, a platoon of Company E, 2/9, was carefully making its way back to the combat base when it was ambushed by intense automatic fire. The hidden NVA sprayed the platoon's flank from the concealment of a thick stand of bamboo. Though they couldn't see the enemy soldiers, the patrolling Marines consolidated their position and returned fire vigorously for a quarter of an hour before the ambushers withdrew. Five Americans were wounded and one was killed in this brief exchange.

Helicopters were summoned to evacuate the wounded, and the platoon moved toward a clearing about a hundred yards away, where the Dust Off flights could land. However, before they could cover even this short distance, they ran into a second, even more savage ambush, suffering seven killed and another four wounded. The beleaguered platoon took whatever cover it could find, returning fire while calling in artillery support. Soon shells plunged accurately into the NVA firing positions, but the enemy kept up the pressure as the platoon's ammunition started to run short.

Another patrol from Company B, 1/9, had been sweeping the area about a half mile to the east, and it was quickly ordered to go to the assistance of their comrades. The situation grew more critical as that patrol, numbering only two squads, was pinned down by enemy fire before it could link up with the Company E platoon. With the help of airstrikes and continual artillery fire, the two patrols finally joined forces and started working their way toward the medevac flight's intended landing zone at the summit of a little knoll. Once they attained that elevation, they quickly cleared an LZ and called for the medevac flights.

The first CH-46 landed, collected wounded, and took off again without incident, but when the second of the big helicopters landed, a barrage of mortar fire from hidden NVA tubes struck the hilltop LZ. That chopper made a narrow escape, getting into the air with more wounded, but the two Navy corpsmen serving as medics on the ground were both killed, and other Marines who had been helping to evacuate the wounded were themselves hit. Marine artillery poured a number of rounds onto the site of the suspected mortar position, but the next attempted landing also resulted in casualties from the NVA heavy weapons.

Things went from bad to worse when a CH-46 attempted to insert a reinforcing squad on the reverse slope of the small hill. The helicopter crashed when it missed the small landing zone. The men wounded in that crash were quickly evacuated by another helicopter, but it wasn't until the next Sea Knight came in, bringing Captain Terrill and the 2nd Platoon of his E Company, that more able-bodied Marines were able to make their way to the fight. The new arrivals helped the survivors transport the wounded to the reverse slope LZ, which at least was safe from enemy mortar fire. By nightfall, all but three of the wounded had been evacuated.

Terrill and his fresh Marines stayed overnight with the remaining wounded, and also to protect the damaged CH-46. The next day the last of the wounded, as well as the bodies of the slain Marines, were brought out, and by midday on 18 March a CH-54 Sea Crane had lifted out the wrecked Sea Knight. Captain Terrill and two platoons spent a couple of days searching the area, but the enemy troops had pulled out. In all, 19 Marines had died and 59 were wounded over these clashes; for once the American casualty total was probably higher than the losses the NVA had suffered in the fight.

However, the discovery of significant enemy forces in the Khe Sanh region provided an important wake-up call. General Ryan made several visits to the base from his advance HQ in Dong Ha, and agreed with Captain Sayers's assessment that more strength was needed at the base. Once the road was open, on the 19th, Ryan ordered up to Khe Sanh several tanks, a section of Ontos, and two detachments of US Army track- and truck-mounted weapons, some of which carried twin 40-mm automatic cannon, while the others boasted lethal quad .50-caliber machine-gun mounts.

However, at the same time as the reinforcements arrived, E Company was pulled back to Dong Ha for badly needed replenishment. In early April, when intelligence began to locate two full NVA regiments in the KSCB area, the base had fewer than a thousand men to defend it—and these included a sizable number of CIDG irregulars holding the Lang Vei Special Forces Camp several miles away. Captain Sayers's B Company remained the largest single unit in the garrison, while Battery I was swapped out for Battery F, 12th Marine Artillery. By the end of April, the 3rd Marines had overall control of the base, though most of that regiment was conducting operations farther to the east.

FIRST BATTLE OF KHE SANH: THE HILL FIGHTS

On 23 April, Captain Sayers, CO of Company B, 1/9, sent his 1st and 3rd Platoons to the north of Hill 861. They were to establish a night position and then move out the next day to search a complex of caves. On the morning of the 24th, a detachment from 2nd Platoon, accompanied by a mortar section, took up a position on Hill 700, a short distance to the south of Hill 861's summit. They set up the tubes there, and First Lieutenant Philip Sauer led a small group, including a forward observer (FO), toward the top of Hill 861, intending to set up an observation post to direct the mortars, as well as additional guns from KSCB itself, if necessary.

Before they could draw near to the hilltop, Sauer's party was slammed by an NVA ambush, the enemy quickly killing all the Marines except the FO, who escaped while the doomed lieutenant covered the man's flight with his pistol. When Second Lieutenant Thomas King, commanding the platoon with the mortar section attached, couldn't reach Sauer's party by radio, he sent a squad to see what was happening. That probing unit met the FO, who led them to the ambush site; the party retrieved the bodies of two of the four slain Marines, but heavy enemy fire forced them back to the mortar position before they could finish the search. Lieutenant King then directed a mortar and artillery barrage against the ambushers and led a squad back to the site, to find that the enemy had pulled back.

After carrying the bodies back to the mortar position, the lieutenant called for a helicopter to evacuate the dead. As soon as the chopper came in to land, however, the NVA let loose a torrent of small-arms fire from all along the crest of Hill 861. Two Huey gunships, already on scene to escort the evacuation flight, raked the crest to suppress the enemy fire—but not before the NVA guns put some three dozen holes in the Dust Off chopper.

Marine mortars and artillery again opened up on the enemy positions as Captain Sayers and a recon platoon reached the mortar position. The company CO ordered his 1st and 3rd Platoons, already positioned on the far side of Hill 861, to try to hit the enemy from behind. Those platoons quickly bogged down when they started taking heavy fire from the front and one flank. By that time the mortar ammunition had been exhausted, and every attempt to land helicopters on the position's hilltop was thwarted by strong enemy fire. Captain Sayers, with the mortar section and the rest of his men, moved down from Hill 700 to spend the night.

During that day's fighting, the Marines had lost 12 men killed and 17 wounded, together with two men missing. But their sacrifice had inadvertently forced the NVA to reveal the strength of its presence in the Khe Sanh area, tripping the alarm for a planned offensive that had intended nothing less than the overrunning of the entire base. At least two regiments of the 325C North Vietnamese Army Division were almost in position to launch the attack, but now surprise was gone.

The task of protecting the base and rooting out the enemy threat was given to Colonel John Lanigan's 3rd Marine Regiment. As soon as the fog lifted on 25 April, Lanigan sent the 3/3 Battalion, under Lieutenant Colonel Gary Wilder, and an additional company into Khe Sanh by air transport. By the time they landed, Captain Sayers and his 2nd Platoon were back in the field, working to link up with the still-stranded 1st and 3rd Platoons. By 1500 on the day of his arrival, Wilder already had elements of his battalion moving against Hill 861. Unfortunately, without an opportunity to set codes, radio frequencies, and call signs in advance, radio communication between Wilder and Sayers remained sketchy through the developing fight.

Captain Sayers was able to do little more during the day than to reunite his platoons on the northwest side of the hill. Enemy fire was too intense to allow for helicopter evacuation, so the Marines settled down for a lonely night with their many wounded, knowing the landscape around them teemed with NVA troops.

Company K, 3/3, of Wilder's battalion, under Captain Bayliss Spivey Jr., began an assault against the crest of Hill 861 before 1530. The terrain dictated that he divide his attack, sending one platoon up each of two roughly parallel ridgelines that converged toward the summit. The 1st Platoon took heavy casualties, and was reduced to fewer than a dozen effective men after two hours; the 3rd Platoon, on the nearby ridge, was unable to support its sister formation because of terrain, even though it had not encountered enemy resistance. Reluctantly, Spivey committed his 2nd Platoon; when it, too, encountered stiff resistance, Company K was forced to dig in for the night. An additional unit, Company K, 9th Marines, flew to Khe Sanh from Camp Carroll before nightfall on the 25th, but they arrived too late to move out that night.

The following morning, the NVA opened up on the 3rd Battalion CP and Khe Sanh itself with a barrage of mortar and recoilless rifle rounds. Fortunately, a layer of fog shrouded the hillsides and summits, where the guns were, and the fire was fairly inaccurate—many of the shells lobbed at KSCB did not even strike within the perimeter. At the same time, the Marines of Sayers's company, to the east of Hill 881S, spotted the enemy firing positions through the fog, and were able to call in air and artillery strikes that quickly doused the enemy guns.

Company K/9th moved toward the fighting on the 26th, while Companies K and B of the 3rd Marines resumed their attempts to gain the summit of Hill 861. The NVA fought back from a series of well-concealed bunkers, heavily protected on top and built with cleverly interlocking fields of fire. Some of them were so hard to detect that unsuspecting Marines advanced to within a few yards of the position only to be cut down by a sudden burst of fire. By late in the day, casualties in both companies were so severe that they needed assistance from K/9th just to extricate themselves from the fighting and fall back to the base of the hill. In one unit, every man except the point and rearguard needed to help with the stretchers just to get the wounded out of the firing zone.

Once again it was clear that the Marines would need more men for this operation. General Hochmuth, CO of the 3rd Marine Division, released the SLF battalion, the 2/3rd, for this task, in the process returning it to its parent regiment. In a whirlwind transfer, the men of that unit were plucked out of the field near Hue by helicopters at midday and transported to Phu Bai, where they boarded C-130 transport planes. Four hours after initial alert, three companies and the battalion command group were landing at Khe Sanh. They moved out immediately, settling into a night position 500 yards east of the 3/3rd location.

For two days, the 27th and 28th of April, the Marines on the ground evacuated wounded, rested, and reloaded, while airstrikes and artillery punished the slopes and crest of Hill 861. The two companies that had suffered the most, K/3rd and B/9th, were pulled back, to be replaced by fresher units. Another artillery formation, Battery B, 12th Marines, was flown into Khe Sanh late in the afternoon of the 27th, and was in firing position less than two hours later. The Army's 175-mm guns at Camp Carroll added their heavy ordnance to the shelling; all in all more than 2,000 rounds were expended against the enemy target.

But that was only a fraction compared to the weight of explosives dropped on the hill from the air. For most of both days, flights of USMC attack aircraft were "stacked up" above the hill. Because of the thick vegetation on the target area, the FACs started the attacks with small "Snake Eye" bombs of 250 or 500 pounds. These ripped away the foliage, allowing the larger bombs to plummet straight down and penetrate many of the sturdy enemy bunkers.

With two full battalions in position to attack, the next move for the grunts on the ground was to be an assault on Hill 861 by the 2/3rd Marines, under Lieutenant Colonel Earl Delong, late in the day of 28 April. Lieutenant Colonel Wilder's 3/3rd was to pass through Delong's battalion and move directly against Hill 881S. The 2/3 was to support this attack, and then turn toward the final objective, Hill 881N. The initial attack went off without a hitch, as it turned out that the NVA had pulled off of Hill 861. The Marines moved through the burned and shattered terrain, finding the wreckage of bunkers and enemy bodies, consolidating their position without suffering any further casualties.

The next phase of the Hill Fights began right away on the morning of 29 April, with the 3rd Battalion, operating on the left of the 2nd, advancing toward a hill halfway between Hill 861 and the next objective, Hill 881S. Three companies, M of 3/3rd, and K and M of the 9th Marines, took to the advance, with M/9th moving in the lead. When that company met a small NVA force in a ravine, the other Company M bypassed the firefight and continued toward the intermediate hill. The enemy resistance was overcome with fire support, and shortly after 1900 the Marines held the smaller elevation, with a clear view of Hill 881S.

When the Marines spotted NVA troops setting up a mortar section on the higher hill, they called for artillery strikes, and the enemy hastily abandoned the position. After dark, an NVA attack began to take shape nearby, but lethal artillery strikes broke up the North Vietnamese companies before they could advance. The Marines on the intermediate hill could hear the wounded enemy troops crying out after the deadly bombardment.

The next move of the battle began with dawn on 30 April as the 3/3rd continued toward Hill 881S while Lieutenant Colonel Delong's battalion moved down from Hill 861 toward the third objective, Hill 881N. The battalion's immediate task was to protect Wilder's 3/3rd's right flank. Companies H and G ran into strong bunkers occupied by NVA, with Company H suffering more than 50 casualties, nine of them fatal. The casualties were evacuated while fire support pounded the bunkers. When the attack resumed, Company G was able to take the strongpoint—though some of the NVA troops defended their position with suicidal tenacity.

Meanwhile, the 3rd Battalion moved toward the formidable height of Hill 881S. After moving up the rugged elevation along several ridges and encountering only sporadic small-arms fire, some of the Marines allowed themselves a tinge of optimism. Too soon: at about 1100 the hilltop seemed to burst into flame as hidden NVA blasted small arms and automatic weapons from a whole series of well-camouflaged bunkers. Mortar rounds struck the exposed Marines while additional enemy troops appeared behind them, shooting from bunkers and concealed holes that the advancing riflemen had passed right through without realizing the enemy was there.

Huey gunships and strike aircraft swept in to pound the enemy, often as close as 50 yards from the friendly forces. The order to retreat came at 1230, but it was much later in the afternoon before the embattled Marines could extract themselves from the savage fight. They carried 43 killed and more than a hundred wounded down from the hill, a casualty rate that would knock Company M 3/3rd, which had been leading the climb, out of the fight for the time being.

The pattern that had worked on Hill 861 was repeated for the rest of 30 April, and through 1 May. More than half a million pounds of explosives were directed at the two remaining heights from the air and from the guns of Khe Sanh and the Army tubes at Camp Carroll. Company M was pulled from the line, replaced by the regimental reserve, Company F, 2/3. The division commander, General Hockmuth, also placed Company E, 9th Marines, under control of the 3rd Marine Regiment.

By the 2nd of May, the 3rd Battalion moved out again, and during the course of the day moved up and over the crest of Hill 881S, having to deal with nothing worse than the occasional sniper. Colonel Wilder set up his command post on the summit, while his men looked over the hill. They were astounded by the level of fortifications, which had begun with some 250 bunkers, each covered with multiple layers of logs and a thick coating of dirt. Wilder's men quickly passed the word to Colonel Delong, warning him to expect the same on Hill 881N.

The 2nd Battalion, 3rd Marines, had already encountered fierce resistance on the lower slopes of its objective, first in the form of enemy small arms and mortars, and finally as an assault from Mother Nature herself as an intense squall of pouring rain and howling wind lashed the exposed riflemen. The three assault companies, E, G, and H, hunkered down for the night partway up the hill. A savage NVA counterattack struck them in the early hours of 3 May, during which the enemy penetrated the Marine position and annihilated most of a squad. In a last-ditch effort, a group of 11 combat engineers picked up automatic rifles and grenades and helped to hold the line.

Finally a flare ship arrived, and parachute flares—with the brilliance of two million candlepower—brightened the night. In the clear illumination the Marines on Hill 881S saw a major NVA attack moving toward their beleaguered comrades, and were able to use long-range recoilless rifle fire to rout the would-be enemy attackers. At daylight, a company of Marines worked on eradicating the few surviving NVA troops remaining within their perimeter, a task that took most of the day and resulted in dozens of men killed on both sides.

At 0850 on 5th May, Companies E and F started for the summit of Hill 881N. Company G worked its way around to attack from the northern flank. The Marines encountered fierce resistance and had to stop several times to call in supporting fire against the enemy strongpoint, but by 1500 they had cleared out the last of the snipers and claimed the summit of the hill. Although some pursuit skirmishing occurred as the 325C North Vietnamese Division pulled back to Laos and North Vietnam, the First Battle of Khe Sanh was, for all intents and purposes, over.

The USMC held the high ground north and west of Khe Sanh, but the victory had not come without high cost: 155 Marines had died on those rugged slopes, and more than 400 had been wounded. Enemy KIA confirmed by body count approached a thousand, and there was reason to believe many more NVA troops had died in the fighting, with many bodies presumably hauled away from the battlefield. One further note is worthy of mention: this was the first battle during which the Marines had been armed with the M16 rifle, as opposed to the old reliable M14. The M16 was lighter and fired a smaller—but even more lethal—round, allowing each man to carry more ammunition into battle. But the newer weapon was already developing a reputation for its tendency to jam, and as for a final comparison the jury remained very much out.

AN INTERVAL BETWEEN BATTLES

Once more the North Vietnamese Army seemed to have withdrawn from the Khe Sanh area, though no one was really optimistic that the condition would last. Still, the 3rd Marine Division took advantage of the quiet time to do some shuffling at the base. The two battalions of the 3rd Marine Regiment were pulled out and replaced by the 1/26th Marines. Since the other two battalions of the 26th were currently attached to other units, an undersized regimental headquarters was established at the KSCB. On 13 May, Colonel John Padley, CO of the 26th Marines, took over command of the base.

The 1/26th placed company-strength garrisons on Hills 861 and 881S and a detachment with a radio relay station at Hill 950 on a shoulder of the highest mountain in the area, Hill 1015. This was a stand-alone peak due north of the combat base, separated by the Rao Quan River Valley from the three summits that had cost so much blood during the hill fights. Despite vigorous patrolling, the rest of May passed with only sporadic contact with small parties of enemy troops.

On 1 June 1967, the Marines made their first change in command at the top of the III MAF since deployment to Vietnam two years earlier. General Walt handed the baton to Lieutenant General Robert Cushman

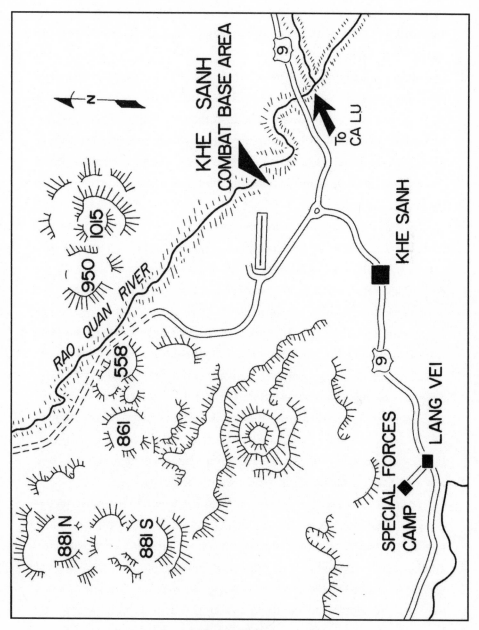

Khe Sanh Area

HISTORY AND MUSEUMS DIVISION, UNITED STATES MARINE CORPS

Jr., a Marine who had been through the attack on Pearl Harbor and had earned the Navy Cross fighting on Guam during World War II. Cushman had been Walt's deputy for some time, and was quite familiar with the situation in Vietnam.

Action picked up in June as, on the 6th, Khe Sanh was hit by a barrage from mortars and rocket launchers. That same day the radio relay station was attacked. The enemy was driven off at the cost of six Marine KIA and two wounded. On the 7th, a patrol was attacked aggressively, resulting in 66 enemy dead and 18 fallen Marines, plus 28 wounded. On the 9th, a Huey was shot down near the base; the pilot died, though the other three crewmen were rescued.

Clearly, the action was increasing in intensity. Throughout the rest of June, the base was subjected to additional mortar and rocket attacks, and patrols in the base's TAOR made increasingly frequent contacts with the enemy. Several sharp firefights occurred until, around the end of June, the NVA seemed ready to stand down again.

Throughout this period, truck convoys had been bringing supplies from Dong Ha to the base along Route 9. These big columns, always escorted by Marine infantry and a few armored vehicles, had been rumbling down the road without molestation. On 21 July, however, a convoy of 85 vehicles started westward from the depot near the coast. Following routine, it halted in Ca Lu so that a rifle platoon could sweep the road ahead. On this day the searching Marines discovered an enemy ambush, and had the trucks wait at Ca Lu while the threat was neutralized.

Over the next two days, several companies swept the roadway, uncovering mines and other enemy ambush positions. It was not until 25 July that the convoy completed its relatively short journey. Two weeks later, another convoy brought in many tons of supplies, but after that General Cushman ordered the road closed down again, deciding that the convoys were too vulnerable and the route too dangerous to keep tempting fate. For the next nine months, Khe Sanh would be supplied by air.

Danger was present at all levels in the Vietnam War, a fact illustrated when General Hochmuth, CO of the 3rd Marine Division, was killed when the Huey in which he was riding was shot down near Hue. His replacement was announced two weeks later: Major General Rathvon Tompkins, another veteran of World War II who had won a Navy Cross for gallantry in the Marianas Islands—on Saipan, in his case. As he took command of the allied operation area that was closer to North Vietnam than any other, he would have his hands full with this new kind of war.

NINE

ALLIES STAND TOGETHER

SOUTH VIETNAM AND THE
UNITED STATES HOLD FIRM AT LOC NINH

This operation is one of the most significant and important that has been conducted in Vietnam. . . . So far as I can see, you made just one mistake, and that is you made it look too easy.

GENERAL WILLIAM WESTMORELAND, PRAISING HIS TROOPS
AFTER THE BATTLE OF LOC NINH, NOVEMBER 1967

When the Americans began to arrive in Vietnam in force, the entire organization of the South Vietnamese Army was teetering on the brink of defeat. Desertion among the rank and file had reached astronomical levels, and the efforts of young men to avoid conscription made replacing the army's losses a very difficult challenge. A series of disastrous and costly defeats inflicted by the Viet Cong—who had begun to seem invincible—had brought army morale to an all-time low. The arrival of US Marine and Army units in the middle of 1965 stemmed the tide of losing, giving some hope of a least holding on in the war against the Communists. But from the summer of 1965 until early in 1967, the ARVN had for the most part been content to let the burgeoning United States military presence in their country take on the conduct of the war.

In addition to fighting the enemy, the Americans had taken a strong role in training, equipping, and otherwise bolstering the strength of their South Vietnamese allies. A string of US victories in the field began to convince the ARVN officers and men that they were not necessarily engaged in a lost cause and that ultimate victory was at least a realistic possibility.

This shift, coupled with the fact that a growing percentage of the population was now living in areas free of VC harassment and raiding, profoundly affected the attitudes of both military and civilian South Vietnam.

By May of 1967, the best MACV assessments of the ARVN indicated that US advisers rated 148 out of 153 battalions as capable of standing toe-to-toe with at least the Viet Cong, and possibly even with units of the North Vietnamese Army, in battle. As if to illustrate the point, in that same month the 2nd ARVN Rangers were helicoptered into an exceptionally rugged region of the Central Highlands. They concluded their mission successfully, and with considerable flair, a fact that frankly astonished their American advisers, who only a few months earlier had never suspected that the unit could perform such a mission.

By autumn, the South Vietnamese were making significant contributions to their own defense, with an ARVN unit even defending a portion of the Demilitarized Zone. On October 27, the 88th NVA Regiment made a vicious night attack on the 3rd Battalion of the 9th ARVN Regiment in Phuoc Long province. Not only did the South Vietnamese stand firm, but they drove off the attackers and inflicted heavy casualties.

Two days later, the enemy target was a South Vietnamese base at Loc Ninh, which included an airstrip and an adjacent Special Forces camp. The base was the northernmost outpost on Highway 13, and was garrisoned by an assortment of troops, none of them regular army. The defenders included three Civilian Irregular Defense Group (CIDG) companies, a company of Regional Forces (RF), and a platoon of Popular Forces (PF) soldiers. All of these units lacked the equipment and training of a regular ARVN unit. The 5th ARVN Regiment, which had a history of less than stellar performance in combat, was stationed nearby and considered as a potential, but not a reliable, reinforcement.

Loc Ninh was the district capital, a city of some 10,000 people and the center of huge plantations of rubber trees. It was in an area of low, rolling hills, and the well-ordered trees of the plantations marched over those hills like lines of soldiers in an old-fashioned, precision-drilled army. The most prominent features of the town were the regal villas of the French plantation managers, with their red-tile roofs, lush green lawns, and the grand country club with its huge swimming pool and tennis courts paved with hard red clay. Gardens of bright flowers blossomed around the splendid colonial-era buildings, and if one looked in that direction one might conclude that this was a town entirely at peace.

The harsh reality of the present war, however, was visible in the military airstrip and fortified compounds on the outskirts of the city. The largest compound contained the garrisons of the irregular companies of CIDG and the RF and PF units. A rickety control tower rose next to the long airstrip, and another compound of French-style bungalows and stables, now reinforced into bunkers, contained the district headquarters, all surrounded by barbed wire. The Special Forces camp, farther down the airstrip, was marked by low, solidly built bunkers and a diamond-shaped perimeter protected by barbed wire, all surrounded by a cleared area extending out to where the rubber trees loomed.

The CIDG (pronounced sid-jee) troops were drawn mostly from the country's ethnic minorities. They had been trained and equipped primarily through the Green Berets, and because of a history of racial bias against them, they tended to be more loyal to their American advisers than they were to the South Vietnamese government. Both the Regional and Popular Forces were essentially militia formed from recruits drawn from the local population, often men older than the typical soldier, less fit, and lacking the training and equipment of regular ARVN units. But they were at least equally motivated to defeat the Communists.

In addition to guarding the district capital, the base at Loc Ninh occupied a key location near where Highway 13 met the Cambodian border. Due to this important placement, Loc Ninh was an important component of the border interdiction plans that the Americans and South Vietnamese were attempting to implement—they could not completely seal the border with Cambodia, but at least they could try to monitor the comings and goings of enemy formations. Since as early as September 1967, a variety of intelligence reports had indicated that enemy forces might be planning an attack on the camp. By early in October, those estimates had been tightened to the point where the attack was predicted to occur between 22 and 30 October. The new president of South Vietnam, Nguyen Van Thieu, was to be inaugurated during that week, and the Communists knew that the capture of a district capital while this ceremony was going on in Saigon would have a huge morale and propaganda impact.

The enemy was on the move, too: observers at Loc Ninh and elsewhere throughout the border region and War Zone C had been keeping track of the 272nd VC Regiment, which, short one battalion, was known to be active nearby. The 273rd Regiment had been tracked moving steadily northward, leaving War Zone C in August to approach Dong Zoai. A month later it was still farther north, and by the last week of October it would be located just a few miles northwest of Loc Ninh. The 165th VC Regiment had engaged in a battle at Tong Le Chon on 7 August in the so-called Fishhook stretch of borderland, but it, too, had been moving north, and by November was suspected to be lurking in the Loc Ninh district. The overarching headquarters would presumably be the 9th VC Division, which had moved west and north out of War Zone D to bring itself into proximity with units near Loc Ninh.

A preliminary round in the battle for Loc Ninh actually occurred about 35 miles south of the base, near a town called Dau Yeu. By 11 October, a unit of the 1st Infantry Division, the 1st Battalion, 18th Infantry, under the command of Lieutenant Colonel Richard Cavazos, had been patrolling in the area for a week, seeking contact with some part or another of the 9th VC Division, the most important main-force Viet Cong unit in the area. Each day they would sweep a new area of the jungle and at night they would retire to a night defensive position (NDP) complete with roofed bunkers, remote sensors, and carefully aligned fields of fire.

On the 11th, the battalion's Companies B and C were in the field. The point (i.e., leading) squad in the search was accompanied by a handler and a scout dog, one of many canines who were being employed in the field to help with searches and serve in their time-honored roles as watchdogs. The dog quickly indicated an alert, and the infantry column immediately went into the cloverleaf search pattern that General Dupuy had instigated for the Big Red One during the previous year.

After advancing the better part of a mile through the thick growth, the companies took some enemy small-arms fire at close range. They had run into a battalion from the 271st VC Regiment, accidently advancing into the Viet Cong's path while the enemy unit was stealthily trying to make its way north. Because of the cloverleaf search technique, however, the Americans had avoided an ambush and were able to pull back and call for air and artillery support.

For an hour the supporting elements pounded the area where the VC had been hiding. At one point, nearly a hundred enemy soldiers charged the American position, but many were cut down by infantrymen who used the terrain as cover. By the time the fighting was over, one American had been killed, while several dozen VC lost their lives. This encounter was one of several suffered by the 271st Regiment as it moved north, and the cumulative effect was that, by the time it reached the area around Loc Ninh, the unit had been so thoroughly battered that it was at far less than full effectiveness.

FIRST PUNCH THROWN, AND PARRIED

As a result of the intelligence estimates, the South Vietnamese soldiers garrisoning the camp at Loc Ninh maintained a very high level of alert as the last week of October passed. Those estimates were proved to be downright uncanny in accuracy shortly after midnight in the very early hours of 29 October. At approximately 0115, heavy mortar rounds crumped loudly into the district headquarters compound to the northwest of Loc Ninh Airstrip, with machine guns and handheld weapons quickly added to the chorus. By sound, the defenders could tell that the initial impetus of the enemy onslaught likely came from the northwest.

More mortar bombs descended on the Special Forces compound, and recoilless rifle rounds were directed at the house of the district chief. The camp immediately went to full alert, and American forward air controllers, plus a Spooky gunship, sometimes known as "Puff the Magic Dragon," were in the skies over the base within 15 minutes. The mortar shelling continued unabated, mostly focusing on the airstrip and Special Forces compound, and at about 0130 a battalion of the 273rd VC Regiment charged out of the jungle to the northwest and swarmed against the camp's defenses. The attackers were supported by an unusual degree of heavy weaponry, including rockets and recoilless rifle rounds. It was later learned that a VC artillery battalion, the 84A, had been attached to the 9th VC Division for the battle at Loc Ninh.

More than 180 mortar rounds pounded the camp over the next several hours as flares illuminated the night sky and the Spooky gunship raked the attackers with its lethal Gatling guns, often called the "Ruff Puffs." Helicopter gunships added rockets and machine guns to the defense, while the irregular South Vietnamese companies garrisoning the camp fought furiously to resist the onslaught. Around 0300, some of the VC fought their way through the perimeter defenses of the Regional Forces/Popular Forces camp and began to ransack the headquarters compound. They set fire to buildings and dropped grenades right through the firing slits of many of the bunkers.

After an hour the only holdout in the compound was the command bunker, which the base CO, Captain Tran Minh Cong, held with 12 men. As this small group was running out of ammunition, the captain radioed his attached artillery battery and ordered the guns to target his own position. When the gunners resisted he assured them that his shelter was so strong it could survive a B-52 bombing raid. So the shells fell on the bunker, and the captain and his men survived while the shrapnel from the exploding rounds cleared the VC off of his roof again and again.

By 0520, the Communists broke off their attacks, falling back from Loc Ninh except for those who occupied the captured camp. As soon as the main attack petered out, however, the defenders organized two companies of the CIDG to counterattack the Viet Cong in the RF/PF camp. A company of the 5th ARVN Division, one of the formations the Americans had previously regarded as less than reliable, was helicoptered 60 miles to Loc Ninh and landed in the Special Forces camp. Soldiers of the 5th Division, it turned out, were more than willing to fight.

Indeed, the ARVN soldiers quickly spearheaded the attack against the enemy position, leading the CIDG companies who pressed home the assault with commendable tenacity. Though it took almost the whole day, by 1600 they had ejected the enemy from the portion of the base they had managed to penetrate. The Communists left 147 bodies in and around the camp. At the same time, a company of the base's garrison had been making an overnight patrol north of Loc Ninh when the men heard the attack. This unit moved through the forest on its officer's initiative to strike some of the attacking formations from behind. The small patrol company managed to kill 23 VC and NVA soldiers before safely returning to the base.

NEXT MOVES

In the garrison of Loc Ninh, those not engaged in the counterattack to recapture the occupied camp spent the daylight hours of 29 October digging their trenches deeper, resupplying weapons, and preparing for another attack. As for an American response, Major General Hay commanding the 1st Infantry Division, had reacted within hours of learning about the attack. He immediately seized upon the idea of inserting four US battalions, drawn from his own and the 25th Division, each with supporting artillery, in a rough square formation around Loc Ninh. He would place those units in such positions as to virtually force the VC to attack if they wanted to move out of the battle area. He also ordered some of his infantry and artillery to make ready for air transport right to the base at Loc Ninh, anticipating that a stiffening of the defense might become necessary.

At 0630, less than six hours after the Viet Cong started their operation, the 1st Battalion, 18th Infantry, under Lieutenant Colonel Cavazos, dropped into a hastily designated landing zone that would form the southwest corner of the square. Within less than six hours, at 1215, the battalion had attacked and defeated a VC company in the midst of the rubber groves, leaving a bizarre after-battle image of hundreds of bullet-punctured trees "bleeding white sap." The clash left 24 VC dead when their survivors fled the field. Exactly 24 hours later, at 1215 on 30 October, Cavazos's men engaged a battalion of the 273rd VC Regiment and killed another 83 enemy soldiers.

Also on the 30th, elements of the 2/28th Infantry and two batteries from the 6/15th Artillery, landed on the Loc Ninh Airstrip and took up positions at one end of the runway. Many of the infantrymen rode in on CH-47 Chinook helicopters, but big C-130 transport planes also came in for landings, often disregarding enemy fire. The Hercules could carry APCs, and delivered several of the armored vehicles to the battle; on at least one occasion the track rolled right out of the plane and opened up on enemy positions with its smaller machine guns (the main gun having been stored for the flight). Another C-130, having dropped off its cargo, was punctured by a friendly 105-mm round as it took off again, the round fused so that it exploded a hundred yards after it passed through the plane. The Hercules completed its flight without untoward incident.

At the same time, tanks of the 1st Division's cavalry squadron raced up Highway 13, roaring toward the battlefield at top speed. The 1/28th Infantry, under the command of Lieutenant Colonel James Cochran III, flew into an LZ a couple of miles to the southeast of Loc Ninh, setting itself up to block the VC from fleeing the battlefield in that direction. It encountered only mild enemy resistance, as the bulk of the VC forces seemed to be on the opposite side of the base.

Just after midnight in the early morning hours of 31 October, the 272nd VC Regiment made its strongest push against the base at Loc Ninh. They attacked in waves through the outer perimeter and charged across the airstrip, making for the CIDG camp and the nearby district headquarters. Apparently they didn't realize that one of the American howitzers was positioned right at the end of the runway. The gunners lowered their barrel to horizontal and took aim; later one would say it was like "shooting down a bowling alley." Though they were not equipped with the lethal fléchette canister rounds, the artillerymen improvised by bouncing high-explosive rounds along the flight line and into the enemy formations with fuses set for short range. The gun fired more than 500 rounds at what was point-blank range for the big howitzer. (The radio call sign for the battery was "Deadly," which probably even the enemy would have agreed was most appropriate.) The attack was repulsed after furious fighting, with the

VC and NVA leaving 110 bodies on and next to the airstrip when they pulled back before dawn.

Some others of the ever-inventive American military personnel had come up with a unique technique to mark friendly positions for the overhead aircraft during a night battle. The idea, supposedly originating with an FAC officer, was that the men on the ground would fill a C-ration can about three quarters full of sand, and then soak the sand with diesel fuel. The cans would then be placed around the perimeter held by the American soldiers, and ignited when action seemed imminent. The fuel would burn for some time in the can, with a low flame that wouldn't flare above the can's rim. Thus it would be visible to pilots and gunners above, plainly marking the friendly position, but undetectable to the enemy ground forces at the same elevation as the cans. Many of these makeshift lanterns were employed around the defensive positions at Loc Ninh.

NAILS IN THE VC COFFIN

After the bloody attack across the airstrip, the 272nd had had enough, and began to move southwestward to get out of the battle area. Just after midnight in the early morning of 2 November, the rest of the Viet Cong regiment came up against the 1/18th battalion, which, like all American units in the area, had gone into a night defensive perimeter (NDP) when the sun went down. Ambush patrols outside the NDP picked up the approach of the VC, and detonated claymore mines that disrupted the initial thrust of the attack. The patrols were pulled back to the perimeter just in time as the VC charged from three directions, northeast, east, and south, only to be met by a hail of small-arms, machine-gun, and artillery fire.

When helicopter gunships reached the scene, they focused their fire on the southern approach to the camp. The choppers were shot at by some VC heavy machine guns on the ground, but they made difficult targets in the night skies, and none of them suffered significant damage. After about three hours, the Viet Cong broke off the attack, leaving more than 200 bodies in the vicinity of the perimeter. The Americans suffered one killed and eight wounded. As an oddity, two of the slain VC were found to be carrying Soviet-made flamethrowers; they had both been killed before they got close enough to employ the frightening weapons.

After daybreak on 2 November, General Hay decided that it was time to close off the rest of his square. The 2/12 Infantry had been attached to the Big Red One for the operation, and he directed the battalion commander, Lieutenant Colonel Rafael Tice, to air-assault into a position four or five miles to the northeast of the base. Lieutenant Colonel Arthur Stigall's 1st Battalion, 26th Infantry, was directed to a blocking position a similar distance to the northwest. Both battalions made quiet, uncontested landings and had established NDPs before dark.

That very night an unlucky party of eight VC from the 272nd Regiment, some of them carrying handheld flashlights, wandered right into the lines of the 2/12 just before midnight. An irate sergeant major grabbed one of the men by the collar and demanded an explanation for the violation of light-discipline, only then recognizing the black uniforms and AK-47 guns carried by the new arrivals. Before the startled enemy could react, four were killed and the others captured. One of the prisoners was physically tackled by a young lieutenant who then knocked him out with a sharp punch to the face. A larger force attacked the position at 0220 of 3 November, but the VC were brushed aside, leaving 28 dead.

Several more days passed without significant contact with any sizable enemy forces. The Americans temporarily stationed at the airstrip maintained their vigilance at night, always prepared for another attack, but none materialized. During the day, they practiced whatever forms of recreation and relaxation they could invent, here in the heart of a war zone with enemy lurking in the surrounding jungle.

One unusual event would become a popular memory for the men at Loc Ninh: a group of infantrymen found a massive python in the jungle just beyond the perimeter, and eight soldiers carried it back to the NDP. The snake had a large "pig-sized" bulge about a third of the way down its body, and was rather torpid at the time of its capture. A lieutenant found a refrigerator-sized cardboard box, and the reptile—affectionately named

"Lurch"—was placed in that makeshift pen. A few nights later the airstrip was the target of a mortar barrage, and as the infantrymen were heading down into their bunker one of them noticed that the box was tipped over and Lurch was missing. After some hesitancy, the men decided that the bunker, even with the possibility that it contained a huge constrictor, was a better option than the airstrip during a mortar attack. Fortunately for all concerned, it turned out that the snake had apparently slithered back into the jungle whence it had come. One soldier later wrote that he hoped Lurch was contentedly squeezing and eating Viet Cong in the jungle.

A final firefight marked the close of the battle of Loc Ninh on 7 November. The 1st/26 Infantry Battalion had been pulled out of its northwest corner of the square the day before, and air-assaulted into a position several miles to the east. After one day in the new position, they encountered the 3rd battalion of the 272nd Regiment. Two American companies and the battalion colonel's command group roughly handled the Communist force with the help of 27 airstrikes, artillery, and helicopter gunships. More than 90 VC lost their lives in that engagement.

The battle for Loc Ninh had resulted in a stunning defeat for a veteran, well-equipped Viet Cong main-force unit. The 9th VC Division and attached formation had suffered at least a thousand men confirmed killed in action, and most estimates suggest that the number is significantly higher. Allied losses were fewer than 50 men killed, and less than half of those came from the American forces. It is likely that nowhere else in the war, at no other time, was the United States doctrine of aerial mobility and crushing superiority in firepower so dramatically illustrated as during the nine days of battle at Loc Ninh.

IN THE SHADOW OF DIEN BIEN PHU

THE SIEGE OF KHE SANH COMBAT BASE

[It was] just like a World War II movie. . . . Charlie didn't
know how to cope with it. . . . We just walked all over him.
CAPTAIN EARLE BREEDING, CO COMPANY E, 2/26 MARINES,
REMEMBERING COMBAT OF 6 FEBRUARY 1968

By the end of 1967, it had become clear that the 325C North Vietnamese Army Division was again moving into Khe Sanh's remote corner of South Vietnam. Reliable intelligence also fixed a second division, the 304th, in the area just west of the Laotian border. General Westmoreland, who still harbored a desire to use Khe Sanh as the base for an eventual American incursion into Laos, was keen to make sure that the Marines held the position at all costs. To that end he ordered III MAF commander General Cushman to reinforce the KSCB. The order was passed down to General Tompkins, commanding general of the 3rd Marine Division, who elected to dispatch the 3rd Battalion, 26th Marines, to Khe Sanh, reattaching it to its parent regiment and doubling the number of Marine riflemen holding South Vietnam's most remote outpost.

MEMORIES OF DIEN BIEN PHU

As the pivotal year of 1968 began, Khe Sanh remained very much on General Westmoreland's mind. As discussions of holding the base continued, it was impossible not to think of an earlier event that bore at least superficial resemblance to the Marines' situation at the remote combat base. West-moreland, like every other professional American military man, knew the story of the French disaster at Dien Bien Phu 14 years earlier.

In one of the pivotal battles of the 20th century, the Viet Minh insurgents in Vietnam, a mixed organization of both Communist and nationalist loyalists commanded by the brilliant revolutionary General Vo Nguyen Giap, won a pitched battle against a French Army that was desperate to maintain a hold on its resource-rich colonies in Southeast Asia. It was the first time in history that an army of former colonists had used Western tactics and equipment to win a decisive victory over their former colonizers.

Like the Americans at Khe Sanh were hoping to do with the North Vietnamese, the French at Dien Bien Phu had very much tried to goad the Viet Minh into attacking an impregnable position by building a base in a remote, hilly region of the country and practically daring the insurgents to assault. The colonial-minded French, trying to regain the empire that had mostly withered during World War II, were confident that their modern doctrine, training, weaponry, airpower, and artillery would allow them to annihilate vast numbers of the enemy, and bring the French Indochina War to a satisfactory close.

In reality, the Viet Minh were able to move a huge amount of heavy artillery to within range of the French base, a fact that absolutely stunned the French, and most of the world's other military experts. Sometimes digging tunnels right through mountaintops, the Viet Minh guns fired from concealed and well-protected bunkers that were virtually impervious to counterbattery fire and air attack. Giap's guns outperformed the French artillery to the extent that the French artillery commander committed suicide by hand grenade when he realized he had no effective means to match the insurgents' firepower.

The Viet Minh closed in on the base, overrunning the nearby outposts until they could bring their guns to bear directly on the runway of the air base, thus negating the French ability to support Dien Bien Phu by air. The result of the battle was the loss of all French Southeast Asian colonies, and the division of Vietnam into two countries along the line of the 17th Par-allel as a result of the Geneva Conference of 1954.

Clearly, the similarities between the base and battle at Dien Bien Phu and Westmoreland's cherished outpost at Khe Sanh were apparent to any-one who cared to think about it. And the Marines did think about it. But the MACV commanding general was as determined as his French fore-runners had been to force the insurgent enemy into a decisive battle, and he believed Khe Sanh was the place to do it. In fact, the American general knew that the parallels between Khe Sanh and Dien Bien Phu would not escape General Giap, who as North Vietnam's defense minister was now the supreme commander of the North Vietnamese military. Dien Bien Phu had been Giap's greatest triumph—surely he would wish to repeat that accomplishment against this new, American foe.

And in fact, the Americans in 1968 had some significant advantages that the French, in 1954, had lacked. American airpower was unparalleled in its ability to deliver ordnance on ground troops during battle, and also in its ability to carry a massive tonnage of supplies. A great variety of heli-copters, with their vertical takeoff and landing capability, added an ele-ment to airpower that the world had never before seen. And the Khe Sanh Combat Base was within range of powerful American artillery batteries from other locations, including the Rockpile and Camp Carroll—a capa-bility for external support that Dien Bien Phu had not enjoyed.

Any doubts as to whether the enemy would ignore or attack Khe Sanh were laid to rest by a curious incident in the early evening of 2 January 1968. The sentries at one of the Khe Sanh Combat Base's checkpoints watched curi-ously as six men in Marine fatigues sauntered out of the jungle and began an earnest conversation just outside of the concertina wire ringing the perime-ter. When the men didn't walk any closer, one of those sentries issued a chal-lenge. Something about the strangers' reaction triggered a mental alarm, and the sentries opened up with their M16s, killing five of the men. The sixth man, though wounded, snatched a portfolio from one of his slain comrades and vanished into the undergrowth.

Perhaps the survivor had made away with some important papers, but the Marines found plenty of illuminating documents on the corpses. Apparently, this daring reconnaissance party had included an NVA regimental commander and key members of his staff. To Colonel David Lownds, the new CO of the 26th Marines and current commanding officer at Khe Sanh, the probe gave clear proof that the NVA intended to attack the base. No less a personage than General Westmoreland himself absolutely agreed.

Immediately MACV ordered a major increase in American strength in the I Corps area. Many Army units, including the 1st Cavalry Division (Airmobile) and the 101st Airborne Division were transferred north. Additional ARVN divisions and even the Korean Marine Corps brigade also transferred into the I Corps area. These reinforcements allowed the III MAF to focus much more of its strength on the defense of Khe Sanh, and General Cushman did not hesitate to do so.

In the first three weeks of January, the Marines put two more battalions into the KSCB, the 1/9th and the 2/26th. (The latter meant that the 26th Marines was now the only Marine regiment in Vietnam to operate with all three of its battalions on the same battlefield.) The South Vietnamese Army would send the 37th Ranger Battalion to Khe Sanh by the end of the month. In addition, the Marines added four more artillery batteries, bringing the total to five, as well as six tanks, 10 Ontos, and two Army M42 mobile gun platforms with the twin 40-mm cannon, and two M50s with quad .50-caliber machine guns. By the time the reinforcements had stopped arriving, the KSCB was filled almost to bursting. The Marines pushed out the perimeter in several directions just to get a little more elbow room.

Colonel Lownds had posted companies on the hills to the north and west of the base, with an additional outpost on Hill 558 to watch for enemy incursion down the Rao Quan Valley. In addition to the 325C NVA Division and the nearby 304th, two regiments of the 320th Division were spotted some 20 miles to the northeast. Furthermore, an enemy front headquarters (the equivalent of an American corps) was rumored to be joining the 304th Division just a few miles away, in the Laotian sanctuary.

Obviously, the attack was coming. Colonel Lownds, General Westmoreland, and everyone else just wanted to know when.

THE SIEGE OF KHE SANH

On 17 January, a small Marine patrol was ambushed as it swept the southern face of Hill 881N. It was a small sign of things to come.

At the westernmost of the Marine outposts around Khe Sanh, atop Hill 881S, Captain William Dabney made sure that his Company I, 3/26, was as well prepared for action as possible. His camp was surrounded by multiple layers of barbed wire, with plenty of antipersonnel claymore mines placed to blast their shrapnel across every likely approach path. In addition to an abundance of machine guns, mortars, and recoilless rifles, Dabney even had a detachment of three 105-mm howitzers to defend his position. The captain made a point of proudly proclaiming his unit's presence on the hilltop, the highest elevation held by United States troops in the Khe Sanh area: every morning he would gather his men at attention and hold a formal flag ceremony, raising the Stars and Stripes on a tall flagpole so that the banner could be seen by everyone for miles around.

On 20 January, Captain Dabney was authorized to take his entire company on a sweep toward Hill 881N. He moved out with 185 men while a replacement force from Khe Sanh—including the 3rd Battalion command group—was airlifted to 881S to protect the camp during the patrol. The Marines had to wait out a period of the very dense fog that was common in these hills during the wet season, but by 0900 they could move with good visibility. Following a rolling barrage of artillery, the company advanced toward the neighboring hill. As they moved up two ridgelines toward the summit, still following the barrage of artillery, intense NVA fire ripped into the columns.

Dabney's men kept up the pressure, carrying one ridge in a dramatic uphill charge that cost the life of platoon leader 2nd Lieutenant Thomas Brindley, who was subsequently awarded the Navy Cross. But despite the support of artillery, bombs, and napalm, the enemy force was too strong for Dabney's company to move any farther. By 1730, the captain ordered his men to fall back to 881S. They did so, carrying seven dead and 35 wounded with them. This firefight can be regarded as the opening salvo of the Siege of Khe Sanh.

At about the same time as Company I was fighting for its life, an NVA deserter waving a white flag appeared outside the perimeter of the combat base itself. He turned out to be Lieutenant La Thanh Tonc, commander of an antiaircraft company. He wanted to defect to the south, and he was happy to provide information about his former comrades' plans for Khe Sanh—including the fact that the attack would begin that very night. He also provided a list of the NVA formations near the base, which corresponded to the three NVA divisions the Americans already knew about. Though some Marines were skeptical of the chatty turncoat and his very detailed report, Colonel Lownds took him seriously; and when a courier carried the information to 3rd Marine Division HQ, General Tompkins, and soon III MAF CO General Cushman, also took him at his word.

THE ATTACK BEGINS

Company K, 3/26, atop Hill 861 about two miles east of Hill 881S and three miles northwest of the KSCB itself, received the opening salvos of the enemy offensive shortly after midnight in the early morning of 21 January 1968. Two red star shells burst over the summit, and several companies of NVA soldiers charged into sight 100 yards away and hurled themselves at the northwest arc of Company K's perimeter. Using bangalore torpedoes to blast gaps in the concertina wire and supported by heavy mortar bombardment, they rushed right into the Marines' positions.

Company commander Captain Norman Jasper Jr. immediately realized that he had a savage fight on his hands. His 1st Platoon was quickly overrun, and moments later the attackers occupied the hilltop landing zone, Company K's only link to reinforcement—or retreat. As he tried to rally a defense, Jasper suffered a series of wounds, leaving him disabled. His company XO, 1st Lieutenant Jerry Saulsbury, immediately took over command. The young lieutenant had recently washed out of flight training and had no infantry experience. He was advised over the radio to make use of his veteran NCOs, but he replied that in short order the company gunnery sergeant and first sergeant had also been killed. Thus Saulsbury was forced to make do with his own confidence and skills.

Having pushed the 1st Platoon back, the NVA started to move through the 3rd Platoon bunkers, attacking from the flank. They threw satchel charges into Marine strongpoints and continued forward until a determined counterattack, spearheaded by Sergeant Mykle Stahl, broke the enemy momentum. Stahl, who would receive a Navy Cross for his heroism, manned a .50-caliber machine gun while his fellow Marines grimly fought to regain their lost position.

The Marines on Hill 881S could only watch the nearby battle while warily maintaining vigilance against attack on their own position. The members of the battalion command group, which had been transported to the hill earlier when Dabney's company had moved out, had elected to remain, and could easily follow Saulsbury's efforts on the radio. Some of the mortars—and later all of them, as it became clear that Company I would not be attacked this night—on 881S lent support to Company K's battle, overall launching 680 rounds. The tubes became so hot that they had to be cooled by water and, when that became too scarce, direct urination in order to keep them functional.

By 0530, the attack's impetus was broken, and the NVA fell back, leaving 47 dead on the battlefield. In the savage fighting the Marines had suffered four killed and 11 wounded. The young lieutenant, who had not succeeded in flight school, had proved more than capable of leading a company in a desperate battle for survival.

Even as the hill attack petered out, the enemy commenced a huge bombardment against the Khe Sanh base itself, utilizing artillery, mortars, and rockets launched from many directions. The Marines of Company I stared upward in astonishment as waves of 122-mm rockets erupted from west of their position, arcing directly overhead to plummet down onto the airstrip and base.

Almost immediately as the bombardment began, an enemy round landed on the base's main ammo dump, known as "ammunition supply point (ASP) Number 1." Ironically enough, on a tour of the base several weeks earlier, General Cushman had noted that the dump was not adequately protected from bombardment. Whatever remedial steps had been taken were clearly insufficient as some 1,500 tons of ordnance went up in one of the largest explosions any of these Marines had ever seen, felt, or heard. Making matters worse, unexploded rounds, some of them burning, flew through the air under the force of the blast, tumbling to the ground across much of the Khe Sanh base. Some Marines, ignoring concerns for their own safety, picked up these smoldering shells and bravely moved them away from occupied positions.

Meanwhile, the punishing barrage of enemy shells and rockets continued unabated. Huge holes were torn into the sheet-metal plates that smoothed the runway, also wrecking several helicopters. A mess hall and the base's small PX were destroyed, while hundreds of riot control grenades—basically tear-gas canisters—erupted at ASP Number 1 and sent clouds of choking gas billowing down into the trenches where Marines sought protection from the enemy shells. A few intrepid Marines managed to scrounge up gas masks, but most could only try to protect themselves with wet towels.

One battery commander, Captain William O'Connor, had a unique experience as the gas filled his trench. He had earlier noted a very mangy dog hanging around and had ordered his men to destroy the filthy animal; instead, they had cleaned it up and kept it hidden from their CO. When the tear gas rolled in, according to O'Connor, "I found myself sharing my gas mask with the dog." (Later, the fortunate animal would make its way to the United States when one of his Marine owners rotated home.)

Four hours later, another huge explosion shook the base as a supply of C-4 plastic explosive erupted. The tremors were so severe that a battalion command post nearly collapsed, sinking downward a foot before holding. At the first shudder of collapse, the members of the command staff threw themselves to the floor, entirely convinced they were about to be buried alive.

The Marines tried to retaliate with counterbattery fire, but it was hard to do so with any accuracy since the enemy fired from positions on the rear slopes of the surrounding elevations and thus were concealed from direct observation. Furthermore, with the main ammo dump destroyed, the base's guns were quickly running low on ammunition. More supplies would have to be flown in, a task complicated by the fact that more than half of the 4,000-foot runway was rendered unusable by the barrage. Until the strip was repaired, there would be none of the huge C-130 Hercules bringing in supplies.

After dark on 21 January, the NVA made a small probing attack against the west end of the base, but the Communist soldiers were quickly repulsed. The long day of combat resulted in 14 Marines killed and 43 wounded. The amount of damage, to the runway but also to facilities and equipment, was huge. That same night, star shells illuminated the shortened runway and six C-123 Provider cargo planes landed, bringing in 26 tons of ammunition and carrying out the wounded.

Also on the first day of the siege, the NVA attacked Khe Sanh village, which was defended by a small Regional Force company and some American advisers. After stiff resistance, these defenders were forced into a narrow defensive perimeter. A day later, the Americans would be brought out by helicopter, while the Regional Force fighters who had survived, mainly Bru tribesmen, made their way through enemy lines and reached the KSCB on foot.

On the 22nd, another 20 C-123 flights brought in more supplies, and then hauled out wounded Marines and some civilian refugees. Despite intermittent bombardment, repair efforts continued through the day. At noon, the 1st Battalion, 9th Marines, helicoptered in to reinforce the garrison, arriving amid volleys of mortar fire. An hour or two later, the 1/9th, under Lieutenant Colonel John Mitchell, moved out of the base to establish a strongpoint near a rock quarry, about a mile west of the perimeter.

Repair and resupply continued as fast as the Marines could manage, always subject to enemy bombardment. On the 23rd, enemy antiaircraft (AA) fire shot down a helicopter and ground-attack jet in short order. Several FACs remained in the air during the hours of daylight, and attempted to direct counterbattery fire, but the enemy targets remained aggravatingly elusive. In another disturbing development, the NVA attacked a Royal Lao Army battalion on Route 9, a short distance west of the Laotian border. Employing tanks in battle for the first time ever outside of their home country, the North Vietnamese easily overran the outgunned Laotians.

Another reinforcement flew into the combat base on 27 January. Both the ARVN I Corps commander, Lieutenant General Hoang Xuan Lam, and General Westmoreland felt that there would be a psychological benefit to having a South Vietnamese Army unit helping to defend Khe Sanh, and the choice of the 37th Ranger Battalion was a good one. The ARVN Rangers established a defensive position some 200 yards outside the base perimeter; their performance under combat over the next months would gain the full respect of the Marines.

THE RING TIGHTENS

The Americans introduced a new, high-tech wrinkle into the battlefield as January drew toward a close. Aircraft scattered an array of highly sensitive noise and motion detectors across the ground, trying to concentrate the devices in areas where the enemy was likely to gather forces before an attack. Using small radio transmitters, the sensors would send data to intelligence monitors who would attempt to make estimates of enemy intentions based upon the signals received. No one had any idea whether they would really work in practice.

By the end of January, normal intelligence channels indicated that the massing of NVA forces around Khe Sanh was continuing unabated. Third Marine Division commander, General Tompkins, ordered that patrols around the combat base perimeter be limited to a distance of 500 yards. The annual Tet holiday, a great universal celebration in Vietnam, had been the occasion for a general cease-fire during previous years. In 1968, this short truce was scheduled to begin at 1800, 29 January, and last for 36 hours.

Even before the truce was to commence, however, word came down from above that the cease-fire had been canceled in I Corps, though it was intended to remain in effect in the rest of South Vietnam. Of course it would turn out that there would be no cease-fire anywhere this year, as all across South Vietnam the massive Tet Offensive erupted in the shape of a stunningly broad series of attacks by the Viet Cong and North Vietnamese. (See Chapter Eleven.) Huge numbers of Viet Cong attacked hundreds of targets, in most of the provincial capitals, all of the airfields, even the US embassy in Saigon, in a wave of battles that consumed the country and compelled the attention of the world.

Khe Sanh, however, remained quiet for those few days, though up to five NVA divisions were now located in the vicinity of the combat base. General Westmoreland, analyzing the enemy strategy and getting it almost exactly backward, decided that the Tet attacks represented a Communist attempt to divert American attention from the key position at Khe Sanh, a base he still regarded as the linchpin to his defense of South Vietnam. In point of fact, Westmoreland's massive commitment of forces to the northernmost provinces of South Vietnam had thinned the defenses in the areas that would get the most attention from the Communist forces attacking during Tet.

Not until 4 February did the enemy make another move against the combat base. On that night, the electronic sensors in the field suggested a huge enemy infantry force moving toward Captain Dabney's company in its fortified position atop Hill 881S. Fire control officers carefully plotted the target area, and some 500 HE shells pounded the suspected enemy formation. Whether or not they disrupted an enemy formation, no attack against 881S developed.

However, early in the morning of 5 February, the NVA made an aggressive attack against Company E, 2/26, on the nearby elevation of Hill 861 Alpha, an extension of Hill 861. In a furious onslaught, commencing with bangalore torpedoes blasting apart the concertina wire, enemy soldiers poured into the camp, forcing the Marines out of a section of their fortified lines. The company may have been saved by a classic battlefield conundrum facing the commanders of troops who have just driven home a successful attack: the North Vietnamese soldiers swarming through the American bunkers were amazed at the assortment of cigarettes, C rations, weapons, and other equipment they found there. Despite the exhortations of their leaders, they stopped to gather loot instead of pressing home the attack, giving the Americans time to rally. In a brutal counterattack led personally by company commander Captain Earle Breeding, the Marines ejected the interlopers, often with the use of knives, shovels, and even bare fists.

The next enemy move was made against the Lang Vei Special Forces Camp, which was defended by a small detachment of American Army personnel and nearly 500 indigenous South Vietnamese irregulars, all under the command of a former Marine who was now an Army officer, Captain Frank Willoughby. The NVA struck the wire at about 0200 on 7 February with at least 12 Soviet-made light tanks of the 202nd Armored Regiment. Infantry of the 304th Division also finally appeared on the battlefield. Though the defenders knocked out several of the tanks with recoilless rifles, the camp was overrun.

Colonel Lownds declined to send a relief column from Khe Sanh, believing that the position was already lost and that any expeditionary force from the base would be rolling into an ambush. Though this decision didn't earn Lownds any points for Army/Marine cooperation, even General Westmoreland later agreed that it was sound. Nearly 300 of the base's garrison, including 10 Americans, were killed, captured, or missing. Fourteen American personnel, 13 of them wounded, were eventually evacuated by helicopter back to Khe Sanh, while some of the surviving CIDG forces were able to reach the Marine base on foot.

The next night, the NVA 101D Regiment launched an attack against a Marine outpost of the 1/9 called Alpha 1, some 500 yards west of the rock quarry. A reinforced platoon of 66 men fought a desperate battle against a much larger force, and was nearly overrun. With the help of another platoon, and supporting fire from artillery, and direct fire from recoilless rifles from several Marine companies overlooking the battlefield, the Alpha 1 position held out. At least 150 NVA troops, probably many more, were killed;

but the small Marine units suffered grievously as well, with 24 killed and 27 wounded.

After this fight, the NVA stood down from direct assaults against the combat base for a while. Instead, they worked diligently to extend trenches toward the perimeter, and to try to interdict the aircraft that were Khe Sanh's only link to the outside world. And every day the base was subjected to sporadic shelling, usually at least 100 rounds per day. By the end of February, the firing increased significantly, with more than 1,300 rounds striking KSCB on the 23rd, killing 12 Marines and wounding more than 50.

On 23 February, a Marine platoon departed the perimeter and probed a little farther than usual on its patrol, advancing about a thousand yards, to the south. Spotting several enemy soldiers, the Marines gave chase, and ran right into a trap. The patrol was savaged by an ambush at point-blank range. A second platoon sent to rescue the first was also ambushed, 300 yards short of its objective. Six Marines KIA and 17 wounded were carried back to the base, but the 25 missing were presumed dead, and in a rare setback the Marines had been unable to recover their bodies.

On the night of 29 February/1 March of that leap year, the NVA made an attack against the ARVN 37th Ranger Battalion. In this case, the highly classified sensor system gave advance warning of the attack. Artillery and airstrikes pounded the Communists before they reached the wire, and a stout ARVN defense stopped the survivors in their tracks. One ranger was wounded in the fight, while the enemy left nearly 80 bodies, and a great degree of sapping equipment, on the field. The NVA would make seven more attacks against their countrymen during March, but the rangers fought off each and every one—of course, aided by all the supporting artillery and air that could come to bear.

Also during March, and in compliance with General Westmoreland's orders, the Marines and the US Army began planning for Operation Pegasus, which was to be an overland expedition to reclaim Route 9 and allow ground resupply of the Khe Sanh base. With the monsoon season ending during the month, aerial supply was able to increase, though this transport was not without risk. At least three transport planes were destroyed, two of them on the runway, trying to keep the combat base supplied. Naturally, the focus remained upon ammunition, so the Marines within the perimeter got used to going hungry, some of them reduced to two or, occasionally, one C ration per day.

Despite hunger and fatigue and the stress of daily bombardment, the Marines were for the most part not happy about Operation Pegasus, and did not want anyone to get the impression that they were somehow in need of rescue by the Army. They believed, with complete justification, that they could take the worst the enemy could dish out, and give it back to him in spades. Some of them even resented terming the battle a "siege" since, unlike at Dien Bien Phu, the base had never been cut off from support via air transport. Though it had not been the Marines' idea to make a stand at Khe Sanh, they were determined that the record reflect that they had done so with flying colors.

By late March, signs—including North Vietnamese propaganda— began to indicate that the North Vietnamese no longer considered Khe Sanh a vital objective. Radio broadcasts even proclaimed that Ho Chi Minh himself would be displeased if his army devoted significant efforts against "only 6,000 Marines at Khe Sanh." Intelligence reports further suggested that two of the nearby divisions, the 325C and the 304th, were being pulled back into Laos. By the second week of March, General Westmoreland had advised President Johnson that he no longer believed the enemy was determined to capture the remote combat base. Then, on 10 March, the news broke that the general was going to request 200,000 more combat troops in Vietnam, and Westmoreland's professional fate was sealed.

An expedition from Khe Sanh ventured out on 30 March and, under heavy artillery support from nine batteries, closed in on the site where the earlier patrol had been so savagely ambushed. They were able to recover the 25 bodies that had been left, and remained undisturbed, from the previous patrol on this mission. This marked the first significant offensive action by the Marines since the siege began. They wiped out an enemy bunker complex, killing 114 NVA in the process, while losing 10 killed and suffering 100 wounded.

On 1 April, Operation Pegasus commenced with a great deal of fanfare and publicity. Marines at Cam Lo charged west down Route 9 while the helicopters of the air cavalry division began leapfrogging from LZ to LZ along the highway. Neither force encountered any opposition as they slowly advanced toward the KSCB. During the first week of April, the Marines made several attacks from the combat base, pushing back the NVA positions each time. On 8 April, the advance elements of the 2nd Battalion, 7th Cavalry, of the US Army rolled up to the gate of the camp and the siege was officially over.

One last attack remained, and it was an eerie echo of the action that had signaled the start of the siege nearly three months earlier: Companies K, L, and M of the 3/26 would move off of Hill 881S and capture the neighboring summit, Hill 881N, that had been in enemy hands throughout the battle. Artillery preparation began at 0400, 14 April—Easter Sunday. Scores of cannon and hundreds of aircraft pounded the elevation, and when the Marines moved onto the slopes around 0600, they were ready for revenge. Scout dogs barked and signaled the alert to indicate enemy positions, and the Marines set into the enemy with a rare savagery, employing bayonets, grenades, and small arms, driven almost to the point of frenzy to defeat this persistent foe one last time. By 1430, they had cleared the summit and driven out the last of the enemy troops, killing more than a hundred while suffering six killed and 32 wounded in the attack.

The siege of Khe Sanh was over. Colonel Lownds would turn over the base to a new CO of the 26th Marines, Colonel Bruce Meyer. Lownds would be awarded the Navy Cross for his leadership during the siege. For the rest of the Marines, they were ready to be done with the place once and for all. If it had been left to the Corps, they would have destroyed the camp and marched out of there as soon as the battle was over. General Cushman remained a strong advocate for closing the base.

But there were niceties still to be observed. The long struggle at Khe Sanh, coupled with General Westmoreland's request for several hundred thousand more soldiers in country, had finally broken the president's confidence in his field commander. Westmoreland would be replaced by his lieutenant commander, General Creighton Abrams Jr., in early June, and the departing general asked that the base be maintained at least until he was out of the country.

On 17 June, General Abrams authorized the abandonment and destruction of the Khe Sanh Combat Base. Very much glad to be rid of the place, the Marines went about the destruction with a vengeance, filling in trenches, wrecking the airstrip, collapsing bunkers, and hauling away anything useful. Each of the thousands of sandbags marking the long, serpentine edge of the perimeter was slit open and drained. A few days later, the last Marines at Khe Sanh boarded trucks and the convoy started rolling east on Route 9. They stopped at every culvert, bridge, and carefully graded stretch of road, destroying even that as they passed east. General Cushman would establish a new base at Ca Lu, which would be out of range of enemy artillery based in Laos, and was blessed with much better flying weather than was Khe Sanh. The northern border of South Vietnam would remain well defended.

Khe Sanh was abandoned so completely, the site scoured so thoroughly, that it might never have existed—except that it would live on in the memories of the men who had given so much to gain and hold that place that had come to symbolize so much of the American cause in Vietnam. Khe Sanh would remain a controversial battle, an epic fight, a symbol of courage and futility, a valiant part of the valiant history of the United States Marines. It was all this, but there was one thing it was not:

Khe Sanh was *not* another Dien Bien Phu.

ELEVEN

TET OFFENSIVE 1968

COULD THE VIET CONG WIN BY LOSING?

What the hell is going on? I thought we were winning the war!

VETERAN CBS NEWSMAN WALTER CRONKITE, REACTING OFF CAMERA TO NEWS OF THE TET '68 OFFENSIVE (ATTRIBUTED)

As 1968 began, General Westmoreland remained firmly fixed on the perceived threat to South Vietnam presented by the NVA divisions gathering around Khe Sanh (see Chapter Ten), but the Viet Cong had a very different focus of attention. For the better part of a year, the COSVN staff had been preparing for a stunning blow that was intended to do nothing less than grab the world's attention, unite the people of South Vietnam under the Communist banner, shock the United States into giving up, and win the war in one dramatic series of offensives—offensives on a scale and scope several orders of magnitude greater than anything the Viet Cong had attempted before.

The decision to make these attacks was the climactic result of the political battles that had been raging since 1965 between the zealous, passionate revolutionary commander of the Viet Cong, General Nguyen Chi Thanh, and the more conventional military commanders in Hanoi, represented by the national hero, former general and current minister of defense, Vo Nguyen Giap. These two had clashed before (see Chapters Four and Six) regarding Giap's preference for a small-scale guerrilla war versus Thanh's determination to meet the US Army and Marine Corps in large-scale battles, with the expectation that American losses would become unacceptable to Americans more quickly than Vietnamese losses, even if much greater in actual numbers, would to the Vietnamese.

Beginning in April 1967, General Thanh had commenced planning for a nationwide offensive to occur early the following year. The plan was drawn up by COSVN headquarters and forwarded to Hanoi in May. The general traveled to North Vietnam in July to argue his case in front of the Politburo. On 6 July, the plan was approved. Ironically enough, Thanh, drinking heavily as he celebrated the decision that night, apparently suffered a heart attack. In any event, he died right then and there.

But the plan did not die with him. Indeed, any further resistance on the part of Giap's faction was forestalled by a series of arrests of North Vietnamese functionaries so comprehensive, ruthless, and stunning they would have made Joseph Stalin proud. Beginning in late July and continuing through the fall, a complete purge scythed through the country's leadership. Those arrested included military officers, educators, and party members who had been slow to embrace Thanh's plan for a decisive countrywide offensive. Buoyed by a lack of popular support for South Vietnamese president Nguyen Van Thieu in the fall election, and antiwar protests in Saigon and other southern cities—as well as in the United States—the staff of COSVN planned a huge offensive, and expected very big results. The target date for the operation was picked as the Tet holiday, the lunar-new-year celebration that would fall at the end of January 1968.

Although Giap did have input into the plan, much of his staff had been arrested during the recent purges, and he obviously knew better than to tinker too much with COSVN's ideas. Thanh's former deputy, General Pham Hung, was the ultimate authority as the operation came together. It would require massive logistical and personnel support from the north, with a great infusion of supplies and men.

The operation was to be breathtaking in its scope, as it would involve hundreds of attacks at targets ranging throughout South Vietnam. The main forces engaged would be Viet Cong units, though some significant North Vietnamese Army formations would lend a hand against some of the most critical objectives. It was hoped—and, in many cases, assumed—that the widespread attacks would be so stimulating and convincing to the citizenry that the people of South Vietnam would rise up en masse, throw off the yokes of their capitalist oppressors, and embrace the glorious future promised by the Communist revolution. A simultaneous propaganda campaign would convince the ARVN troops to desert the government army and join the winning side.

By the month of January 1968, with the offensive only a few weeks away, the VC had assembled more than 80,000 tons of supplies in South Vietnam. In addition to the more than 100,000 Viet Cong forces already in country, additional formations totaling no fewer than seven infantry regiments and 20 separate battalions had moved south along the Ho Chi Minh Trail from North Vietnam to take up positions prior to the attack. The Viet Cong had been extensively rearmed with the high-quality AK-47 assault rifles and the lethal B-41 RPG launchers. The latter, known to the allies as the RPG-7, were much more powerful weapons than the VC had been using previously, and would prove capable of destroying fortified bunkers and damaging or destroying armored vehicles as powerful as main battle tanks.

The primary battlefield foe of the VC in this campaign, according to the plan, was to be the South Vietnamese Army. The Americans would be dealt with as they inserted themselves into the fighting, but this time they did not constitute the main focus of the enemy's offensive power. Through the ranks of Communist forces, optimism and confidence in a successful outcome reigned supreme. The Tet Offensive, it was widely believed, would be the tipping point, the operation that at long last would win the war.

ALLIED PERCEPTIONS

General Westmoreland had been spending much of 1967 moving his forces northward, in an attempt to reinforce the I Corps area and be ready to meet the incursion he so confidently anticipated across the DMZ, or from the enemy sanctuary in Laos. He did not expect a major offensive to occur around Saigon or in other parts of the south, though he was also worried about an enemy invasion in force from Cambodia. As a consequence, many of his battalions had been moved away from the cities and posted to South Vietnam's frontiers.

A notable dissenter to this view was General Frederick Weyand, who as II Field Forces commander had responsibility for the area around the capital. He prevailed upon his commanding officer to bring some of the forces back from the north, and on 10 January Westmoreland agreed to return 15 battalions from the borderlands to the area around Saigon. Within a month, this would prove to be a brilliant, possibly lifesaving, decision.

But, much like the American and British commanders in Europe during December of 1944—just before the Nazi Ardennes Offensive achieved complete tactical surprise, resulting in the Battle of the Bulge— the high command in South Vietnam simply didn't consider the possibility of a huge enemy offensive. To them, such a plan just didn't make any sense, and they didn't believe the Viet Cong were capable of doing anything of the sort. In retrospect, they fell victim to a classic military blunder, and spent their time thinking about what the enemy was *expected* to do rather than what he *wanted* to do.

American forces in Vietnam just prior to Tet included more than 330,000 US Army personnel and nearly 80,000 Marines. They were organized into nine divisions, an armored cavalry regiment, and two separate brigades. Also aiding the allied cause was a Royal Thai Army regiment, the 1st Australian Task Force, and two infantry divisions and a marine corps brigade from South Korea. Furthermore, the South Vietnamese armed forces had improved considerably since the near-disastrous year of 1965, and now included some 350,000 effective soldiers, enhanced by another 300,000 Regional and Popular Forces. Communist assumptions about the lack of loyalty of the latter forces were to be proved wildly optimistic.

There were many intelligence analysts, both in Saigon and back in the United States, who had been reading the tea leaves in late 1967 and suspected that the enemy was up to something. The Ho Chi Minh Trail through Laos and Cambodia could not be interdicted, but it could be monitored. The number of trucks heading south through Laos along that route, for example, jumped from fewer than 500 per month through the first 10 months of the year to more than 1,000 in October, and to more than 3,000 in November and 6,000 in December.

Still, despite these suspicions, there were few signs of heightened alertness during January. The ARVN had granted leave to nearly 50 percent of its forces for the upcoming Tet holiday, and a 36-hour truce had been declared from the evening of 29 January through the morning of the 31st. General Westmoreland decided to cancel the short truce in the northern I Corps Zone, but President Thieu, citing army morale and fuel for potential enemy propaganda, refused to make this decision countrywide.

Even though they suspected that some kind of enemy operation was in the works, the American military community did not think the danger was truly imminent, certainly not in the form of any large-scale enemy action. In a scene that has to evoke American complacency on 6 December 1941—as so many United States Army and Navy officers enjoyed a Saturday night in Honolulu while the Imperial Japanese Navy's aircraft carriers approached Oahu, and Pearl Harbor, from the north—several hundred American officers of the MACV intelligence staff attended a lively pool party at their quarters in Saigon on the night of 30 January.

Not one of them had any idea of what was about to happen.

A NATIONAL HOLIDAY, AND WAR

There is some dispute as to whether the initial Tet attacks were launched prematurely or according to plan, but there is no doubt when and where they occurred. During the early morning hours of 30 January, a full 15 hours before the Tet Nguyen Dan holiday would mark the lunar new year, the provincial capitals of all five provinces in II Corps, as well as Da Nang in I Corps, were attacked by battalion-sized Communist forces. The attacks were all preceded by rocket or mortar attacks against key headquarters, government buildings, and radio stations. However, with the exception of the battles at Kon Tum and Ban Me Thuot (see below), none of the attacks was pressed home with much determination, and by daylight the attackers had been driven off in almost all locations.

It was later speculated that the offensive had originally been scheduled for 30 January, but North Vietnamese Defense Minister Giap had ordered it postponed one day in order to make sure all units were in position. However, because of the somewhat patchwork communication network employed by the insurgents, not all VC commanders "got the memo." Those who didn't learn of the change attacked a day early, an error that could have resulted in more significant readiness for the actual offensive on the part of the Americans and the ARVN.

Yet even these premature attacks did not trigger a sense of urgency, especially among the South Vietnamese—who were clearly anticipating the important holiday and assuming that the insurgents shared their festive mood. General Phillip Davidson, the recently arrived MACV intelligence chief, warned Westmoreland on 30 January to expect more attacks in the upcoming days, and the commanding general ordered American forces placed on full alert. The Americans did a better job than their allies of making ready for action, but they were hampered by lack of knowledge as to when and where the enemy would strike.

Certainly no one expected the offensive to consume the whole country, and most of the high-ranking US officers assumed that the VC would not initiate action until after the holiday. Furthermore, and this assumption was perhaps colored by General Westmoreland's views, most American officers did not expect the enemy to strike the heart of the big cities, but thought the VC would make strong attacks against more isolated, rural locations.

Perhaps distracted by his own family's holiday plans, which included spending a couple of days out of the city at a rural resort, President Thieu only urged a few more halfhearted preparatory moves before he left town. Some additional ARVN leaves were canceled as the South Vietnamese, too, made a pretense of preparation, even to the point of requiring most units to maintain 90 percent of their personnel on base. But the holiday spirit was upon them; many soldiers simply ignored the orders to return to service, or didn't receive them in time to respond. As the offensives erupted, the average strength of the South Vietnamese Army formations in the country hovered at about 50 percent.

A full 24 hours passed from the preliminary attacks until the dramatic explosion of a full-blown crisis. The evening of 30 January was a wild one throughout South Vietnam, and nowhere more so than in the national capital. Saigon was convulsed by revelry, as firecrackers, rockets, and other traditional symbols of celebration filled the night with explosions and brightened the sky with fireworks and sparks. People in bright costumes danced in the streets, and in places the serpentine dragons so emblematic of East Asian celebrations twisted their way through the crowds, fabric heads bobbing in a festive dance.

The people of the capital city shared a universal sense of optimism and good cheer—perhaps with good reason, since Saigon had not previously been the scene of any significant fighting. To the city dwellers, the war seemed a long way off. They barely took notice of the dark-clad, serious-faced men who moved among them with intent purpose—some wondered if perhaps the government was facing another coup—and even the first volleys of automatic weapons fire sounded like nothing so much as exceptionally loud, exciting fireworks.

But that elation would be very short-lived. For very many South Vietnamese, the war had come to their doorsteps with a vengeance.

SAIGON, LONG BINH, AND THE AIR BASES AT BIEN HOA AND TAN SON NHUT

The South Vietnamese capital city and environs were a primary focus of the Communist offensive. At 0200, a bus rolled up to a gate leading to the Joint General Staff compound, near the great Tan Son Nhut Airport on the west edge of the city. More than a dozen VC carrying explosive charges rushed out of the bus toward the gate, which had just opened to allow an ARVN general to pass, but in a confused shootout triggered by the saboteurs reacting to the coincidental passing of a US Army jeep carrying military policemen, the guard slammed shut the gate. More American MPs opened fire and the initial attempt to rush the compound was temporarily stymied.

On the other side of the city, a company of Viet Cong sappers, many of them local taxi drivers, rushed the compound of the United States embassy. This huge six-story building had been finished less than six months earlier, and stood as a proud symbol of the American presence in Vietnam. Prior to Tet, it had never been targeted by the insurgents.

On this night, however, the Viet Cong attacked with a vengeance. They killed the guards and blew holes in the brick walls with their explosive charges. The Marine Saigon Guards, a full company strong, closed the embassy building's solid wooden doors and opened fire from the windows with submachine guns, pistols, and shotguns. The VC in the courtyard returned fire enthusiastically. More VC from the same unit took up positions in the framework of an unfinished, multistory hotel, using the vantage to launch rockets at the national Independence Palace. Other VC attacked the Korean embassy, shelled the hotel where many American officers lived, briefly occupied the Philippine Chancery, and were blocked in a fierce fight from entering the headquarters compound of the South Vietnamese Navy.

A detachment of VC charged into and took over the national radio station. They had brought with them a tape of no less a personage than Ho Chi Minh, delivering an address announcing that Saigon had been "liberated" and a call to action for all South Vietnamese, urging them to rise up against the regime. Fortunately, the station's transmitter was located several miles away, and technicians shut down the station's power supply and remotely shifted the broadcast to prerecorded content so smoothly that listeners had no idea anything was amiss. The station occupiers were forced out later in the morning.

Nevertheless, as the night wore on, VC soldiers in palm-leaf helmets and black rubber sandals began to appear on many of the city's streets, shocking residents who, up until this night, had considered the war to be a distant menace. In Cholon, which was sort of Saigon's "Chinatown," two police stations were occupied by the attackers, who also established control over several key streets and sections of some neighborhoods. They began to consolidate their defenses, and would be able to hold off the South Vietnamese counterattacks for some time. Later, the allies would learn that Cholon had been the epicenter of the VC power in Saigon, and contained the operational headquarters for the Communist high command in the whole area,

Just outside the huge Tan Son Nhut Air Base, hard by the northwest edge of Saigon, companies of VC from three separate battalions took over the large Vinatexco textile mill complex. Posting antiaircraft weapons on the roof and machine guns and recoilless rifles in the windows of the big building, they opened fire on the air base. Waves of Viet Cong from the D16 and 267th Battalions, as well as the 271st Regiment, charged three of the gates leading onto the base. With rockets from the textile mill shattering the defenses, they broke through at Gate 51 and swarmed toward the runway.

Fortunately for the government, two companies of the 8th ARVN Airborne Battalion were sitting around waiting at the airport for transport to I Corps. In response to General Westmoreland's urging, the South Vietnamese had reluctantly agreed to send them north, but there had not been any aircraft available to move them. Now they joined the airport security forces in halting the throng of VC before they could shut down the runway, meeting the black-clad attackers in a wild melee of hand-to-hand combat right on the flight line.

Northeast of the city, the big American II Field Force headquarters complex at Long Binh was better prepared to receive an enemy attack than most nearby locations. At 0300, a savage bombardment of mortar and rocket fire rained down on the complex, and at 0330, the 275th VC Regiment charged across Highway 1 against the northern flank of the American position, while the U-1 VC Battalion attacked from the east and tried to divert the defenders' attention from an attempt to blow up the ammunition depot. The US Army's 199th Infantry Brigade had garrison duty and counterattacked vigorously, including a sally by a mechanized company that managed to mount its APCs and roared toward the attackers with machine guns blazing.

A VC flanking attack was slowed as the insurgents fought their way through a thick stand of bamboo that impeded their progress so much that American troops were in position to gun them down when they finally emerged into the clear. Some of the sappers did profit from the diversion to reach the ammunition supply, and managed to set charges that blew up several bunkers after dawn. But the men defending the complex's multitude of buildings held firm.

At nearby Bien Hoa headquarters and air base, the 274th VC Regiment, supported by mortar fire, attacked in the wake of a fast rocket barrage. A platoon of ARVN infantry and a reaction force of American MPs met them with concentrated firepower, blocking the attackers from reaching the airstrip. Still, both Bien Hoa and Long Binh, located as they were in the midst of densely populated suburban areas, provided the enemy with plenty of opportunities for hiding, dispersing, and commencing future operations.

Meanwhile, the adjacent III Corps ARVN HQ was holding off an attack by the 238th VC LF Battalion when a column of South Vietnamese APCs from a reserve mechanized battalion came roaring down Highway 1. It shattered a VC regiment trying to close the highway, then slammed into the flank of the regiment trying to enter the air base. The tracks, with .50-caliber machine guns spewing tracer streams through the night, disrupted the attacks of both enemy units even as they came under fire from recoilless rifles and RPGs.

By dawn, other regular ARVN and American units were responding to the attacks. The South Vietnamese Army mechanized unit counterattacking at Bien Hoa was soon joined by a mechanized cavalry troop from the American 9th Infantry Division. It rumbled down Highway 1 toward the base complex, fighting its way through a VC roadblock, then maneuvering around a bridge that had been destroyed. Several tracks were knocked out and casualties suffered, but the cavalry dished out more damage than it took. Just short of the objective it was joined by the 2nd Battalion, 506th Infantry, and some tanks of the 11th Armored Cavalry.

Just beyond the Bien Hoa base, the 58th RF Battalion of South Vietnamese irregulars gathered at the edge of the village of Ap Than, which had been occupied by the VC, and moved in to fight for the neighborhood. Supported by tanks of the armored cavalry, American infantry cleared the village in close combat that lasted throughout 31 January and into the first day of February, but by the end of the second day of fighting all the attackers had been killed or driven out.

Meanwhile, at nearby Long Binh, an American infantry company, B of the 4/39, flew in on Hueys to assault a hot landing zone adjacent to the II Field Force headquarters. The building complex, ably defended by the 199th Brigade and military police, was still under attack but had not been breached. With the air-assault unit coming in behind them, the VC attacking the base broke and fled, and the base was cleared of enemy troops during the morning of 31 January—though, as at Bien Hoa, the retreating VC occupied a nearby village. More tanks and tracks of the 11th ACR arrived to reinforce, and by nightfall the village, too, was reclaimed.

Heavy fighting continued at Tan Son Nhut, where General Westmoreland's MACV headquarters had come under direct rocket fire. The South Vietnamese paratroopers had broken up the attack by their surprise rush across the runways, and they were joined by a USAF police unit, the guard unit protecting MACV headquarters, and several South Vietnamese police and service units. They held their own through the night, and help was on the way in the form of more American cavalry.

The main base camp of the 25th Tropic Lightning Infantry division had been established at Cu Chi, some 15 miles north and west of the city. The original idea for this placement had been to protect the capital against an enemy incursion from Cambodia, but it turned out that it was fairly well placed to come to the city's internal defense as well. The reconnaissance unit of the 25th Division was the 3rd Squadron, 4th Cavalry, and the squadron's Troop C happened to be posted to the base at Cu Chi when the offensive began. Even before the sun came up, the squadron's commander, Lieutenant Colonel Glenn Otis, had the troop on the road, bound for Tan Son Nhut. Colonel Otis escorted the column by helicopter, issuing orders to the tanks and tracks to veer around potential ambushes while still making good time.

After a short, furious dash, the cavalry troop roared up to the battle raging at ruptured Gate 51. The well-equipped VC, firing RPGs from the base and heavy weapons from the windows of the textile mill across the highway, shot up the cavalry, but the Americans returned fire, tank guns ripping through the exposed Viet Cong with volleys of canister while the heavy machine guns on the APCs added their chatter to the din of combat. Several of the vehicles began to burn, including four tanks, as testament to the VC resistance, but the cavalrymen dismounted and took cover beside the road, continuing the fight with their M16s.

The position of the embattled troop, which eventually suffered the loss of nearly half its vehicles, completely blocked the retreat of the VC who were being driven off by the ad hoc collection of ARVN, police, and American security guards on the air base itself. As the morning blossomed into full daylight, flights of helicopter gunships swarmed through the air, punching rockets and machine-gun rounds into the increasingly battered Vinatexco plant. When Troop B, 3/4th Cavalry, arrived to support its sister formation, the attack was broken for good. With the textile mill in flames, the defenders on the air base drove the surviving VC against the armored cavalry blocking position at the gate. The air base was declared secure early in the afternoon of 31 January.

Adjacent to the air base stood the ARVN Joint General Staff compound, where the initial attack against a compound gate had been thwarted by an alert guard closing the gate and the fortuitous presence of some American military police. Here another attack commenced at 0930 on the 31st. Two battalions of Viet Cong charged a different gate and blasted it apart with the powerful B-41 rockets they had recently received. The VC charged through the breach and swarmed into the giant compound.

However, the attackers appeared to have been poorly briefed, since they seemed confused by the array of the targets before them. The compound's military defense consisted of the Honor Guard ARVN Battalion of infantry, supported by a company of tanks. While these two formations were mustering for a counterattack, the VC took a guess as to which buildings to occupy. Passing by some vital communications centers, they charged into and fortified the large barracks and maintenance building of the headquarters support company.

But however insignificant the complex they had captured, the VC weren't about to give it up without a fight. The buildings of the support HQ were solid stone and sturdy. The VC knocked out windows to make firing positions and resisted stoutly as the guard battalion and its supporting tanks tried to gain entrance. The South Vietnamese garrison was soon joined by the ARVN airborne troops who had recently helped to win the fight at the nearby Tan Son Nhut base. During the day, several companies of ARVN marines, supported by additional armor, joined the efforts to clear the Joint General Staff compound, though it wasn't until midmorning on 1 February that the last of the VC had been driven out of the compound.

In the city proper, the VC had been thwarted at some of their most important objectives. The sappers who had broken into the compound of the US embassy had not been able to enter the building, but a lively firefight raged between them and the Marines defending the installation. Just before dawn a helicopter tried to land on the roof to bring in a squad of airborne infantry, but the Huey was driven off by heavy ground fire, with one of the crewmen wounded. A few hours later, however, around 0800, the helicopters returned with a gunship to suppress the ground fire. The troops landed and counterattacked, and with the help of the Marines all of the attackers were killed in short order.

Though the VC in the unfinished high-rise hotel had been unable to seriously damage the Independence Palace with their rocket attacks, they were not easily displaced. They defended the structure with machine guns and small arms as well as the rocket launchers as city defense forces gathered in the blocks around them, cutting off access to and from the hotel. By the end of the day on 31 January, the Presidential Security Brigade, aided by national and American military police, supported by a couple of tanks, closed in on the hotel and pressed the attack. The VC resisted furiously, and it wasn't until late on 1 February that they were finally eradicated.

THE PHU THO RACETRACK

The most significant Communist stronghold in the Saigon area was quickly established at this huge facility in the Cholon district, which was taken over on the first night of the offensive by the 6th VC LF Battalion. With the Viet Cong controlling much of the surrounding city sections, neighborhoods that were inhabited primarily by Chinese, the huge concrete structure of the grandstand could be turned into a formidable fortress. Located at the intersection of several of the city's main roads, and widely known throughout Saigon, it became a natural centerpiece for the attackers' operations.

At the same time, the wide fields of the track, infield, and surrounding spaces would have made for probably the best natural helicopter landing zones in the city proper. The Viet Cong control made certain that no allied reinforcements would be choppered in to the racetrack grounds. Given the strong VC control in the surrounding streets and the sturdy nature of the massive grandstand, the racetrack was destined to be the site of the most furious firefights of Tet in Saigon proper.

The task of counterattacking would fall to the 3rd Battalion, 7th Infantry—the "Cotton Balers," a name the 7th Infantry had claimed since their initial action during the Battle of New Orleans in 1815. The battalion CO, Lieutenant Colonel John Gibler, had been one of those American officers with a strong premonition before the Tet holiday that something unpleasant was brewing. In part, his suspicions were fueled by the fact that in mid-January his unit had made several contacts with the VC, but the enemy had quickly vanished, showing none of his usual propensity for combat. Gibler had the foresight to order all three of his companies back to the base just before the Tet holiday.

Gibler's 3rd Battalion operated out of Binh Chanh, a hamlet about 30 miles south and west of Saigon. Early on the morning of 31 January, the battalion was ordered to move into Saigon and go into action in the Cholon district, with the objective of recapturing the racetrack. Since there were no good landing zones in the vicinity—aside from the already captured racetrack—the

infantry rolled toward the city in two-and-a-half-ton trucks, the type of ubiquitous Army vehicle famously known as the "deuce-and-a-half." Company A,
under Captain Tony Smaldone, rode in the lead. Before they left Binh Chanh,
they were joined by a platoon of six tracks from the 17th Cavalry. Two of the
M-113 APCs led the column, while two occupied a middle position and the
other two trailed the file of trucks.

The reinforced company made good time as it raced up Highway 4 to
the capital city. Overhead, Major James MacGill, the battalion operations
officer, followed along in a light observation helicopter with a careful eye
on the ground below. In barely an hour the column reached the Cholon
district and slowed to a crawl. Initially they encountered no resistance, but
saw plenty of combat aftermath, including dead Vietnamese sprawled next
to wrecked mopeds, and even the bodies of Americans as they moved
closer to the racetrack. The grunts, dressed in khakis and full of gunshot
wounds, had been massacred in their jeeps, presumably as they had been
returning to their duty stations.

Fully alerted now, the Cotton Balers rolled on narrow streets between
wooden, mostly two-story buildings. They took a few shots from overhead
snipers initially, but quickly drove them off with a few rounds from the
106-mm recoilless rifle mounted on top of one of the APCs. They were still
six blocks from the racetrack when the first significant action struck: an
RPG rocketed into the front of the leading track, killing three men including the cavalry platoon leader.

Immediately after the rocket explosion, the buildings on both sides of
the column erupted in fire as Viet Cong in the upper floors and on the
roofs poured devastating volleys into the Americans. Gibler's infantry, in
the soft-skinned trucks, were particularly vulnerable. Most of them
quickly dismounted and charged into the nearby buildings, while others
returned fire with their M16s, using the bulky armored personnel carriers
for cover. The cavalrymen in the five remaining APCs opened fire with
heavy machine guns and the recoilless rifle.

Smaldone wasted no time in bringing order to his company's response.
He was fortunate in that he had become familiar with this area on one of

his several previous tours in Vietnam. He started his men working through the buildings one by one, clearing each with the help of supporting fire from the APCs. Meanwhile, Major MacGill directed target acquisition for some helicopter gunships that quickly arrived on the scene. Windows, walls, and roofs broke apart under the intense firepower, while inside the buildings the infantry used C-4 explosives to blast holes directly from one structure into the next. Fleeing civilians would periodically throng the street, and the combatants tried, not always successfully, to hold their fire to let them escape the battle.

After two hours, the column had forced its way down five blocks, but met furious resistance while still a block away from the racetrack—though they could see that formidable grandstand rising beyond the intervening structures. The VC took cover behind concrete benches lining the streets while heavy machine guns and rocket launchers zeroed in on the Americans from concealed firing positions on the towering grandstands, shooting through gaps in the concrete facade that rendered the place a natural fortress.

Major MacGill's small helicopter landed on a sturdy rooftop, and the major joined several MPs who were using the building as a firing position. When the officer saw a VC emerge from a building and remove the red armband that identified him as an insurgent, the major shot him as he approached a group of civilians with his hands up. But one sprawling building, occupied by VC who had used the place to set up multiple machine-gun nests, blocked the column's access to the racetrack proper. Automatic weapons blazed from a multitude of doors and windows, and there was no ready way around the obstacle.

Smaldone worked out a plan to knock the strongpoint out with the heaviest weapon at his disposal: the 106-mm recoilless rifle mounted on one of the tracks. His company laid down a barrage of fire against the building from rifles, machine guns, and grenade launchers while the APC rolled into position. A series of rapidly fired rounds from the big gun sent the building up in a spectacular explosion. The wreckage of the wooden structure, obviously packed with a lot of ordnance, continued to burn, popping now and then with secondary explosions.

The Cotton Balers didn't stop to watch, however—instead they charged across the street and right onto the grounds of the racetrack, firing furiously at the embrasures from which the VC had been targeting them. But the destruction of the machine-gun position had apparently demoralized the insurgents; they retreated out the other side of the racing facility and spread out into the streets of Cholon, effectively vanishing into the local population. The men of Smaldone's company owed a lot to their captain's tactical acumen—despite the gauntlet of fire the column had endured, the infantrymen had suffered only one man killed and a few more wounded.

With the track and its infield secured, Lieutenant Colonel Gibler's battalion now had a landing zone, and he wasted no time in airlifting his B and C Companies onto the grounds. On the following day, 1 February, two mechanized companies of the 5/60th Infantry and the 33d ARVN Ranger Battalion joined the Cotton Balers at the racetrack. The multinational force immediately set out to clear the VC out of Cholon, a fight that would involve the Americans for five more days. In bloody street fighting more reminiscent of World War II than Vietnam, the infantrymen worked their way from house to house, supported by the tracks rumbling through the ruined streets. During the fighting, much of the Cholon district was destroyed, and great numbers of insurgents were killed.

After five days, the two American battalions departed Cholon, as the ARVN was determined to finish this fight on its own. Much of the city lay under a pall of smoke as huge fires at a government rice depot and a blazing paper mill couldn't be extinguished. Enemy resistance had been gradually wiped out in most areas of the city under the pressure of the South Vietnamese military—but in Cholon, the VC stubbornly held on.

Finally, the ARVN high command asked for additional American help, and once again the 3/7 traveled to Cholon. This time they choppered right into the racetrack in flights of Hueys, only to discover as they landed that the VC had regained control of the massive grandstand and they were coming to ground in a hot LZ. Fortunately, the helicopter door gunners were quick to respond, laying down suppressing fire so that the grunts could leap out and seek whatever cover they could find. Fortunately as well, the enemy troops showed little stomach for an extended fight, and quickly retreated into the city district again. This time the battalion stayed in the city for four days, eventually finding and destroying the main VC command post in Saigon. For its actions in Cholon during Tet '68, the 3/7th Cotton Balers were awarded the Valorous Unit Citation, the second highest award for combat given to American units.

THE PROVINCIAL CAPITALS AND OTHER URBAN TARGETS

The two major cities assaulted during the Tet Offensive were Saigon and Hue, but lots of other areas in the country were subjected to the coordinated attacks. Overall, the Viet Cong struck 36 of the 44 provincial capitals, five of six autonomous cities, and 64 of the 242 district capitals. Many of the attacks began, as in Saigon and Hue, in the dark hours before dawn on 31 January; in a few places, the enemy made his move later, and, as noted, a few locations were actually attacked prematurely in the early hours of 30 January.

The cities attacked in the first wave, generally planned and implemented at 0300 on 31 January, included the major targets of Saigon and Hue, but also Gia Dinh in the Saigon area; to the north, in I Corps, the cities of Quang Tri, Tam Ky, and Quang Ngai and the American bases at Da Nang, Phu Bai, and Chu Lai were attacked initially; in the II Corps Zone, Phan Thiet and Tuy Hoa cities and the US installations at Bong Son and An Khê suffered enemy offensive action; while in the south, in IV Corps zone, Can Tho and Vinh Long were subjected to initial attacks.

During the daylight hours of 31 January, additional attacks against major targets commenced at: (III Corps) Long Thanh and Binh Duong; and (IV Corps) Kien Hoa, Dinh Tuong, Go Cong, Kien Giang, Vinh Binh, and Ben Tre. The final target to be attacked did not see violence until 10 February; that was Bac Lieu, in the southern (IV Corps) zone. In all, more than a hundred cities were hit, and every allied base or airfield was at least subjected to a mortar or rocket barrage. Dozens of smaller towns were also struck.

For the most part, the defense in all of these wide-ranging locations was the responsibility of the South Vietnamese. The ARVN played a major role, of course, but the Regional Forces (RF) and Popular Forces (PF) as well as the Civilian Irregular Defense Groups (CIDG) and many units of the national police were all called upon in some form or another to join the fight. Considering that the attackers numbered more than 80,000 men, and that they were defeated in every location, generally in less than a week, the South Vietnamese response can only be considered as remarkable. Despite the nationwide calls for people, including soldiers, to change sides and join the Communist cause, no units defected, nor did any of them abandon their posts during the fighting.

Some of the more significant battlefields of the Tet Offensive include:

Kon Tum, in the II Corps, was one of the cities attacked prematurely, on 30 January. Operating together, the 24th NVA Regiment and the 3/4 VC Battalion combined forces to attack the town with significant strength. In addition to government offices, the Communists sought to destroy the headquarters of the 24 ARVN Tactical Zone and a strong MACV compound. The first units to defend the city were two companies of CIDG scouts, both of which were quickly overwhelmed. The 2nd Battalion, 42nd ARVN Regiment, held out for a little longer, but it was outnumbered and was soon forced to retreat to defensive positions around the airfield. A Special Forces compound was compromised, though never completely overrun; it would hold out with some of the South Vietnamese forces until relieved.

By midday on the 30th, an American force under the umbrella of the 4th Infantry Division was mustered to drive the enemy out of the city. Under the command of Lieutenant Colonel William Junk, commander of 1st Battalion, 22nd Infantry, it also included the 7th Squadron, 17th Cavalry, and a company from the 1/69th Armor. Mustering north of the city, the task force moved into Kon Tum that afternoon. One of Colonel Junk's companies air-assaulted into an LZ beside a key bridge south of the city, and soon the battalion CO had established his field headquarters there. Meanwhile, the cavalry and armored elements of the task force moved south to clear the area around the airfield. That afternoon the NVA renewed its efforts to capture the airfield, but the North Vietnamese were driven off by helicopter gunships.

At around 0400 on 31 January, the NVA renewed its efforts to capture the city, but were halted on all fronts—though a rocket attack struck an ammo dump and destroyed most of the South Vietnamese artillery rounds. After daylight, more South Vietnamese troops, regulars and RD/PF forces, entered the city to hold the places that were in friendly hands. The Americans continued to press forward, with M48 tanks leading small teams against pockets of resistance. Overnight the enemy once more pressed the attack, this time against the MACV compound, but again the NVA was repulsed.

On 1 Feb, another 1/22 company moved into the city, and the initiative shifted to the allies. Highway 14, connecting the city to Pleiku and Dak To, was reopened by the end of the day. By midday, the MACV compound was relieved. Later that afternoon, some 100 NVA soldiers, apparently panicking, fled across an open swath of ground, and many of them were gunned down by intense automatic fire. On 2 February, two companies of the US Army's 1/12 Infantry were airlifted to Kon Tum, adding to the pressure, and by the next day the surviving NVA troops were trying to escape the city as best they could. Many could not.

Pleiku, also in the II Corps area, was attacked in the dark hours of early 31 January by the 15H LF and 40th Sapper Viet Cong Battalions. The attackers charged across a broad open area to close in on the city, and suffered heavily from alert defenders who mowed many of them down with automatic weapons. The city was garrisoned by the 3rd ARVN Cavalry Squadron, the 22nd ARVN Rangers, and a company of tanks from the ARVN 1/69th Armor.

The element of surprise was lost almost immediately, and the VC found themselves significantly outgunned from the start. While rockets rained down on the Pleiku Air Base just outside of town, the city's defenders formed a pair of strike forces, each spearheaded by tanks. A company of American Special Forces soldiers took to the streets to help clear the enemy out of the area in house-to-house fighting, while engineers of the 4th Battalion armed themselves and fought beside the rest of the infantry.

An AC-47 Spooky gunship circled overhead, adding firepower to the city's defenders, and the Viet Cong could only try to desperately hold on to the few parts of the city they had occupied. By 3 February, organized resistance by the attackers had ceased, and the South Vietnamese and American defenders had reclaimed the city, completely defeating this prong of the Tet Offensive.

Ban Me Thuot was the largest city in the Central Highlands of South Vietnam, and was the capital of Darlac province in the II Corps zone. Like Kon Tum, it was struck a day before the mass of the Tet Offensive, on 30 January. The primary attacking unit was the 33rd NVA Regiment, reinforced by the 301E VC LF Battalion. The city's targets included an MACV compound, a small dirt airstrip right in the city, and local government buildings; a larger, paved airfield a few miles east of the city was also targeted.

In the early hours of fighting, the enemy pretty much had its way, as the only defenders available were the trainees and their instructors at a Regional/Popular Forces school and a small Special Forces detachment. These units were stunned by the sudden attack, but managed to hold without breaking, and by noon on 30 January reinforcements were rolling onto the scene. First to arrive was the 8th ARVN Cavalry Squadron, with tanks and APCs. The 45th ARVN Regiment was close behind.

By that night the city was being torn by house-to-house combat as the two forces, approximately equal in strength, fought a savage, close-range battle. A day and a half later, on 1 February, the 23rd ARVN Rangers arrived, and started to turn the tide. On the 2nd, a company of American paratroopers from the 1/503rd Infantry (Airborne) were airlifted into the fight. The NVA kept up the pressure, launching new attacks each day of the battle, but finally the enemy's back was broken and the survivors were driven into the highlands.

The city was declared secure on 6 February. The fighting had been so intense that many blocks, over a third of Ban Me Thuot's total area, had been destroyed.

Dalat, a resort town in the pleasantly forested highlands of Tuyen Duc province, seemed like an unusual target for a military operation. It did contain the elite Vietnamese Military Academy, many other exclusive private schools, and the prestigious Pasteur Institute, but it was known mainly as a resort town where people could enjoy the fresh scent of the lush pine forests that surrounded it. It was garrisoned by two RF companies and the engineering cadets of the academy, supplemented by two armored cars staffed by military policemen. It had not been attacked by the end of 31 January, when the Tet Offensive was rocking so much of the country.

Nevertheless, the Viet Cong sent two battalions, the 145th and 186th, against Dalat in the early morning hours of 1 February. They swiftly entered the city during the hours of darkness, and by morning were stationed in the city's central marketplace. Despite the inexperienced nature of the defenders, however, after dawn broke they quickly rallied to the cause. A helicopter gunship arrived overhead to provide air support, and with the two armored cars leading the way, the ad hoc force of engineering students and RF trainees attacked with vigor, forcing the VC out of the marketplace.

The attackers withdrew to the stone buildings of the Pasteur Institute and fortified their position there. When no action was immediately forthcoming, the VC sallied forth and fought a brief, violent clash in the town, driving the defenders into fortified buildings on the other side of town. On 5 February, an understrength battalion of ARVN Rangers, the 23rd, accompanied by American

Special Forces soldiers from Trang Phuoc, arrived and helped the engineers and Regional Forces reclaim the marketplace and town center. Once again the VC fell back to the school.

It was not until 11 February that a strong reinforcement arrived, the 11th ARVN Ranger Battalion. They provided the impetus to defeat the VC aggressors, eventually killing some 200 of them while the rest were forced to flee. When the city was declared secure that night, the attackers of the Tet Offensive had been defeated in every location except Saigon and Hue.

THE DEVASTATION OF HUE

The bloodiest battle of the Tet Offensive, and perhaps of the entire Vietnam War, was the struggle for the ancient Vietnamese imperial capital city of Hue, in the I Corps area just a few miles inland from the South China Sea. The city was a focal point of the nation's radical Buddhists, and the loyalty of the population was viewed skeptically by the government in Saigon. Since it was a cultural landmark, cherished by all Vietnamese, north and south, it had been spared from combat through the early years of the Vietnam War. The important main national road, Highway 1, ran right through Hue, extending all the way to the DMZ only some 30 miles to the north.

The city was dominated by two massive structures: the Citadel, which, as the name suggests, was a massive fortress with high walls, defensive positions atop those walls as well as positioned throughout the structure, all surrounded by a moat; and the Imperial Palace, a beautiful and hallowed building cherished by all Vietnamese as the seat of the country's most recent independent leaders. The Citadel was a walled city unto itself, modeled on the Forbidden City of Beijing, shaped in a square with walls almost two miles long on each side. On a map it looks to be tilted at an angle, with the points of the square oriented to the north, east, south, and west. The Imperial Palace lay within the Citadel, and was a smaller but still huge structure adjacent to the Citadel's southeast wall.

The city was bisected by the poetically named Song Huong, or Perfume

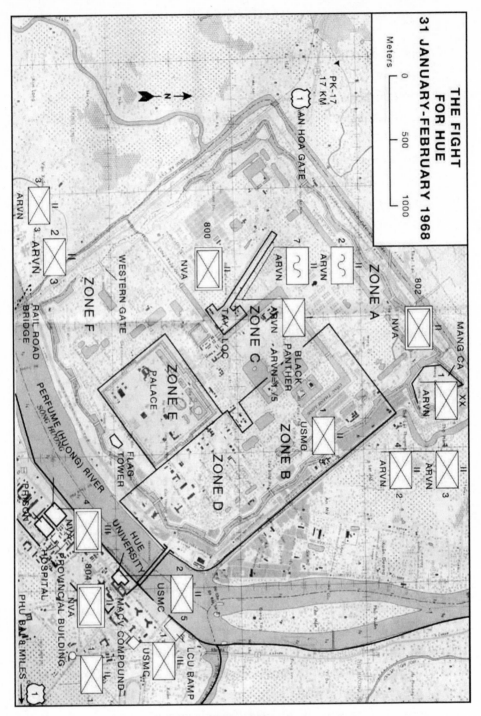

Battle of Hue

HISTORY AND MUSEUMS DIVISION, UNITED STATES MARINE CORPS

River, which flowed right through the middle of Hue, passing almost adjacent to the Citadel's southeast wall. The city's modern neighborhoods were all in the south, across the river from the medieval-looking Citadel. Two long bridges, the Truong Tien to the east and the Bach Ho to the west, spanned the river and connected the two parts of the city. Prominent buildings lined the river on the south bank, including the university, a hospital complex, and many government buildings.

Because Hue was not considered a military objective for either side, very few allied forces were actually posted there. Only two small installations, in fact, contained military personnel, and both of them were administrative offices, not combat unit barracks. North of the river was the headquarters of the ARVN 1st Division, including the division's commanding officer, Brigadier General Ngo Quang Truong, his headquarters staff, and the high-quality Hac Bao, or "Black Panther," reconnaissance company. Both ARVN units were only at about half strength because of the holiday. The HQ occupied a compound in the northwestern corner of the Citadel, nestled in a niche of that fort's high stone walls. To the south of the river stood the only American military presence in Hue, an MACV compound with about 200 mostly rear-echelon military personnel, including a mix of Army and Marines. Their primary purpose was to serve as advisers and liaison between MACV and the 1st ARVN Division.

Before the attack, many VC were already present in the city either because they lived there, or they had recently infiltrated Hue by joining the throngs coming to the ancient imperial capital to celebrate the Tet holiday. Hundreds of weapons and many tons of ammunition and other supplies had been patiently smuggled into the city during previous months, often hidden under the bags of rice that were routinely carried through the gates by supply wagons.

All in all, the attack on Hue was probably the most carefully prepared and efficiently executed operation of the entire Tet Offensive. The objective in the Tet attack on Hue differed significantly from the enemy's goal with other targets in that the VC and NVA fully intended to occupy the city and were prepared to defend it against all challenges. The initial attackers were expected to hold on for just a few days, and then they were to be reinforced by strong North Vietnamese Army units that would move in to consolidate the occupation. Because of the city's long tradition of liberalism and antigovernment sentiment, the Communist leadership sincerely expected that Hue's residents would cheer the arrival of the Viet Cong and willingly embrace the new regime. This, in turn, would presumably have a profound effect upon the morale and desires of citizens all across South Vietnam.

The signal to commence the attack was a flare firing upward from within the city at a minute or two after 0230 on 31 January. Firing immediately commenced from many locations as the hidden VC in the city emerged to claim their objectives while external forces swarmed from the countryside into the attack. As soon as the go signal flared, two battalions of the 6th NVA Regiment attacked the Citadel from the west. They were preceded by a sapper team, dressed in ARVN uniforms, who attacked the gate guards by surprise, killing them and opening the huge portal to one of the fortress's eight access routes. They used flashlights to signal the 6th Regiment battalions to advance.

A file of North Vietnamese soldiers quickly moved into the Citadel through the opened gate. One of the battalions, the 800th, swung north and tried to occupy the Tây Loc Airport, which spread out in the western corner within the walled city. At first the attackers were slowed by the Black Panther company, but when the other battalion, the 802nd, charged against the 1st Division HQ compound at Mang Ca, General Truong called the reconnaissance company back to the compound to aid his 200 clerks and staff officers in defending the command center. The NVA was in control of the airport before dawn, and Communist soldiers swarmed all over the walls and through the streets within the Citadel. At 0800 hours, they proudly raised the huge red-and-blue Viet Cong flag, emblazoned with the bright gold star, on the massive flagpole before the Imperial Palace.

South of the river, the 4th NVA Regiment advanced through city streets, welcomed by the VC forces waiting for them. Local insurgents joined by the score and quickly swelled the numbers of the North Vietnamese formation. Their objectives included the MACV compound, government buildings, utilities, and university that were located throughout the modern section of the city. All of these facilities except the MACV compound, where staff officers, clerks, and others put up a stiff resistance, were in the attackers' hands by morning. The VC also captured the city jail and released some 2,500 prisoners. Many of these were pressed into service as laborers, but at least 500 of them volunteered to serve in the ranks of the Communist forces.

Just about the time the VC flag was raised over the Citadel, the ARVN high command was beginning to react to the attack on Hue. Information was limited, and Lieutenant General Hoang Xuan Lam, the commander of all South Vietnamese forces in I Corps, didn't know that virtually the entire city was already in enemy hands. In fact, Lam had originally had a hard time believing that the Tet Offensive was anything more than a few skirmishes, insisting that the telephoned reports a subordinate colonel was giving him early on 30 January couldn't possibly be true.

But now he was convinced, and even without a detailed map of dispositions, Lam began to dispatch his forces to the city. The closest unit was his 3rd ARVN Regiment, which was about five miles away to the northwest of Hue. He decided to send half of it by boat down the Perfume River, and send the other half by road. The waterborne portion of the regiment off-loaded at piers practically in the shadow of the Citadel walls by evening of the 31st, but the battalions traveling by road were trapped and surrounded by an ambush, and lost a great deal of their strength just fighting to extricate themselves.

Another column, with a troop of the 7th ARVN Armored Cavalry leading two truck-mounted airborne battalions, sped south on Highway 1 from a base about 10 miles away. They pulled to within a few hundred yards of the Citadel, but before they could connect with General Truong's compound, they were halted by an enemy roadblock. The relief column finally forced its way into the HQ compound on the morning of 1 February, having lost 40 men killed and a third of their vehicles in the fighting.

Meanwhile, the Marine command of the III MAF wanted to come to the rescue of the embattled MACV compound on the south side of the

Perfume River. The large base at Phu Bai was not far away, but it was mostly a supply depot and had no combat units currently stationed there. The base had been hit by rockets and mortars overnight as part of the Tet attacks, and given the conflicting signals about combat all across the country, the officers commanding headquarters at Phu Bai, Task Force X-Ray, didn't prioritize the MACV call for help. Finally, however, III MAF ordered X-Ray to see what was going on, so it dispatched first one, then a second company, controlled for the moment by 1/1st Marines, toward the city by helicopter and truck. They had to fight their way through the streets of southern Hue, but reached the MACV compound by midday on the 31st. Taking fire from enemy troops positioned along every block, the Marines did well just to reach the compound.

However, they couldn't believe it when the remote commanders at Phu Bai, who still didn't grasp the seriousness of the situation at Hue, ordered them to advance all the way to the north side of the city to link up with the 1st ARVN headquarters. Lieutenant Colonel Marcus Gravel, the senior Marine officer in Hue, argued against the unreasonable order, but was overruled on the basis that it had come all the way from III MAF HQ in Da Nang.

One company of Marines, G of 2/5 under Captain Charles Meadows, tackled the much tougher task of securing the long Truong Tien Bridge spanning the river. The bridge began near one corner of the MACV compound on the south bank, and ended at a corner of the Citadel on the north. It was a formidable objective, more than a thousand feet long and offering no cover for the incredibly courageous men fighting their way across, into the teeth of intense automatic weapons fire. Despite heavy casualties, however, the intrepid Marine riflemen had gained control of the important span by 1615 that afternoon. However, when they tried to follow orders and move north along the wall of the Citadel, they were pinned down and pounded by NVA small-arms fire from three sides. It took Meadows two hours to extricate his men and bring the company back to the MACV compound; fully a third of his Marines had been killed or wounded.

The counterattack to regain control of Hue commenced in earnest on the morning of 1 February. Both American and ARVN commanders, still out of touch with the situation, expected the battle to last a couple of days. Two ARVN airborne battalions, escorted by tanks, entered the Citadel and gained control of the Tây Loc Airport, which filled the western corner of the square. The rest of the city within the walls was a dense maze of buildings, courtyards, alleys, and streets where the NVA were very well dug in. The South Vietnamese made no headway into this stronghold, though on 4 February a battalion of the 3rd ARVN Regiment did clear the northwest wall, which allowed the 1st Division HQ position to link up with the airport. A battalion of the 2nd ARVN Regiment moved down the southwest wall on the 5th, clearing most of it. But the NVA counterattacked at night, using grappling hooks to scale the wall and drive off the South Vietnamese. The bold attack regained that section of wall for the Communists on the night of 6 February.

Meanwhile, south of the river, the Marines trying to recapture that part of Hue engaged in a kind of urban, building-to-building combat that the Corps had not experienced since the USMC had driven the North Koreans out of Seoul in September of 1950. They adapted quickly, however, learning to toss a grenade into every room before entering, spraying M16 rounds ahead of them. They employed tanks for fire support and fought their way, yard by yard, down the riverbank to the southwest. Gradually, III MAF realized that the fight to retake Hue would be a major battle. By 3 February, a full battalion was in the city, and by the 5th, another had arrived.

The first major objective gained was the university. By the 6th, the Marines had pushed the NVA out of the prison, where the enemy had been firmly entrenched, and other buildings of the central government compound. Most of the combat in Hue had been fought under conditions of cold, wet rain, mist, and drizzle, which made for a low cloud ceiling and impeded aerial observation of the battlefield. Even if the skies had been clear, however, the counterattacking Marines and South Vietnamese were initially not allowed to call in airstrikes because of General Lam's insistence that the landmarks of the hallowed city be preserved as much as possible. Even artillery support was limited to very precise objectives.

By 5 February, given the grueling and bloody nature of every inch of ground gained, the restrictions on bombardment were lifted for the battle in the southern part of the city and the Citadel, though Lam insisted that the Imperial Palace not be attacked by anything larger than handheld small arms. The increased offensive punch had an immediate effect. Not only did the normal air and artillery support enjoyed by the Marines return, but they also benefited from the huge guns of United States Navy vessels cruising just offshore. Before the battle was over, nearly 5,000 rounds of naval gunfire would fall on Hue. In some cases, the Navy used armor-piercing (AP) rather than the standard HE rounds, since the delayed fuse on the AP ordnance allowed the shell to plunge deep into something like a bunker complex before exploding.

In another unusual aspect of the battle, the Marines started using tear gas to clear areas of enemy defenders. The idea had come from a staff major who was visiting the front lines prior to ending his tour and returning to the United States. Upon observing the challenges the riflemen were facing, he collected a bundle of tear-gas grenades and asked permission to use them. After the battalion commander on the scene made sure that the Marines had gas masks and knew what was coming, permission was granted. No doubt many American lives were saved as the Marines, even visually impaired as they were by the gas masks, were able to advance through buildings where the enemy troops had literally been blinded or forced to flee. Naturally enough, the NVA in the Citadel across the river responded by launching tear-gas bombs from their mortars.

Of course, in the end it all came down to the Marine, his rifle, bayonet, hand grenades, and the support of his squad, platoon, and company mates. The battle at Hue invoked some of the hardest, nastiest fighting ever done by the USMC; and it is safe to say that the Marines of 1968 did their forefathers proud. By 11 February, the southern half of Hue was free of Communist control, though much of the formerly beautiful residential, commercial, and government sections had been reduced to rubble.

In the Citadel, the ARVN had been making slow but steady progress.

In some cases, units allowed themselves to get bogged down, with battalion commanders reluctant to advance and risk casualties, while General Truong railed against this attitude. Other units, however, fought and advanced—and suffered—with considerable élan. The 3rd ARVN Regiment, in particular, distinguished itself, even though it began the battle at only half strength and two of its battalions had suffered grievous losses just trying to fight their way to the city. But the NVA continued to resist with a fanaticism not encountered in other parts of the country during Tet. On 10 February, the Communists launched a powerful counterpunch, more or less annihilating a battalion of the 1st ARVN Division and pushing the South Vietnamese out of several days' worth of hard-won yardage.

Other American and ARVN units had established blocking positions outside of Hue to try to interdict any enemy efforts at reinforcement or resupply. Several battalions from the 3rd Brigade of the 1st Cavalry Division had been fighting their way toward Hue from the west since 2 February. The VC used boats and small units to continue to infiltrate, and throughout the course of the battle were able to at least maintain contact and communication between their units in the city and those beyond Hue.

At one point, while the battle still raged on both sides of the river, the VC used swimming sappers to plant floating mines along the key Truong Tien Bridge, blowing up two spans of this beautiful and important structure and breaking the most important link between the two halves of Hue. The allies began using boats to bring supplies into the city, coming up the Perfume River from the coast. They also employed amtracs and other amphibious vehicles to connect the two banks of the river. Two South Vietnamese Marine Corps battalions were carried by boats into the city to land just outside the fortress walls north of the river.

As the Marines finished clearing the south bank, the ARVN was rather thoroughly stymied in the maze of fortified streets and structures within the Citadel. General Truong controlled the operation there, and by the second week of the battle, he had some fifteen battalions under his command, including those of his 1st Division, 3rd Airborne, three from the South Vietnamese

Marines, and two battalions of ARVN Rangers—though it should be noted that even at full strength the ARVN battalions tended to contain only about half as many men as a USMC battalion.

The North Vietnamese and Viet Cong remained firmly entrenched in the area around the Imperial Palace. They still held the southeast wall, half of the northeast wall, and a large stretch of the southwest wall, stubbornly resisting all ARVN efforts to push into the last corner of the bastion. For reasons of prestige, General Lam had very much wanted his countrymen to be the soldiers who reclaimed the landmarks of Hue City, but after the setback suffered by the 1st Division, he set aside his pride and asked the Marines to help clear the last strongpoints of enemy from Hue. South Vietnamese pride was assuaged when it was agreed than only ARVN forces would actually enter the Imperial Palace.

Almost immediately the 1st Battalion, 5th Marines, which had been responsible for road security along Highway 1 around Da Nang, was airlifted directly into the Citadel and placed on the left flank of two South Vietnamese battalions moving generally southeast toward the palace. The Citadel wall would be the left flank of the Marine formations' advance. On the very first morning of action, Company A, 1/5, with Captain James Bowe in command, moved down a street just a short block away from, and parallel to, the wall. He expected to advance about halfway down the northeast bastion, where he would relieve an ARVN paratroop battalion that had gained that much ground before being halted.

About 200 yards short of the rendezvous point, however, the column of Marines was savagely attacked by NVA soldiers lying in ambush. Rockets, mortars, and hundreds of rounds from AK-47 rifles ripped into the Americans, who had assumed they were safely behind friendly lines. Two men were killed and more than 30 wounded, a casualty count that wrecked the company's combat effectiveness for the next few days. Company C moved forward to take on the mission, as the Marines learned, to their dismay, how the mistake had happened: when the ARVN paratroopers learned that their allies were going to replace them, they simply abandoned their position, allowing the Communists to move right back in—and allowing the Marines to walk, unsuspecting of danger, into a deathtrap.

But the battle continued. Company C, under the command of 1st Lieutenant Scott Nelson, pressed forward against stubborn opposition. As on the south bank of the river, the fighting was house to house—and here the houses were smaller and more tightly packed. Making this worse, the NVA had had nearly two weeks to dig in, getting to know the layout of streets, buildings, and allies. They had sandbagged machine-gun nests in many locations, and stored plentiful ammunition within easy reach.

The Marines of 1/5 had no experience in urban fighting, but like their comrades on the south bank of the Perfume River, they quickly learned on the job. Tanks accompanied the point position on many assaults, their 90-mm guns adding a powerful punch to Marines storming buildings or attempting to reduce bunkers. But even the armored behemoths were not immune to enemy attack, as the new B41 RPGs had proved to be a lethal threat. More than one armored vehicle was knocked out, only to have a replacement crew take over and put the tank back into operation.

The Ontos vehicle, unique to the Marine Corps, also proved its worth in the city fighting. With three recoilless rifle tubes to each side of the driver, the Ontos was capable of delivering a devastating blast against enemy strongpoints. Not as heavily armored as a tank, however, the Ontos became a favorite target of enemy gunners who had learned to fear its lethal volleys. With continued bad weather, artillery remained the only external fire support available to help in the attack. The prohibition on striking the Imperial Palace limited the effectiveness of the big guns, however, and for the most part the Marines fought with the weapons they could carry, or that could drive down the streets with them—and in fact, the tanks had difficultly working their way between obstacles on some of the narrow lanes.

On Valentine's Day, the Marines, now three companies abreast, approached a key obstacle: the tower above the Citadel's Dong Ba Gate. After two days of savage fighting, scrambling over piles of rubble, firing every weapon they had, the Marines carried the tower and the gate below it. At 0430 on the 16th, the NVA swarmed forward in a fanatical attempt to retake the tower, and for several hours the two sides fought at hand-to-hand and pistol range until, shortly after dawn, the North Vietnamese were pushed back.

And that day, for once, dawned clear. Immediately the sky over the battle-scarred city filled with American attack planes. Napalm and high-explosive ordnance tumbled onto the Communists' position, while helicopter gunships opened up on targets of opportunity with rockets and machine guns. But the fighting inside the buildings remained a matter of one man versus his enemy. The Marines used satchel charges to blow holes in walls, entering the next building without having to use a door. They used hundreds, thousands of grenades, throwing the explosive devices into every space they prepared to enter.

By the 17th, the 1/5 Marines had worn themselves out. In the last few days of combat the battalion had suffered 47 KIA and 240 men wounded badly enough to require evacuation. An untold number of Marines had been wounded and continued to fight, unwilling to abandon their buddies in this urban hell. The battalion commander, Major Robert Thompson, decided to give his weary Marines a day of rest on 18 February. Replacements were brought right into the front lines, including some Marines still wearing the shiny boots they had been issued at Camp Pendleton, California—a few short weeks, and a whole world, away from Hue.

Two more days of bloody fighting followed the brief rest, as the NVA troops had naturally taken advantage of the respite to strengthen their own positions. Enemy strongpoints atop the Imperial Palace particularly aggravated the Marines, as they were not able to direct any heavy ordnance against those enemy troops. By the evening of 20 February, Major Thompson and his men were sick of the entire ordeal, and the idea of several more days of bloody, inch-by-inch advance was demoralizing in the extreme. The major brought up the bold idea of a surprise night attack, something the Marines rarely did. First Lieutenant Patrick Polk, CO of Company A, volunteered that his men, who had been the battalion reserve for a couple of days, would make the attempt.

The objective was a large building obstructing access to the Imperial Palace, and also providing the enemy a commanding view of the advancing Marines' positions. Personally leading an understrength platoon of his company, Lieutenant Polk surprised even himself as the American strike force crossed the open space before the fortified structure while remaining unseen. By 0300, his men had taken the building not only without firing a shot, but without being discovered.

Before dawn, Polk observed groups of NVA moving forward to reoccupy the building, and he was able to call down a crushing mortar barrage that caught the enemy in the open. Buoyed by news of this startling victory, the rest of the battalion surged forward, advancing to the very end of the wall that day. Now the allied forces occupied the eastern corner of the Citadel and all the walls except for the southeast, which was the stretch above the riverbank and adjacent to the Imperial Palace.

Overnight on the 22nd/23rd, the most battered Marine company, B of 1/5, was pulled out of the battle, replaced by the fresh Company L, 3/5, commanded by Captain John Niotis. The Marines were ready to get this fight over with once and for all. On the 23rd, they pressed forward, but were halted by intense fire on the wall, and down in the city streets. But finally even General Lam had had enough, and the next morning he authorized airstrikes against the Imperial Palace. As soon as the Marine jets began to plaster the once-hallowed structures, the last NVA resistance began to crumble.

It turned out that the NVA had been slowly pulling out of the city over the past few nights. When companies of the 1st ARVN Division assaulted the bombed, smoldering palace later on the 24th, they forced their way inside against only light opposition. Only one stretch of wall, the place supporting the huge flagpole and the VC banner that had taunted the city of Hue since 31 January, remained in enemy hands. On the morning of the 25th, part of the 3rd ARVN Regiment, the unit that had demonstrated such valor and suffered so many casualties during this battle, charged down the wall, eliminated the last of the NVA, and raised the flag of the Republic of South Vietnam once more over the city of Hue.

The battle had been one of the most savage in a savage war, and the toll in lives and property was staggering. Among the combatants, the VC and NVA had suffered at least 5,000 killed, and quite possibly more. Marine Corps casualties numbered 147 killed and nearly 1,000 badly wounded; the ARVN had lost nearly 400 killed and an untold number of wounded. The once-glorious city, hallowed by generations of Vietnamese, was a heap of rubble. Thousands of civilians had lost their lives, and tens of thousands were homeless.

As the Americans and South Vietnamese took stock of their victory, they learned of another horror, one that was unprecedented even in a war as brutal as this. After the Communists had taken control of the city, many VC agents had gone around with lists of "reactionary" individuals. Some were professors or government officials, others merchants, or simply people known to favor the government. Those people were forced from their homes, their families told they were being taken to camps for "reeducation." In reality, a great many of them were shot or clubbed to death and buried in mass graves, graves that were discovered and excavated after the battle. No one knows how many victims died in this manner, but the estimates range from as low as 2,800 to as high as 8,000. It was a war crime that would forever mark the tragedy that was the Battle of Hue and a crime for which no one has ever been held accountable.

Eventually, in Hue as in everywhere else during the Tet Offensive of 1968, the Communist forces were thoroughly defeated. Their losses across the country were so staggering that the campaign effectively broke the back of the Viet Cong—the insurgent organization would never again approach the strength, capabilities, or numbers that it had before. It was a battlefield victory for the Americans and South Vietnamese without parallel.

But Americans were beginning to realize that battlefield victories might not be enough to win the war.

TWELVE

PUSH FROM THE NORTH

NINE HUNDRED MARINES STOP
6,000 NVA AT DONG HA

I started out with 123 men and by the time I got through
[Dai Do] I was down to 41. . . . Every trooper had a captured
AK-47.

CAPTAIN MANUEL VARGAS, CO COMPANY G, 2/4 MARINES,
DESCRIBING 1 MAY 1968

The base outside the city of Dong Ha was a major supply depot for the 3rd
Marine Division, and for all the American and ARVN forces in the northern I Corps area of Quang Tri province. But it was much more than that as
well. It was the forward headquarters of the 3rd Marine Division and the
main headquarters of the 9th Marines, just a few miles south of the DMZ
and North Vietnam. In fact, it was so close to the border that Dong Ha lay
in range of, and was occasionally targeted by, NVA artillery batteries in
the DMZ and in North Vietnam itself. The Dong Ha base also controlled
the key crossroads where Highway 9, the famous serpentine route leading
westward to Khe Sanh, began its winding journey toward Laos.

Dong Ha was just south of a wide river, the Bo Dieu, where Highway
1—the major South Vietnamese artery extending all the way to the DMZ—
crossed an important bridge. Around Dong Ha, the waterways themselves
served as important links in the Marines' supply routes. The Navy transported supplies from oceangoing ships to an off-loading port at the mouth
of the Cua Viet, a broad river and estuary, and the Marines and Navy

used smaller craft to transport those supplies along the wide waterway a short distance inland. These supply ships were protected by small, fast gunboats of the US Navy's Task Force Clearwater, which was responsible for the security of the waterway.

The Cua Viet curved south about two miles to the east of Dong Ha, but the nautical supply continued westward on the slightly smaller river, the Bo Dieu. This was a major tributary of the Cua Viet, and was also easily navigable by small boats and AmTracs. The nautical supply route extended westward a mile or so up the Bo Dieu to the wharves and ramps of the supply depot. During April 1968, more than 60,000 tons of supplies were off-loaded at the port facility beside the river's mouth and moved up the river by an assortment of large and small shallow draft vessels, and even AmTracs, to Dong Ha.

Naturally, it was important to protect the river route from interdiction by enemy forces, since any kind of heavy weapons established on the northern bank of either waterway could effectively block the route to water traffic. To that end, the Marines and South Vietnamese Army had units posted north of the Cua Viet and Bo Dieu to keep the enemy away from the rivers. The 2nd ARVN Regiment, four battalions strong, maintained a headquarters in Dong Ha and was responsible for the security and defense of Highway 1, from the bridge leading northward over the Bo Dieu all the way to the DMZ. To the west of the ARVN unit and the highway, the 9th Marines, three battalions strong, patrolled and conducted search and destroy missions north of the Bo Dieu River and south of the DMZ.

The area east of Highway 1, extending all the way to the sea, was assigned to the 3rd Marines. That regiment had deployed north of the Cua Viet, in order from east to west, the 1/3 Battalion, the 1st Amphibian Tractor Battalion, and BLT 2/4. The Americans had a longer stretch of front to protect, though it should be noted that the ARVN regiment's four battalions together, in terms of personnel, included fewer fighting men than two Marine battalions. The South Vietnamese roster allowed for about 300 men per battalion, while the Marines, at full strength, put 900 men in a single battalion.

With all these forces in the field, the Marines did not have much of a reserve at the Dong Ha base. Most of the personnel there were support and service types, not combat soldiers. The only mobile reaction force that Major General Rathvon Tompkins, commander of the 3rd Marine Division, had available was Task Force Robbie. This TF, commanded by Colonel Clifford Robichaud, included one rifle company, one armored company, a platoon of Ontos recoilless rifle vehicles, and a platoon of engineers. Task Force Robbie was also augmented by four US Army armored vehicles, including two tanklike M42 "Dusters," boasting twin rapid-firing 20-mm cannon in its small turret instead of a tank's main gun. Though originally designed as an antiaircraft weapon, the Duster had proven very effective at supporting infantry in battle.

The I Corps region just south of the DMZ had been active in the early months of 1968. The major focus for both sides had of course been Khe Sanh, at the far west of the short border region, but the Marines and ARVN had also worked vigorously to push the enemy back from intrusions into South Vietnam. By the end of March, these operations had been fairly successful, especially in the east. There, the 3rd Marines had begun to focus more on pastoral activities rather than battle, including projects to improve the hamlets and villages of their TAOR and returning farmers and other citizens to the lands they had been forced to flee during earlier months of combat.

The boundaries between the various units remained fairly static during this time, and the Marine commanders suspected that the ARVN regiment, whose boundary with the 3rd Marines ran north and south along an unnamed stream flowing several miles to the east of Highway 1, might represent the easiest path for enemy infiltration. By April, the 3rd Marine Division headquarters was aware that the 320th NVA Division had been working its way south from the DMZ, and the 3rd Marines patrolled diligently, seeking signs of this intrusion. Other sources from US Navy intelligence had gathered indications that the enemy might attempt to close the import supply conduit along the Cua Viet and Bo Dieu Rivers, thus focusing the threat onto the north bank of both rivers.

The first overt sign of trouble in the Battle of Dong Ha began on the afternoon of 29 April, when enemy troops from what was later determined to be the 320th Division blew up a culvert on Route 1 near the village of An Binh. Following up on reports that the NVA was moving into that village, the ARVN 2nd Regiment deployed two battalions to approach the position from different directions to try to trap the enemy between them. However, both battalions ran into heavy resistance, and the ARVN regimental commander, Lieutenant Colonel Vu Van Giai, called General Tompkins to report more enemy activity to the west of the highway.

The 3rd Marine Division CO dispatched Task Force Robbie, reinforced with an additional rifle and an armored company, to investigate and support. The task force ran into a strong NVA position about three miles west of An Binh and the two sides engaged fiercely, fighting a savage, eight-hour battle that didn't break off until midnight. During the fight, the Communists held firm, and revealed a surprising strength in numbers, as well as real tenacity in refusing to retreat.

In the early morning hours of 30 April, both Task Force Robbie and the ARVN battalions pulled back to the south. Even before that maneuver, however, General Tompkins had become alarmed by the enemy strength north of the river. He contacted Colonel Milton Hull, CO of the 3rd Marines, and told him to make ready to send a company west to help defend Highway 1. Hull arranged for Company E of the 2/4 BLT to move west and keep an eye on An Binh and Highway 1. The general also brought in another battalion of Marines, the 3/9, from the western sector of his TAOR and attached it to Task Force Robbie.

The next day, the 3/9, reinforced with some tanks from TF Robbie, moved out to retrace the route followed by the task force the previous day. They encountered an ambush set by the NVA, but the powerful Marine force fought off the attackers and soon drove them north. The enemy displayed remarkable discipline and professionalism as he retired under the cover of a barrage from North Vietnam–based artillery. Twenty Marines died in this sharp action, with a little more than twice that many NVA slain. But despite its intensity, this clash would turn out to be merely a sideshow, as the 320th NVA Division was ready to throw a powerful punch right at the supply base at Dong Ha.

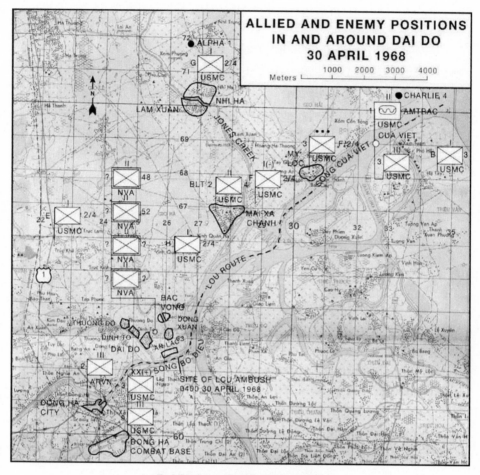

Dai Do Area; Battle of Dong Ha

HISTORY AND MUSEUMS DIVISION, UNITED STATES MARINE CORPS

THE DAI DO VILLAGE BATTLE—DAY ONE

The name Dai Do applied to a collection of five small villages, of which the largest is actually Dai Do. They were lined up along two tributary streams flowing from the north into the Cua Viet River. The lesser waterways combined to form a small peninsula, almost at the junction where the Bo Dieu also flows into the major river. The southernmost of the hamlets was An Lac, which was right on the north bank of the Cua Viet river and allowed for a commanding view along all three channels: the Bo Dieu westward, and south and east along the surface of the Cua Viet as it flowed past the village through its great curve. Four of the five hamlets, including An Lac, were in the ARVN TAOR, while the fifth, Bac Vong, lay to the east of the unnamed stream that formed the boundary between the 3rd Marines and 2nd ARVN areas of responsibility.

In the predawn darkness of 30 April, at about 0330, a US Navy patrol boat from Task Force Clearwater cruised from Dong Ha, out of the Bo Dieu, and onto the Cua Viet River. As it passed An Lac, the boat took fire from enemy automatic weapons, including a heavy machine gun. The small boat quickly turned around and skimmed back to the base. A short time later a larger vessel, a Navy landing craft utility (LCU) traveling down the river toward the sea was struck by several RPGs. The ship took some damage and casualties, with one sailor killed; it, too, turned about and returned to Dong Ha, reporting the attack over the radio as it did so.

Lieutenant Colonel William Weise, the commander of BLT 2/4, heard about the incident from his headquarters staff, which routinely monitored the naval communication. At the same time one of his company commanders, Captain James Williams of Company H, reported that Marines from one of his patrols had seen the attack. The reports went up the chain, and the 3rd Marines commanding officer, Colonel Milton Hull, ordered Weise to have his men investigate. Hull would take care of getting the operational boundary shifted at the division level so that Weise's battalion wouldn't be treading on ARVN turf.

At the time the matter seemed like nothing more than an enemy nuisance patrol that would have to be cleared out, but Colonel Weise began to worry that it might be a sign of bigger trouble. He decided to start concentrating his battalion, which was spread out over several miles of territory north of the Cua Viet. The 2/4 HQ and most of Company F were located at Mai Xa Chanh, some three miles east of where the shots had been fired; one Company F platoon was another two miles east, at My Loc. Company G was several miles to the north, around the hamlet of Nhi Ha on Jones Creek. Weise did not have his Company E as it had been op-conned to 3rd Division and was currently stationed on Route 1 around the hamlet of An Binh. Because they were on station to guard against enemy infiltration, Wiese could not move either the My Loc platoon from F Company, or G or E Companies, without permission from the division HQ.

Making the best of what he had, Weise ordered Captain Williams to prepare Company H to move toward An Lac, and he told Captain James Butler, CO of Company F, to load his two platoons in AmTracs and start them chugging up the river. By 0830, the advance platoon of Company H, with Captain Williams accompanying, moved through Bac Vong and prepared to cross the creek. Immediately beyond the little waterway was the hamlet of Dong Huan, with An Lac—the site of the shots fired across the river—just beyond.

Before the platoon even reached the stream, intense enemy fire erupted from Dong Huan. Mortars, RPGs, and fixed machine guns amplified the chatter of AK-47s as the enemy fired from a multitude of well-concealed positions. The platoon quickly pulled back to await reinforcements as the other Company H platoons hurried toward the sound of the guns. The enemy strength in Dong Huan, both in numbers of men and the quality of the prepared positions, was startling. In response, Lieutenant Colonel Weise also called up the battalion's recon platoon, which included two M48 tanks and several AmTracs, two of which, as a "field expedient," were topped by 90-mm recoilless rifles protected by sandbags.

Although the Marines would not find this out without the expenditure of considerable blood, sweat, and ammunition, they had ventured into a powerful and well-prepared NVA bastion. At least four battalions, including several of the 320th NVA Division, had infiltrated the village complex right under the noses of the 2nd ARVN Regiment, which had responsibility for the area. And this was not just a recent incursion: the enemy had built solid bunkers—strong enough, according to Weise, to support the weight of a tank—and surrounded them with trenches and barbed wire. They had carved out firing positions in the multitude of hedgerows that surrounded each hamlet, and stockpiled plenty of ammunition. The Marines later learned that the villagers had been coerced to construct the fortifications so that the NVA soldiers could simply move in and set up in the established firing positions.

Back at battalion HQ in Mai Xa Chanh, Lieutenant Colonel Weise was eager to get closer to the action. After sending a message up the chain to division asking permission to move his Company G and the last platoon of Company F, he boarded a US Navy LCM 6 "Mike Boat," also called a monitor, with a small group from his headquarters staff. The boat was a formidable craft in its own right, armed with a mortar, two automatic cannons, and machine guns, with a bow ramp that dropped to allow for fast debarkation onto a beach or shoreline. The monitor roared upstream from Mai Xa Chanh and quickly brought the battalion CO to the scene of the developing battle.

While Weise's extra units moved into position, machine gun bursts and rockets from helicopter gunships, fighter-bomber airstrikes, and artillery thundered into the suspected enemy positions in all five hamlets of the Dai Do complex. Just before midday, the assaulting units were in position, and Company G, which had been released back to battalion control, was to be heli-lifted to Mai Xa Chanh, where it would board a landing craft and come up the river as soon as possible. The attack was to begin with Captain Williams's H Company crossing the stream just north of Dong Huan while the tank guns and recoilless rifles added firepower to Company F, which was to cover the initial assault. With artillery rounds creating a smoke screen, Company H pushed across the stream and cautiously advanced across nearly a mile of flat, open rice paddy. The Marines crawled much of the way and that, coupled with the smoke, allowed Williams's company to reach its assault position just outside of Dong Huan.

Now it was H Company's turn to lay down covering fire as Captain James Butler advanced his F Company, with the riflemen riding atop the big AmTracs, into position on Williams's right. The two companies were to attack simultaneously, H taking Dong Huan and F advancing on Dai Do proper. The attack kicked off about 1400, and Company H made remarkable progress against fierce opposition. The softening up of the air and artillery bombardment had made a difference, though the remaining NVA troops fought with a vengeance. One enemy soldier wounded Captain Williams with a grenade before the officer shot him dead with his .45. First Lieutenant Alexander Prescott took over the company, and after an hour of intense combat Dong Huan was in American hands.

The attack on Dai Do ran into trouble right away, however. NVA artillery fired well-aimed supporting rounds from north of the DMZ, and intense fire from both infantry weapons and emplaced recoilless rifles and machines guns brought Company F to a halt just at the edge of the hamlet's first buildings, with one platoon pinned down in a cemetery 300 yards short of the objective. Two AmTracs were destroyed in the attack.

The expected reinforcement of Company G might have made a difference, but in yet another surprising sign of a strong enemy force in the area, that unit's exit from Nhi Ha had been compromised by a heavy mortar attack on the intended LZ. The flight of choppers coming to get the Marines couldn't even drop safely to the ground, much less lift out the riflemen. Instead, the company commander, Manuel Vargas, elected to lead his men on a night march back to battalion HQ on the river.

Meanwhile, on the small nameless creek east of the village complex where Company H had just secured Dong Huan, regimental CO Colonel Hull arrived at the scene in a small, fast boat. He told Lieutenant Colonel Weise that he would have operational control of Company B, 1/3, which was currently just south of the Bo Dieu. Fortunately, B Company had a platoon of LVTPs (Landing Vehicle, Tracked, Personnel) attached, which were essentially armored personnel carriers that could move over land or water. With H Company poised to move on An Lac from the north, Weise decided to use the fresh company's amphibious capability to deposit it right on the riverbank, southwest of An Lac so that he could hit the hamlet from two directions.

By 1630, with the support of a flotilla of Task Force Clearwater gunboats, the LVTPs of Company B's first wave lurched from the water to deposit half of Company B on a small beachhead just outside of An Lac. The big, blocky vehicles rolled back into the water, churned to the south bank, and delivered the rest of the company about 45 minutes later. With First Lieutenant George Norris in command, B 1/3 held a narrow beachhead, but was taking fire from both An Lac close by to the right and Dai Do, a little more than a half mile away to the left. Nevertheless, Norris pushed his men off the beachhead and into An Lac, clearing about half the village before he was shot and killed by a sniper. The attack lost momentum, and as darkness approached, the company formed a small perimeter in the western half of the hamlet.

At the same time, in the gathering dusk, Captain Butler was finally able to extricate Company F from the outskirts of Dai Do. He and his men pulled back to join Company H in Dong Huan. The enemy probed their perimeter several times during the night, but the advances were quickly turned away by riflemen firing their M16s, with supporting artillery adding a few well-placed rounds. During the long day of battle, the Marines of Weise's battalion (and attached Company B) had lost 16 men killed and more than a hundred wounded badly enough to require evacuation. Enemy losses were estimated at around a hundred killed.

THE DAI DO VILLAGE BATTLE—DAY TWO

General Tompkins was concerned that G 2/4's pullout from Nhi Ha had opened up a potential enemy infiltration route along Jones Creek—one that the NVA had previously exploited with some success. Believing that the ultimate objective of the 320th NVA Division was nothing less than the key depot and crossroads at Dong Ha, the 3rd Marine Division commander asked for reinforcements from the Corps reserve. He was quickly provided a battalion of Army infantry, the 3/21st of the 196th Light Infantry Brigade. By 0900 on 1 May, the soldiers of the 196th were aboard transport choppers, flying into the battle zone. Within a few hours they would be placed under the operational control of the 3rd Marines.

Before dawn on 1 May, scouts probing from An Lac's Company B perimeter discovered that the enemy had pulled out of the village overnight. The Marines quickly occupied the rest of the village, bringing the three easternmost hamlets of the complex—from south to north, An Lac, Dong Huan, and Bac Vong—under American control. From Dong Huan, at first light, H Company Marines noticed some 50 or 60 NVA soldiers crossing an open space on the far side of Dai Do. Quickly the Marines called in supporting fire and targeted the exposed troops with their own weaponry. Casualties among the surprised NVA were significant.

Artillery continued to try to soften the Dai Do defenses as Company G, having reached Mai Xa Chanh after a night march, boarded Navy landing craft and moved up the river to disembark into Company B's position in An Lac. Two more tanks accompanied G Company. Many of Company B's LVTPs fired up their engines and roared forward and back to conceal the sounds of the two tanks as they rolled ashore from inside the landing craft. The fresh company formed up, two platoons abreast with the third trailing, for the attack, the tanks preparing to advance side by side between the two lead platoons.

Artillery, including big guns from Navy ships, pounded Dai Do until the Marines moved out. As soon as the guns ceased firing, a pair of USMC A-4 Skyhawks screamed overhead, dousing the hamlet with napalm and dumping in more high-explosive bombs. More artillery rounds laid a smoke screen across the 500 yards of clear space the Marines would have to cross.

But the well-protected enemy troops in Dai Do had not been destroyed or driven out, and instead opened up a fierce barrage of fire from automatic rifles, supported by mortars, as Company G advanced. The left platoon was forced to take cover about 200 yards short of the objective, but the platoon on the right flank made it all the way to the NVA bunker line. These they attacked with grenades and satchel charges, bypassing the strongest defensive positions as they pushed through the shattered, smoldering village.

No sooner had the Marines (mostly) cleared that stubbornly defended hamlet, however, than the NVA organized a battalion-strength counterattack from both the north and the west. Supported by accurate artillery fire from the remote batteries outside of South Vietnam, the mortars intrinsic to the attacking units, and additional enemy soldiers who emerged from some of the bypassed bunkers in the southwestern quadrant of Dai Do, the Communists pushed the Americans out of some of their gains, though Captain Vargas finally halted his retreating men in the eastern half of the village. From there, they spotted a number of NVA moving across the open ground some two miles to the north. Airstrikes pounded these exposed soldiers and managed to kill many, including an entire forward artillery control party. The loss of the latter significantly degraded the enemy's fire support for the rest of the day.

Lieutenant Colonel Weise wanted to support the partial occupation of Dai Do made by Vargas's men, and the only force of significant strength he had available was Company B, 1/3, which had been op-conned to him for the battle. In the last 12 hours the unit had received some reinforcements from south of the river, and a new CO, First Lieutenant Thomas Brown. Riding on top of their LVTPs, the Marines of Company B rolled toward Dai Do at 1700—only to be stopped by a veritable hail of lead that wounded many men, including the new company commander. When a young officer, the next in line for command, sounded close to panic on the radio, Captain Vargas was able to "talk him down," calming him enough for him to pull his company back to An Lac in reasonably good order.

Fortunately, by 1730, Weise's own Company E, released from its road patrol on Highway 1, arrived at the village complex—though not without some difficulty. The company had to ford a fast-flowing stream west of Dai Do that was deeper than some of the Marines were tall. The inventive company captain, James Livingston, had six of his tallest Marines strip down and stand in the deep middle channel, where they could safely pass their shorter, heavily laden comrades from one man to the next and get them past the water barrier.

The second night on the battlefield was another restless period. That day the Marines had lost 24 men killed and had evacuated 44 wounded, while again killing an estimated 100 or so of the enemy. The Marines now had three perimeters, one at An Lac with Companies B and E, one with Company G in half of Dai Do, and the position in Dong Huan held by Companies F and H. The middle of the night passed with only limited probing by the enemy, and no serious contacts—though none of the Marines actually got a decent night's sleep.

THE DAI DO VILLAGE BATTLE—DAY THREE

Upon hearing reports from interrogated prisoners of large numbers of NVA pouring into Dai Do, Lieutenant Colonel Weise decided to attack the village while it was still dark on the morning of 2 May. He sent Company E forward at 0500 with Company G providing covering fire. After E passed Captain Vargas's position, he pulled E around to hit the enemy troops holding the south side of Dai Do in the flank. Savage fighting raged for several hours, with grenades, satchel charges, and bayonets all coming into play; handheld M72 light antitank weapons (LAWs) proved especially effective at destroying enemy bunkers. By 0930, Dai Do was at last secured by American forces.

Although Colonel Weise knew his men were reaching the point of exhaustion, no more reinforcements were available, and he sensed that his battalion had the NVA at the breaking point. He ordered 1st Lieutenant Prescott to take his Company H and try to capture the next hamlet up the line of villages, Dinh To. The company pushed its way into the fringe of that village, but then was threatened with annihilation by an intense NVA counterattack. As Prescott radioed for assistance, Captain Livingston acted on his own initiative, moving north from Dai Do with his 30 remaining effective Marines. That was enough to rally the defense against the first counterattack, but the next wave of enemy soldiers hit them even harder. Prescott was wounded and evacuated; Captain Livingston was shot through the legs and unable to walk, but waited until the rest of his men had been evacuated before allowing himself to be carried back to the new forward battalion HQ in Dai Do.

With assurances that an ARVN mechanized battalion was now moving up on his left, Lieutenant Colonel Weise assigned the two freshest of all his badly depleted companies to another attack. Companies G and F had barely 120 men between them, but they made another valiant effort to clear Dinh To. They pushed through the hamlet and approached the sixth and final village of the complex, Thuong Do. But this attack was broken when an NVA counterattack hit them in the flank, where the ARVN unit—which never materialized—was supposed to have been guarding them.

An enemy AK-47 round hit Lieutenant Colonel Weise and put him down with a serious wound. The battalion CO would later credit Captain Vargas with saving the stranded companies and bringing them back to the Dai Do perimeter, saying, "He was everywhere at once." As night fell, and Weise lay on a litter chewing on a fat cigar, he couldn't know that the NVA had broken before the Marines. The day's bloody fighting had cost the lives of 40 of his men and more than 100 had been seriously wounded. But the enemy had lost something like 400 soldiers killed, and he had also lost the stomach for any further fighting.

DONG HA SECURED

With three of the Marines' bloodiest days in the Vietnam War behind them, the weary leathernecks of the 2/4 BLT carefully moved out on the morning of 3 May to find that the enemy had gone. Parties of NVA were spotted moving north through open terrain, and airstrikes were called in. For the most part the survivors of the three-day slugfest were just in need of a decent meal and, perhaps, a good night's sleep. By midday, the 1st Battalion, 3rd Marines, arrived in Dai Do and took over responsibility for the area; by nightfall, the battered companies of Weise's men had returned to the battalion's original command post at Mai Xa Chanh.

Though they had paid a high price in blood, with 2/4 suffering 81 KIA and some 250 to 300 wounded—there are discrepancies in the wounded total among several official Marine Corps sources—the Marines of Lieutenant Colonel Weise's Battalion Landing Team 2/4 had turned aside a major enemy push by a force that outnumbered them by at least 6:1. Weise would be awarded the Navy Cross for his leadership, and both Captain Vargas and Captain Livingston would win the Congressional Medal of Honor, America's highest military award, for their contributions to this significant victory.

And this was more than just a battlefield victory. The battle of Dong Ha forced the NVA to abandon its plans to strike southward from the DMZ during the summer of 1968. The 320th NVA Division had engaged the Americans and South Vietnamese at several locations, including the battles on Highway 1 and farther west, where the 3/9th Marines near Cam Phu had held firm against aggressive probes. The Army battalion from the 196th LIB, the 3/21st, fought some intense battles along Jones Creek north of the Dai Do battlefields, and these, too, helped to send the NVA packing back to the north.

But if in those other fights, the 320th NVA division had been stopped, and even beaten, when it fought the Marines of 2/4 in the Dai Do area, it had truly been broken.

THIRTEEN

BREAKING POINT

THE SCREAMING EAGLES PAY
FOR HAMBURGER HILL

The only significance of Hill 937 was the fact that there were North Vietnamese on it. My mission was to destroy enemy forces . . . and that is where we fought them.

MAJOR GENERAL MELVIN ZAIS, COMMANDER, 101ST AIRBORNE DIVISION, COMMENTING ON OPERATION APACHE SNOW, 10–20 MAY 1969

The A Shau Valley lay in the very western part of the I Corps Tactical Zone. Inhabited only by an isolated tribe, the Katu, who were known to be staunch supporters of the insurrection, the valley was significant because it provided an easy access route for Communist infiltration from Laos. The Army had established a Special Forces camp there, barely two miles from the Laotian border, in the southern portion of Thua Thien province. In early 1966, this was the only allied presence in the area, as the previous December the South Vietnamese had abandoned the two outposts they had established there to monitor the border.

On 9 March 1966, the camp and its 430 defenders were struck by an intense and destructive mortar barrage that lasted for more than two hours. An attack by two NVA companies was repulsed during the day, but not before the attackers and their supporting heavy weapons had inflicted heavy casualties. Furthermore, the camp was well beyond the range of any supporting artillery. Low clouds restricted the number and effectiveness of airstrikes, and to make matters more challenging for the fliers, the enemy had brought significant AA artillery into the battle zone, enough to shoot down a USAF AC-47 Spooky that had been circling at low altitude and lending fire support to the camp's defenders.

Air Force pilots attempted throughout the day to fly in supplies, including water, and to carry out wounded, but the effective antiaircraft fire seriously impeded these operations, with a second aircraft, a helicopter, shot down as it tried to land. The Americans next made attempts to drop supplies by parachute, but many of these landed outside the perimeter where they could not be retrieved by the camp's defenders. Finally, at sunset, a big Air Force CH-3 helicopter did manage to land and evacuate 26 wounded.

The second night the NVA bombarded the camp with an even more intense barrage than the first, leaving most of the buildings, weapon emplacements, and defenses damaged. The North Vietnamese swarmed against the camp in the last hours of full darkness, and this time, as the Communist attackers reached the wire, many of the CIDG members who were part of the camp garrison turned their guns on their comrades and the American Special Forces men who were their advisers. Taking advantage of this betrayal, the enemy poured into the camp and drove the defenders from their initial positions. After a retreat and a desperate fight to hold the communications bunker—the last position remaining in friendly hands—the camp's commander, Captain John Blair IV, decided the only remaining option was to try to evacuate the survivors.

A wave of 26 Marine Hueys came roaring in late on 10 March to pull the garrison out. Antiaircraft fire knocked down two, and a chaotic scene developed in the LZ as panicked South Vietnamese trampled over the litters of the wounded who were to be loaded aboard the helicopters first. The mob was held at bay only by Marine crewmen firing their side arms into the crowd. A second flight the next day was met by similar chaos, though eventually nearly 200 men, most of them wounded, were rescued.

The camp was abandoned, and the valley, for all intents and purposes, was left to the North Vietnamese for the rest of 1966 and all 1967. Remote and inaccessible by land, and relatively far from other significant objectives, the A Shau was one of the most rugged areas in all of South Vietnam.

The mountains to either side, rocky links in the chain of the Annamite Range, rose more than 5,000 feet above sea level, and were surmounted by knife-edged ridges and steep, tree-covered slopes. Though the valley floor was for the most part flat, it was covered with a sea of elephant grass far taller than a man's head. An abandoned village, Ta Bat, occupied a clearing generally in the middle of the valley.

To the east of Ta Bat a rocky elevation rose like a monolith from the flat land all around. It was not attached by ridge or other elevation to the mountains to the north and south of the valley. The height was called Ap Bia Mountain (or Dong Ap Bia) by the South Vietnamese, while the American military, per usual practice, designated it as Hill 937 because of its height, in meters, on their maps. To the local tribesmen, the solitary elevation was known by a more ominous sobriquet: they called it the "mountain of the crouching beast."

AIR CAVALRY OPERATIONS

After the Battle of Hue during the Tet Offensive (see Chapter Eleven), General Westmoreland concluded that the A Shau Valley had been the conduit for much of the NVA support that had made its way to that city in the coastal lowlands. Since the 1st Cavalry Division (Airmobile) had moved into the I Corps TZ during the early part of 1968, Westmoreland ordered it to conduct reconnaissance into the valley.

Remembering the intense AA fire employed in the area by the NVA when they had driven the Americans out early in 1966, Major General John Tolson III's air cavalry division proceeded with cautious speed. Flights of Hueys, escorted by fast Cobra helicopter gunships, chattered through the skies above the A Shau Valley as the 1st Squadron, 9th Cavalry, commenced sweeps. They took advantage of perfect weather in the middle of April to photograph as many enemy positions as they could— admittedly a challenge given excellent NVA camouflage and the dense vegetation—and also drew enough fire from the ground to confirm the presence of significant antiaircraft defenses.

Nevertheless, after tremendous pounding from tactical jet aircraft and a number of B-52 Arc Light runs, the air cavalry division sent its 3rd Brigade into the attack on 19 April 1968. Given the strong AA positions in the middle of the valley, the initial landings of the assault, called Operation Delaware, went into the valley's northern slopes. Over the next week the Americans slogged their way to the abandoned village of Ta Bat as heavy rains again became routine. An ARVN regiment flew in, as did a battalion of engineers. The latter attempted to repair an old airstrip for use by cargo planes, but the soggy weather rendered those efforts fruitless. Though the Americans and South Vietnamese uncovered many depots and captured much NVA matériel, they did not engage in significant combat, as the enemy forces chose to withdraw into Laos rather than fight. The Americans and South Vietnamese withdrew from the valley by the middle of May, generally frustrated by the lack of contact.

Such incursions were repeated several times over the course of the next year, usually with combined American/ARVN forces occupying the valley for a week or two. After Operation Delaware, however, they found relatively little in the way of enemy supplies and installations, and each time the NVA who were present simply pulled back across the border into Laos and waited for their enemies—who relied entirely on helicopters for movement and supply—to get tired and once again leave the A Shau Valley to the Communists.

ENTER THE SCREAMING EAGLES

It wasn't until the first few months of 1969 that the Americans took another crack at seriously disrupting the NVA presence in the valley. General Westmoreland had been replaced in June of 1968 by his West Point classmate General Creighton Abrams. Abrams was a legendary tank commander who had helped lead the armored columns of General Patton's 3rd Army across France and Germany in the last year of World War II. After his death in 1974, the Army would name its next-generation, radically redesigned main battle tank the M1 "Abrams" after him.

In 1969, however, General Abrams was in the unenviable position of beginning the drawdown of American forces in Vietnam, forces that numbered more than 500,000 when he took command, and would number fewer than 50,000 when he left the country in 1972. Abrams had served as Westmoreland's deputy for a little more than a year when he assumed the top job in MACV, and while he placed more emphasis on small-unit pacification operations than his predecessor, he was also willing to send his men against tough objectives when the opportunity presented. The A Shau Valley was one such objective.

During the first two months of 1969, signs began to indicate to both American and ARVN intelligence that the NVA was increasing its level of activity in the remote valley that provided such ready access from Laos. Aerial reconnaissance showed that the NVA had gone to the unusual extent of building a new road leading through the region. The 101st Airborne Division, the legendary "Screaming Eagles" who had constituted one of America's premier paratrooper units during World War II, had been operating in the I Corps Tactical Zone in Vietnam for some time. They were the next unit to be assigned the task of entering the A Shau Valley, learning what the enemy was doing there, and clearing him out—if he didn't, as he always had before, fall back under his own volition.

This time, it turned out, the enemy would stand and fight.

As March began, the 101st had built and manned two new firebases on the eastern edge of the valley. The initial sweep, called Operation Massachusetts Striker, was conducted by the 101st Division's 2nd Brigade, and began on 1 March. Five battalions dropped into landing zones on the valley's southern side and began moving through dense jungle. They encountered the NVA and fought several scattered firefights, and in the process discovered a wealth of enemy logistical support—starting with more than a dozen trucks, hoisted up on jacks with the tires removed. In short order they discovered mechanical depots, major caches of food supplies, and several communications stations. Soon thereafter, following the directions of an NVA defector who had been treated there, they found a major field hospital. By the time the operation concluded, on 8 May, the haul of captured supplies had grown significantly, and the frequent contacts with enemy troops had whetted the Screaming Eagles' appetite for more.

The result was a larger operation, Apache Snow, scheduled to begin just a couple of days later. This time the 3rd Brigade of the 101st Division, under the command of Colonel Joseph Conmy Jr., would lead the way. Though the airborne troops would do most of the fighting, they would receive support from the 9th Marines, the 3rd Squadron, 5th Cavalry, and the 3rd ARVN Regiment, a total of ten battalions working together. The target area would be the northern side of the A Shau Valley, and Colonel Conmy and the 101st Division's commander, Major General Melvin Zais, planned to try an aggressive tactic to force the enemy to fight: instead of entering the operational area from the east, north, or south, a massive helicopter assault would place the two battalions right on the Laotian border, from where they would push eastward, hopefully driving the enemy troops away from their international sanctuary.

Operation Apache Snow began on 10 May with the helicopter assault of companies from 1st Battalion, 506th Airborne, and from the 3rd Battalion, 187th Airborne. The men of the 187th Airborne were known as the "Rakkasans," a word coined by the Japanese who had fought the paratroopers in the Philippines during World War II. The term is an offshoot of the Japanese word for "umbrella," and reputedly grew out of awkward attempts to translate "parachutist," resulting in a phrase meaning "falling-down umbrella man." The 187th embraced the nickname; and the unit, which had participated in the Army's major World War II Pacific campaigns from New Guinea to the Philippines, bore it proudly into the future, to service in Korea and now Vietnam.

In May of 1969, that future lay in the A Shau Valley.

APACHE SNOW

After a preliminary bombardment of some 30 potential LZs to disguise the actual target landing sites, Companies A and C, 3/187, were transported by 65 Hueys and landed uncontested near the border with Laos shortly after 0800 on 10 May 1969. As more paratroopers were flown in on later lifts, Company D took responsibility for the security of the battalion HQ, and the initial units began to move east. At the same time, the Marines and the armored cavalry squadron entered the valley from the southeast end while the ARVN regiment moved to block the exit from that end of the valley.

A new artillery base was established at the abandoned Ta Bat village location. The batteries from this FSB could reach all targets in the operational range. Many aircraft were available to support as well, but it was already obvious that the tall tropical forest canopy would make close air support a difficult proposition at best. Two roads, national Route 922, which connected the valley to Laos, and the enemy-constructed Highway 548, which ran the length of the long A Shau Basin, were to be denied to the enemy.

Moving into the valley from the LZs to the west, the Rakkasans encountered only light resistance on the first day. They did discover an extensive network of enemy huts, or "hooches," and fortified bunkers, all within a few hundred yards of their landing zone. Sensing that many enemy troops could be in the vicinity, battalion CO Lieutenant Colonel Weldon Honeycutt asked for his B Company to be released to him from the brigade reserve, and before the end of 10 May, the fourth company landed in an LZ east of the others. Company B began advancing west while A and C pressed eastward. Directly between the converging American infantry units rose the looming height of Ap Bia Mountain.

Company B ran into a nest of North Vietnamese near dusk and the two sides exchanged sharp volleys of small-arms fire. Lieutenant Colonel Honeycutt ordered the company to settle into a secure night defense perimeter east of the mountain while the other two companies set up a perimeter a short distance to the west. In the meantime, Companies B, C, and D of the 1st Battalion, 506th Airborne "Currahees," swept through the A Shau Valley to the south of Honeycutt's battalion, but only a couple of miles away. The 506th was another legendary airborne formation, having earned extensive accolades for their performance in the European theater during World War II, including a drop into Normandy the morning of

D-Day. They took their motto and nickname from a Cherokee word meaning "stand alone."

The troops moved out early the next morning, with all units converging on the base of the high, tree-blanketed summit labeled on the map as
Hill 937. Company B approached from the east and Company A from the
west. Both units sought a route that might work for climbing the hill, while
Company C, 3/187, worked its way around for a look at the north slope of
the steep, thickly overgrown mountain.

The airborne troopers of the first two companies each began to make
their way up one of the many ridges that snaked toward the top of the elevation. Company B had been making good progress when the leading
American soldiers abruptly reeled back or fell under a sudden outburst of
automatic weapons fire, underscored by the explosive blasts of rocket-
propelled grenades. Immediately the Rakkasans took cover from the withering attack and returned fire, though in the dense tropical forest they had
difficulty making out exactly where the enemy shooters lay hidden.

From his 3/187 command post, Lieutenant Colonel Honeycutt contacted his other two companies and ordered them to move up in support
of embattled Company B. He also called in air support, which would be a
tricky prospect given the dense foliage overhead. But a flight of rocket-
equipped Cobra gunships chattered closer, ready to fire an explosive volley
in support. Tragically, the pilots and forward air controller somehow
mixed signals on targeting the support, and the rockets slashed into the
very command post that had summoned them to the battle. Two men were
killed and nearly three dozen, including Lieutenant Colonel Honeycutt
himself, were wounded.

In the chaos of the destruction and casualties, the battalion HQ lost
contact with the three companies working their way onto the mountain.
Company B had made the most progress, advancing to within perhaps a
thousand yards of the summit, but it had also encountered the fiercest
resistance. Without further orders, the men of the embattled unit formed
a defensive perimeter on the mountainside and waited out the night.

By the next morning, the third day of the battle, Lieutenant Colonel Honeycutt had been patched up enough to remain in the field. Believing that the NVA held the summit with, at most, a company of soldiers, he deployed his three companies on the hill onto three separate ridgelines, all of which converged on the tree-covered crest. After a few hours of pounding by artillery and airstrikes, he ordered the Rakkasans forward. He also dispatched his Company D, which had been providing security for the headquarters element, to advance in support. The latter did so against surprising opposition, covering only about a hundred yards per hour over the course of a five-hour fighting advance to the base of the hill.

Meanwhile, farther up the slopes of Ap Bia Mountain, all three assault companies fought against the deeply entrenched enemy, as well as the steep grade and the vegetation-choked terrain. The NVA occupied well-designed bunkers with interlocking fields of fire, protected by stout roofs of many layers of logs and dirt. The solid overhead protection stood a good chance of surviving even a heavy bombardment.

By the evening of 13 May, the fourth day of the battle, the Rakkasans were stymied on three different ridges, in each case blocked by heavily defended and fortified NVA positions. The 3rd Brigade commander, Colonel Conmy, was convinced that the 3/187 faced much more than a company of enemy soldiers, and consequently ordered his 1/506th battalion to march toward the base of the hill from its position in the jungle, less than three miles to the south of the eminence. He expected the Currahees to be ready to attack by the morning of the 15th, but this expectation, like many others, would prove too optimistic for the actual conditions on the field.

Knowing that reinforcements were on the way, Lieutenant Colonel Honeycutt wanted to keep the pressure on the enemy positions. He felt his men were on the verge of cracking the bunker lines and carrying the summit. On the 14th, he ordered his three companies on the hill to press fresh attacks against the summit. Company B, still clinging to its lofty position on the main ridge, was to push toward the top from the northeast as it had been doing. Company C would charge up a neighboring, smaller ridge barely 150 yards to the south, while Company D, currently hunkered down in a ravine, was to try to move laterally to the right until it could reach another avenue where it could advance against Ap Bia Mountain from the north.

Moving off in the morning, B Company entered a zone the enemy had covered with numerous claymore mines. The airborne troops suffered a large number of casualties from the spray of lead as the mines were detonated by remote control. The Rakkasans held their positions, but were raked by automatic fire from a number of hidden bunkers. The extensive air and artillery bombardment of the slopes above them had done little to suppress the defenders.

And as was becoming clear by now, the defenders were many in number, with their units made up of tenacious veteran soldiers. Emplaced on the hill would turn out to be two whole battalions, the 7th and 8th, of the 29th NVA Regiment—a unit known as "the Pride of Ho Chi Minh." They had moved into the area from Laos much earlier, and had spent months preparing their sturdy, interlocking defensive positions, clearly anticipating that one day the Americans would try to wrest the Mountain of the Crouching Beast away from them.

Now, as Company C paratroopers started to make good progress up the small connecting ridge, just south of their comrades in B Company, the NVA counterattacked. Bursting from their bunkers, tossing grenades and firing their AK-47s as they advanced, the Communist soldiers hit the Rakkasans with a stunning wave of violence. Hand-to-hand fighting tore and tumbled along the ridge crest, men trying to kill each other with small arms, knives, even bare hands. The Americans took heavy casualties and reeled backward, Company B losing its XO, two platoon leaders, six squad leaders, three sergeants, and some 40 enlisted men either killed or badly wounded in the melee. The company also lost the ground it had gained in the morning, and then some.

The last of the Rakkasan companies, D, was raked by machine-gun fire and showered with rocket-propelled grenades as it tried to work its way sideways along the slope of the hill. It wasn't until nearly sunset that the unit was even able to work its way into the position from which it would launch its next attack. That night, the airborne troopers looked up to see a hundred or more enemy cooking fires sparking and glowing all around the rim of the hill. In a clear taunt, the NVA wanted the Americans to know they were staying put, and would be ready for them when they again moved into the attack. The day was also marred by another tragic friendly-fire incident, when a helicopter gunship intending to fire at NVA moving along the slopes of the mountain mistakenly targeted American soldiers, killing one and wounding three.

On 15 May, Honeycutt ordered the Rakkasans to renew the attack, essentially repeating the approach routes of the previous day—though at least D Company was also in position to put pressure on the enemy positions. But that didn't seem to make a difference; the NVA apparently had every approach to the hilltop covered by significant fortifications, and they didn't need to move troops from one defensive sector in order to reinforce another. Further adding to the attackers' misery, for the third time in the battle a helicopter gunship mistakenly targeted American troops, blasting a salvo of rockets into B Company's command post, killing one trooper and injuring the company captain.

Lieutenant Colonel Honeycutt pleaded with Colonel Conmy to get 1/506th, the battalion commanded by Lieutenant Colonel John Bowers, into the action. But there wasn't much the brigade could do to press the Currahees through the rugged terrain, where they also fought their way through numerous pockets of enemy resistance. Though Conmy had wanted his 2nd Battalion in position to attack up the hill on the 15th, the 1/506th Battalion fought hard merely to reach the high ground, with another intervening elevation, Hill 916, standing between the Currahees and the Rakkasans. As one small success, B Company, 1/506th, was able to air-assault the summit of the lesser hill, and as the day ended the Americans held the hill 2,000 yards south of Hill 937.

On the 16th, the Rakkasans were at it again, advancing grimly into a fight that had become such a meat grinder that the men began to call the battlefield "Hamburger Hill." This time the 3/187th battalion was not ordered to reach the top of the hill, but to keep pressure on the enemy, get close to the summit, and wait for the Currahees to come up from the south and west to hit the enemy in the rear. Although the 1/506th had a good position atop Hill 916, they would have to descend and then climb back to an intervening elevation, Hill 900, before they could assist their fellow airborne troopers— and they slammed into the equivalent of a brick wall as they tried to force their way onto Hill 900 in their first round of attacks.

The 3/187th once again fell back into night defensive positions. The morale of the hard-fighting airborne troops was reaching a nadir, and when an intrepid reporter, Jay Sharbutt of the Associated Press, reached the combat zone and conducted interviews, they didn't hold back their questions and criticism of "that damn Blackjack" as they called their battalion commander.

With the two battalions still too far apart to support each other, Conmy ordered the 3/187 to hold in place on the 17th, hoping that the Currahees could make better progress. That day was also spent in a thorough pasting of the hilltop and high ridges of Ap Boa Mountain by aircraft and at least eight batteries of artillery, the latter including huge guns of 175-mm and 8-inch bore. The effects of high explosive and napalm had mostly cleared the summit of vegetation by now, but even so, the enemy bunkers were so well built and camouflaged that they were hard for the Americans to spot until a soldier was right on top of the enemy position.

On 18 May, Colonel Conmy again ordered both of his battalions to assault, with the Rakkasans aiming for the crest of Hill 937 and the Currahees expected to carry Hill 900 and move against the main crest from the south. Beginning at 0800, renewed artillery bombardment and follow-up airstrikes hammered the crest and high slopes of both summits for a full 60 minutes. As soon as the explosions ceased, the weary soldiers, in their sweaty fatigues and heavy flak jackets, laden with grenades and ammunition, pushed upward again. The NVA, as anticipated, had stayed in place to fight, and once again every yard of ground was bought with a price paid in sweat and blood. American and North Vietnamese soldiers frequently fired at each other from just a few yards apart. Grenades, satchel charges, and the handheld light antitank weapon (LAW) all came into play as the airborne troops took on one enemy bunker after another.

As always in this battle, the close-quarters fighting and the rugged terrain made outside fire support a challenge. When yet another incident occurred in which a Cobra gunship mistakenly targeted a squad of Rakkasans, killing one, an infuriated and disgusted Honeycutt ordered the helicopters to keep away from the battle. But on this day, also, there seemed to be at least a promise of success, as D Company fought its way to within about 25 yards of the summit. With C Company nearby, Honeycutt ordered it to move laterally to support the final assault. Unfortunately, with the enemy nearly beaten, nature intervened with a driving, torrential rainstorm accompanied by whipping winds. Visibility was reduced to just about zero, and the flowing water turned the steep, now vegetation-free hillsides into muddy slides.

Once again the Rakkasans pulled back to night positions. The battalion had been severely mauled over the now nine-day battle, the last six of which had been spent on Hamburger Hill. Companies A and B had been reduced to 50 percent of established strength by casualties, while the toll on Companies C and D had reduced both formations to only about 20 percent of normal. Two company commanders were casualties, one of them KIA, and eight of the 12 platoon leaders had been put out of action. On the southern flank of the attack, the Currahees had run into a firmly entrenched enemy position defending the crest of Hill 900, and was pinned down below that secondary summit, still more than 500 yards away from the top of Ap Boa Mountain.

The 101st Airborne Division commander, General Zais, arrived on the battlefield late in the day during the 18th. He gave serious thought to calling off the attack, but the airborne soldiers were so close to victory, and the enemy was now surrounded and virtually trapped, that he made the decision to press on. He did order more troops to the fight, including two additional battalions, 2/501st and the 2/3rd ARVN Regiment, together with a company from the 2/506th. The soldiers began moving toward the hill in an attempt to completely surround it, moving by a mix of helicopter transport and ground march.

The division CO also wanted to pull the badly chewed-up 3/187th from the fight, but Lieutenant Colonel Honeycutt vehemently objected, declaring that his men paid such a heavy toll already that they should be allowed to finish the job. General Mais changed his mind, and assigned the reinforcing company from 2/506th to be attached to the Rakkasans for the final push. The 19th of May was spent moving units into position, ensuring that the base of Ap Boa Mountain was basically surrounded. There were now 10 artillery batteries in range of the summit, and these, along with many flights of tactical ground-attack aircraft, maintained the volume of heavy fire on the high ground.

That pressure continued for several hours after daybreak on 20 May. By 1000 that morning, nearly 300 airstrikes had dropped more than a million pounds of bombs and 150,000 pounds of napalm on the enemy positions during the battle. More than 20,000 rounds of artillery had also impacted the crest, leaving the whole hilltop as barren as a moonscape, resembling the ravaged lifelessness of the no-man's-land between the trenches of World War I warfare.

Honeycutt insisted that his battalion again lead the way, and shortly after 1000, the weary survivors of the 3/187, with the extra airborne company as reinforcement, moved out and up. They found the going a little easier than before, and soon discerned that most of the NVA troops had fled, leaving a couple of platoons right at the top of the hill to hold out until the end. By 1145, that summit was in American hands, though it took until 1700 for the whole hill to be declared secured. In keeping with their almost uncanny ability to withdraw from a battle with speed and stealth, the NVA survivors somehow slipped through the net of surrounding American and ARVN troops and limped back to Laos to regroup. The Rakkasans, with help, had won the hill, and the fight.

The Americans, however, especially the 3/187, which lost 39 men killed and nearly 300 wounded, had paid a dear price for their victory. Total allied losses came to 70 men killed and nearly 400 wounded. More than 600 bodies of slain NVA soldiers were found on the hill, and intelligence reports, supported by Special Forces observations, suggested that at least an equal number, and perhaps as many as a thousand, NVA dead had been carried from the field at the end of the battle. Certainly "the Pride of Ho

Chi Minh" Regiment had been shattered to the point where it needed to be completely rebuilt before it would become combat effective again.

One soldier, shortly after the fighting ended, tacked a makeshift sign to a burned tree trunk near the top of the hill. The sign read "Hamburger Hill." Not long afterward, another grunt wrote "Was It Worth It?" underneath. It was certainly not worth it for the real estate captured, as the hill was quietly abandoned two weeks after the battle, and reoccupied by the NVA a week or so after that. One thing about the Vietnam War had not changed, in that the primary battle objective for American forces remained to kill enemy soldiers, not to hold pieces of ground.

The commanders involved, from Lieutenant Colonel Honeycutt to Colonel Conmy to General Zais, all praised the work of the soldiers who took the hill. It was in fact a remarkable achievement won primarily by the individual infantryman, and it proved the primacy of the American soldier on the modern battlefield. In a press conference, the 101st Division's commanding general called it a "tremendous, gallant victory," completely in keeping with America's mission in Vietnam.

But the strains caused by this strategy, which effectively prevented the Army and Marines from conducting a campaign that could end in victory, were beginning to become plain to all. The new president, Richard Nixon, had vowed to somehow reduce and eventually end the American involvement in Vietnam. The publicity resulting from the Battle of Ap Boa Mountain, which became known as Hamburger Hill in all quarters of American life, caused objections to the war to resonate all the way to the floor of Congress. In a June 1969 issue, *Life* magazine ran a photo spread of 241 American men who had died in Vietnam in a single week—a spread that many viewers interpreted to show all the men who had been killed on Hamburger Hill.

Prodded by the president, MACV Commanding General Abrams issued orders that from this point forward American forces were not to take on any offensive operations that were likely to result in heavy casualties. The question scrawled at the bottom of the cardboard sign on Hamburger Hill was starting to be seriously considered at all levels of American civilian and military society, and the answer seemed to be no.

FOURTEEN

A FIRM STAND

THE SOUTH VIETNAMESE TURN BACK AN EASTERTIDE INVASION AT AN LOC

[The North Vietnamese] were simply trying to pile on and pile on and pile on. They frittered away an awful lot of manpower.

COLONEL WALT ULMER, UNITED STATES ARMY, ADVISER TO
ARVN 5TH DIVISION, DESCRIBING EVENTS OF 14 MAY 1972

By late 1971 President Nixon's program, "Vietnamization," which was intended to turn combat operations completely over to the South Vietnamese, had progressed significantly. American units, with few exceptions, were no longer initiating searches, sweeps, or attacks. United States military force had fallen from nearly half a million in 1968 to around 150,000 in 1971, and would be reduced to about 25,000 during 1972. Naturally, the toll in casualties had decreased dramatically as well.

Nevertheless, American advisers were posted with every large size ARVN unit, and with many smaller units as well. In addition, aircraft of the Army, Marine Corps, and United States Navy played a very active role in propping up the fledgling South Vietnamese Air Force, and in supporting ground operations, much as they had done during the intense battles of the American combat involvement. In Paris, a sort of charade of a peace process, one in which the two sides initially wrangled for almost a year over what shape table should be used to host the talks, inched its way toward nothing.

In fact, the North Vietnamese were as confident of eventual victory as ever, and it was in their interests to stall progress on negotiations. The government in Hanoi was not interested in peace; it remained committed to the conquest and absorption of South Vietnam into the Communist state of Vietnam. Naturally, it was eager to see the United States depart South Vietnam altogether.

Observing the drawdown of American forces in the early 1970s, and holding a certain level of contempt for the fighting qualities of the ARVN, the North Vietnamese Army began in 1971 to plan for an ambitious offensive. This attack would eventually become the world's largest military operation since more than a third of a million Chinese soldiers swept from the rugged terrain of North Korea in late 1950 to drive back General MacArthur's United Nations forces. The trigger for that attack, of course, had been the approach of American, South Korean, and other allied forces to the Yalu River dividing North Korea from China. The memories of that stunning military surprise and the resulting near-disaster had lingered as a stark cautionary tale in America's political leadership throughout the war in Vietnam.

Since the Viet Cong had never recovered from the devastating losses they had suffered all across South Vietnam during the Tet '68 Offensive, most of the burden of attacking—and all of the planning—fell to the regular soldiers of the North Vietnamese Army. The overall commander of the operation would be the chief of staff of the NVA, General Van Tien Dung. He would have 14 divisions available for a massive series of attacks, scheduled to begin shortly after the Tet holiday in 1972. The campaign would be called the Nguyen Hue Offensive, named for a national hero who had won a major victory over invading Chinese in 1789.

The plan proposed three main thrusts, one each against the I Corps, II Corps, and III Corps tactical zones. In preparation for this, which would become the largest single operation of the Vietnam War, the North Vietnamese sought and received an exceptionally large amount of material support from their allies in the Soviet Union—eager to show itself as the "true friend" of Communist North Vietnam, as Hanoi's relationship with Red China was growing increasingly strained.

To prove their backing with more than words, the Soviets sent an astonishing amount of weaponry to the Hanoi government. These included 400 tanks, including T-34 and the modern T-54 models, and another 200 PT-96 tanks, which were lighter than the main battle tanks but also had an amphibious capability. Anti-aircraft weapons were also dispatched in great numbers, including large, truck-mounted surface-to-air missiles, and large numbers of the relatively new SA-7, which was called the Grail by western forces. It was a heat-seeking missile that could be fired by a single soldier aiming and shooting it from a shoulder launcher, and was lethal against low-flying aircraft. The USSR also provided its NVA ally with plenty of wire-guided Sagger AT-3 anti-tank missiles, as well as many tubes of large bore artillery. In conjunction with the delivery of the new armaments, the Soviets also brought nearly 25,000 NVA soldiers to Russia or Eastern Europe for training in the use of the modern equipment.

The Nguyen Hue Offensive would commence a new phase of the war for North Vietnam as, for the first time, the NVA would make a conventional assault, including the use of very many tanks and the backing of significant numbers of field artillery batteries, against the south. They would take advantage of the fact that the ARVN continued to view the DMZ as an area that would not be violated by either side, and—even as peace talks proceeded, albeit at a snail's pace, in Paris—the NVA would flagrantly breach the original treaty dividing Vietnam as they sent powerful mobile forces straight south through the zone. Additional North Vietnamese forces would enter Quang Tri province from Laos, outflanking the northern defensive line altogether. The objective in the I Corps area was to occupy all of Quang Tri province and then continue on to take the ancient imperial capital of Hue.

In the II Corps area the attacks would lunge from both Laos and Cambodia in an attempt to occupy the entirety of the Central Highlands, including the important provincial capital and military depot city of Pleiku. Once that fell the NVA would be in position to drive east through the coastal lowlands. If they could make it as far as the port of Qui Nhon, South Vietnam would be effectively cut in two.

To the south, in the III Corps area, the attackers would emerge from Cambodia in two prongs. One was to drive straight south, and if successful could significantly isolate Saigon from the southern part of South Vietnam. The other would take the border city of Loc Ninh, site of the triumphant American and ARVN victory in 1967, and then turn south to charge down Highway 13 toward the important city of An Loc. If that city fell, the invaders would have an open path down the road, potentially leading all the way to Saigon itself.

The plan was obviously ambitious in scope, employing far more troops in a completely unprecedented scale of maneuver than the North Vietnamese had ever used before. While the leaders in Hanoi dared to hope that the attacks would result in the defeat of South Vietnam, that was not, however, a stated goal of the Nguyen Hue offensive. Instead, the attackers wanted to seize and hold control of significant parts of Vietnam to set themselves up for future campaigns, and to solidify their positions during the Paris negotiations.

Hanoi did have some significant objectives that were rated as very desirable, even if they did not result in the complete surrender of the south. One of these goals was the capture of Hue, which still retained powerful symbolic value to all Vietnamese. The second of these was to make a strike all the way from Cambodia to the coast through the Central Highlands. If South Vietnam was physically cut in half by the offensive, the country would be shown to all the world to be teetering on the brink of defeat.

The final goal was to lay open the road to the nerve center of South Vietnam, the great city of Saigon. Even if the attackers couldn't make it all the way to the capital, if they could fight their way down Highway 13 far enough, Saigon's security would be seriously imperiled. The invaders were confident they could breach the border defenses and begin to drive down that long-embattled road, sweeping through the ironically named "Binh Long," which translates as "Peaceful Dragon" province.

The only real obstacle in their path toward Saigon would be the provincial capital, the thriving city in the midst of tens of thousands of acres of rubber plantations, the place called An Loc.

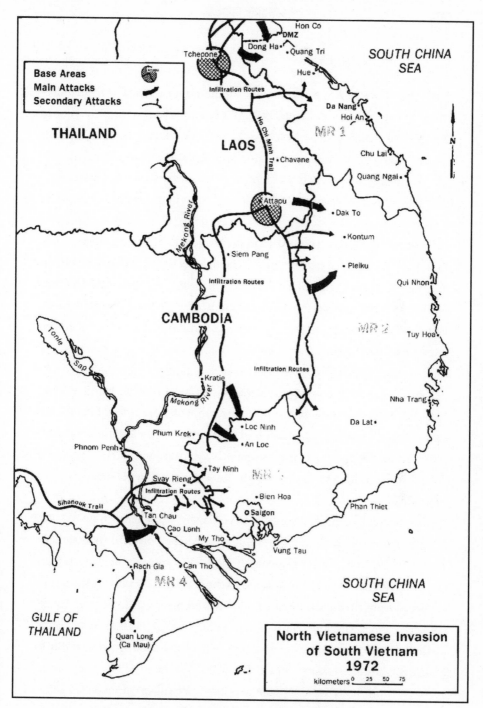

Base Areas
Main Attacks
Secondary Attacks

THAILAND

LAOS

Ho Chi Minh Trail

SOUTH CHINA SEA

Hon Co
DMZ
Dong Ha
Quang Tri
Hue

Tchepone

Infiltration Routes

Da Nang
Hoi An

MR 1

Chu Lai

Quang Ngai

Chavane

Attapu

Dak To

Kontum

Pleiku

Qui Nhon

N

Siem Pang

Infiltration Routes

CAMBODIA

Mekong River

Tonle Sap

MR 2

Tuy Hoa

Infiltration Routes

Nha Trang

Kratie

Mekong River

Loc Ninh

An Loc

Da Lat

Phum Krek

Phnom Penh

MR 3

Tay Ninh

Svay Rieng

Infiltration Routes

Bien Hoa

Phan Thiet

Sihanouk Trail

Tan Chau

Cao Lanh

My Tho

Saigon

Vung Tau

Rach Gia

Can Tho

MR 4

SOUTH CHINA SEA

GULF OF THAILAND

Quan Long
(Ca Mau)

North Vietnamese Invasion of South Vietnam 1972

kilometers 0 25 50 75

Eastertide Invasion of South Vietnam

HISTORY AND MUSEUMS DIVISION, UNITED STATES MARINE CORPS

ATTACKS IN THE NORTH

Both the Americans and the South Vietnamese expected some kind of major enemy onslaught during 1972, though none of the allies envisioned anything as major as the attacks that actually developed. General Abrams warned his chiefs back in Washington that he anticipated an attack during the Tet holidays, and when no such enemy action materialized he and his staff had to endure some ridicule, especially in the press, for being overly alarmist.

Nevertheless, he was only off on the timing, as at about midday on 30 March an artillery barrage opened up from across the DMZ on the northern edge of Quang Tri province. By later that afternoon two full divisions numbering some 30,000 troops, accompanied by at least a hundred tanks, had plunged through the DMZ to surround and overwhelm the northern line of ARVN defenses.

Another NVA division, with a regiment of tanks, attacked along Route 9 from Laos, quickly passing the abandoned base at Khe Sanh and moving into the South Vietnamese flank. By 1 April, the ARVN was blowing up bridges across the Cua Viet River and falling back to try and form a defensive line to the south. Two additional NVA divisions joined the main attack, while a third pushed through the A Shau Valley to strike directly toward Hue.

The second and third prongs of the offensive would launch on 5 April. In II Corps, this involved a preliminary and very powerful diversionary attack on Highway 1 near the coast. The ARVN commander, Lieutenant General Ngo Du, almost overreacted to the diversion by pulling his forces eastward from the Central Highlands down to the coast. It was the American civilian adviser John Vann, former head of USAID and now director of the US assistance group in II Corps, who convinced Du that the first attack was not the enemy's main thrust. Thus, when the NVA did surge eastward from Laos on 12 April, the South Vietnamese at least had some troops in position to slow the enemy attacks—though the NVA spearheads would gain significant ground before the onslaught finally lost momentum.

THE EASTERTIDE OFFENSIVE IN III CORPS

Also commencing on 5 April, the NVA made its move into the provinces north and west of Saigon. The initial objective of this attack was the entirety of Binh Long province, including the key cities of Loc Ninh and An Loc. The ARVN had only a single division, the 5th, to hold the province, and as the offensive began the components of the 5th ARVN Division were scattered all through the Binh Long region.

The Communists attacked with three full divisions, heavily reinforced by armor. Although two of these units, the 9th Viet Cong and 5th Viet Cong Divisions retained their "VC" designations, they were all fully professional formations manned by soldiers who had trained in the north and been sent south for the offensive. Indeed, the 9th VC Division, which would attack directly toward An Loc, was considered one of the NVA's elite formations.

With its position close to the border of Cambodia, the plantation town of Loc Ninh remained a natural target, just as it had been when the enemy attacked it so furiously—and, for the Communists, disastrously—in 1967. This time the result would not be left up to chance.

Loc Ninh was held by about 1,000 men, with an armored cavalry squadron based north of town to support them. The enemy attacked with a full division, the 5th Viet Cong, supported with huge armor and artillery assets. By evening of the first day they had driven the defenders, which included seven American advisers, into two perimeters in the northern and southern sides of the town. American and South Vietnamese airstrikes punished the attackers significantly, and probably were the reason that at least a few of the defenders were able to make a stand.

The next morning the enemy attacked from three directions, north, west, and south, with each thrust supported by about a dozen tanks. The outnumbered and under-armed defenders put up a spirited resistance from both compounds, supported by all the aircraft III Corps generals could bring to bear. These included USAF planes from Bien Hoa and bases in Thailand, and USN aircraft flying from the carriers USS *Constellation* and USS *Saratoga*. A relatively new tool of American air superiority, the super-sized gunship called the AC-130 Spectre, which was built on the platform of the huge C-130 Hercules cargo plane, delivered devastating fire from its powerful Gatling guns, at one point slaughtering the better part of an NVA regiment as the attackers tried to work their way through the barbed wire of a perimeter defense.

For two days the air support and valiant stubbornness of the defenders slowed the enemy offensive at Loc Ninh, but on 7 April sheer numbers prevailed, and the NVA overran the southern compound in the morning. The northern position fell by 1630. Less than 100 of the city's defenders, including only one of the American advisers, made it out of the city and were able to reach An Loc, about 15 miles down Highway 13. (Several other Americans were captured, and would be repatriated after the Americans completed their withdrawal in 1973.) Also on 7 April, the Communists attacked and overran an important airstrip at Quan Loi, a couple of miles northeast of An Loc.

The fall of Loc Ninh, and heavy enemy pressure against a couple of firebases between that city and An Loc, convinced the III Corps commanders, Lieutenant Gen Nguyen Van Minh and Major General James Hollingsworth, that the provincial capital would be the next target of the attack. General Minh ordered the 1st ARVN Airborne brigade, three battalions strong, and the 81st Ranger Group to move north on Highway 13 to protect the city's southern flank. The relief convoy ran into heavy NVA opposition well south of An Loc, and found the road to be completely closed.

By 10 April An Loc had been cut off from overland contact with the rest of South Vietnam. Making matters worse, the area around Quan Loi was a highland that dominated the entire area. From here NVA artillery could pound the defenders in the provincial capital, and artillery observers could see and adjust the effects of their fire. A ring of potent AA weaponry encircled An Loc, making the only allied means to get in and out, the helicopter, a terribly perilous mode of transport. The shoulder-launched SA-7 missiles from the USSR proved to be particularly deadly.

In one small break for the South Vietnamese, the attackers had actually outrun their own schedule by capturing Loc Ninh so quickly. They would need some time to move up their forces to make a serious attack against An Loc. In the meantime, and despite the deadly pattern of AA fire, the ARVN was able to fly some reinforcements into the city, including two battalions and the recon company from the 8th ARVN Regiment. This brought the total number of defenders in the city, and just outside of it, to about 3,000 men in nine battalions, including mostly regular ARVN soldiers but also the Rangers and a sizable number of territorial forces from the RF and LF. They would have to withstand the assault of nearly 20,000 NVA attackers. The city was, and would remain, out of range of any friendly artillery support, so the only external firepower that could be brought to bear would have to come from airstrikes.

THE BATTLE FOR AN LOC

Before dawn on 13 April, the steady but desultory NVA artillery fire against An Loc ramped up dramatically. The attackers employed every kind of weapon in their arsenal, from heavy mortars to field artillery to rockets. They fired massive shells from a battery of Soviet 130mm howitzers, in addition to 105mm and 155mm guns that had been captured from the ARVN earlier during this battle, as well as in previous encounters. For 15 hours the barrage continued, with an average of one shell falling on the city every eight seconds.

Even as this bombardment swelled to a crescendo, Communist troops moved against the northeast side of the city. With the tanks leading the way, the attackers' initial progress was good. The ARVN troops had never faced armor in battle before, and in many places simply broke and ran in the face of the lumbering, tracked behemoths belching fire and steel. However, one remarkable act of bravery changed this attitude in an instant, as Private Binh Doan Quang, a member of the irregular Local Forces, used a hand-held M-72 light antitank weapon (LAW) to destroy one of the tanks that had been leading the attack. This courageous shot was observed by many ARVN soldiers, and word quickly spread, leading many other South Vietnamese soldiers to try and follow suit.

Furthermore, and despite their training in Soviet and Warsaw Pact camps, the North Vietnamese tankers quickly showed that they had not mastered the essential concept of combined arms warfare. The tanks tended to roll on steadily, quickly advancing ahead of their infantry support, and as they moved into the city they became terribly vulnerable to weapons like the LAW, which allowed an ARVN foot soldier to move against the blind spots of the tank without worrying about enemy infantrymen shooting him down.

In addition to having to face the stubbornly courageous defenders of An Loc, the NVA units found themselves pounded by an almost unprecedented level of Allied air support. Fighter-bombers from the Air Force and Navy roamed freely over what has in modern parlance come to be known as a "target-rich environment." An increasing number of B-52 Arc Light raids would be made against the attackers around An Loc, with one bomb run credited with smashing an entire enemy battalion that had been forming up to attack.

Nevertheless, the NVA seemed to be undeterred by heavy casualties, and continued to press the advance into the city. Sometimes the progress would be measured by a gain of one house per day along a certain street. The North Vietnamese might take a whole 12 hours to clear the defenders out of the building, room by room. At night they would fill that house with fresh soldiers, who would press the attack against the next objective on the block the next day.

The attackers had succeeded in capturing the northern neighborhoods in this city that had once held a population of 15,000, but the stubborn resistance prevented them from moving farther into the city center, or southern reaches. The morale of the ARVN troops remained surprisingly high, as they were no doubt encouraged by their own successes, and the massive amounts of airpower flying overhead in their support.

Cobra helicopters proved especially lethal, taking out many enemy tanks in the city with lethal barrages of rocketry. The nimble choppers could quickly line up shots against armored vehicles pinned in the narrow city streets; the pilots quickly learned to destroy the lead and trailing tanks in a column, which often trapped the rest of the AFVs in place, turning them into sitting ducks. During the first week of fighting in the city, one Cobra—piloted by Captain Bill Causey with Lieutenant Steve Shields firing the guns and rocket launchers—was credited with 5 tank kills.

As the fighting progressed, South Vietnamese at all levels of command began to see what was at stake at An Loc: namely, the security of Saigon itself. President Thieu himself authorized the transfer of a division from the Mekong Delta region, and the 21st ARVN Division was airlifted into place south of the battlefield on 16 April. It immediately began to move north along Highway 13, fighting savagely and bogging down as it reached a strong NVA position at the Tau O Bridge.

By this time, the enemy inside An Loc proper were worn down to a state of exhaustion. Two dozen of their tanks, including many of the potent T-54s, had been destroyed, and their timetable—which had called for the city to be declared the capital of the People's Revolutionary Government by mid-April—had been disrupted. But the NVA was not giving up; instead, with uncharacteristic flexibility, the North Vietnamese changed the plan of attack over a matter of days. The new plan shifted the emphasis of onslaught to the city's east side, with the effort to be made by the entire 9th VC Division, reinforced with many other elements. Hanoi also dispatched many more AA weapons to try and counter the American air superiority over An Loc.

In one of those strokes of luck that occasionally happen in war, some ARVN Rangers skirmished with an NVA detachment just outside of the city on 18 April, killing several of the enemy soldiers. On one of the bodies the Rangers found a report detailing the new plan of attack, and predicting that the city would fall in a matter of hours on 20 April. Weary and bloodied, short of food, with many wounded comrades lining up behind them, unable to be evacuated, the South Vietnamese prepared to face this new attack with at least some advance knowledge of what the enemy would try to do.

Early on 19 April an immense artillery bombardment signaled the start of the next phase of the battle. Three NVA regiments hurled themselves against the southeast edge of the shrinking ARVN position, while two other regiments took on the troops of the 1st ARVN Airborne Brigade who maintained several positions outside of the city proper. One airborne battalion southeast of An Loc, the 6th, was virtually wiped out by these incredibly savage attacks. However, the 5th Battalion, fighting west of Highway 13, was able to hold firm with the help of continual airstrikes in support.

The North Vietnamese attacking into the city had a tougher time of it, as they once again encountered stubborn resistance and had to endure a hail of destruction from the skies. By the 22nd, this attack, too, had run out of steam—though the bombardment by enemy artillery rose to a level the Communists had never previously sustained. Great sections of An Loc were reduced to rubble, but the defenders still held firm. That same night the ARVN Ranger Group made a counterattack, the first South Vietnamese offensive action since the Nguyen Hue campaign had begun. They gained back a little ground, but didn't have the numbers to capitalize on their success.

For the next two and a half weeks, until 10 May, the areas of control in the city remained fairly static, though the NVA did press home a small attack to gain a foothold on the west side of An Loc. The survivors in the city lived a hellish life during this period, living almost completely underground in the presence of continual bombardment. The city, and the soldiers' lives, resembled some of the epic battlefields of World War II, such as Stalingrad, Manila, or Berlin. Even parachute drops of supplies had become incredibly hazardous, and more than half of the tonnage dropped from both high and low altitudes seemed to end up in enemy hands.

Around dawn on 9 May, the North Vietnamese began aggressive probing around the ARVN perimeter, which now encircled less than a square mile in total area. When the artillery bombardment subsequently accelerated, General Hollingsworth acted on a hunch that the next attack would come on 11 May: he arranged for 18 B-52 Arc Light raids on that day, and made sure to have a plentitude of tactical strike aircraft standing by as well. The number of B-52 raids would be increased dramatically as the situation developed.

Just after midnight in the early morning of 11 May, the artillery punishment falling on An Loc rose to a new level of intensity. Over the next 16 hours 17,000 rounds fell on the rubble that had once been a city, forcing most of the defenders to stay underground. As daylight broke, the NVA attacked around the entire perimeter, with an emphasis against the defenses on the northern and northwest parts of the ring.

The defenders did their best to cling to the ground they held, and the Americans brought their level of air support to a previously unseen level. Some 30 Arc Light missions wreaked terrible destruction over the 24-hour period at the start of this phase of the attack. These bomb runs, each made by three of the massive Stratofortresses, greatly aided the ARVN morale, as the effects of the high explosive ordnance were easy to see. In addition, all manner of aircraft joined in the ground attacks, pilots braving a level of anti-aircraft fire that had never previously been experienced in Vietnam. At least three FACs were in the air at all times, and at least two or three of the Spectre gunships remained on station, delivering "on-call" fire support wherever the defense was hard-pressed. On the 11th alone, North Vietnamese anti-aircraft blasted one A-37, two Cobras, and two FAC light airplanes out of the sky. One of the massive Spectres took a hit from a Grail missile, but it survived to return to its base.

The axis of the NVA attacks again shifted to the east by nightfall of 12 May. So many of the T-54 tanks had been destroyed that the Communists had to use the lighter PT-76 AFVs to try and break the defenses. When the weather closed in near midnight, the attackers made some progress, and the defensive situation grew critical for several hours. Before daylight, however, additional B-52 strikes against troop concentrations sapped much of the strength from these punches. By dawn on the 13th, the weather improved enough for a couple of Spectres to start circling again, and during the course of that day the North Vietnamese push on the ground slowly petered out.

By the end of May, the situation for the South Vietnamese had begun to improve. The artillery bombardment of An Loc had lessened significantly as enemy supply lines were strained, and American air power continued to attack and destroy NVA gun batteries. Many antiaircraft positions had likewise been knocked out, making it safer to bring in supplies, evacuate the hundreds of wounded, and even bring in reinforcements. On 14 June the 48th ARVN Regiment began to relieve the terribly battered 5th ARVN Division. Within a few days the fresh troops had reclaimed the hills to the south of the city, bringing the period of intense bombardment to an end.

General Minh declared that the siege was broken on 18 June. On 11 July, massive flights of Hueys brought in the entire 18th ARVN Division, which immediately set out to clear the NVA from areas around An Loc. The enemy attack against An Loc had been defeated, just as had their more northern thrusts toward Hue and the Central Highlands. On every front the Nguyen Hue Offensive had been absorbed, stopped, and eventually repulsed.

But the cost had been high, and nowhere was the bill greater than at An Loc. Some 2,300 ARVN troops had lost their lives defending the city, with more than 3,000 wounded. The entire population of the city was rendered homeless, and countless civilians had died during the fighting—including hundreds mowed down intentionally by the NVA as they tried to flee through the embattled perimeter. The entire city was reduced to heaps of rubble, ash, and charcoal.

The defenders, for their part, had wrecked three of the top divisions in the North Vietnamese Army. Estimates of enemy killed ran from 10,000 up to 15,000. Whole regiments were virtually annihilated, and most of the tanks and vehicles that had led the attacks had been destroyed in the fighting. The South Vietnamese Army had fought and won its most significant battle, and the morale effects of such a victory cannot be overstated. It gave the country and its military a real belief that they could stand on their own against North Vietnam.

In the bright glow of that historic accomplishment, made at such a cost, but decisively crushing a much more powerful and well-armed foe, it is perhaps understandable that both American and South Vietnamese chroniclers may have overlooked the crucial importance of American air power in this battle. The victory allowed the United States to continue to draw down its forces, and the Saigon government to believe that it had the military and the resources to stand alone.

It is a historic fact, and to many a tragedy, that the next powerful North Vietnamese attack would come only three years later. And when the NVA charged toward Saigon in 1975, the air power of the United States would not be there to save the day.

ABBREVIATIONS

AA Anti-Aircraft

ACR Armored Cavalry Regiment

AFV Armored Fighting Vehicle

APC Armored Personnel Carrier

ARVN Army of the Republic of Vietnam (South Vietnamese Army)

ASP Ammunition Supply Point

BLT Battalion Landing Team (Marines)

CBU Cluster Bomb Units

CIDG Civilian Irregular Defense Group

CO Commanding Officer

COSVN Central Office for South Vietnam (VC overall headquarters sponsored by North Vietnam)

CP Command Post

DMZ Demilitarized Zone (border between South and North Vietnam)

FAC Forward Air Controller

FO Forward Observer

FSB Fire Support Base

HE High Explosive

HMM Marine Medium Helicopter Squadron

HQ Headquarters

KIA Killed in Action

KSCB Khe Sanh Combat Base

LAW M72 Light Antitank Weapon

LCT Landing Craft Tank

LCU Landing Craft, Utility

LIB Light Infantry Brigade

LOH Light Observation Helicopter

LVT Landing Vehicle, Tracked

LVTP Landing Vehicle, Tracked, Personnel

LZ Landing Zone

MACV Military Assistance Command—Vietnam

MAF Marine Amphibious Force

MEB Marine Expeditionary Brigade

NCO Non-Commissioned Officer

NDP Night Defense Perimeter/Night Defensive Position

NVA North Vietnamese Army

PAVN People's Army of Vietnam (North Vietnamese Army)

PF Popular Forces

PLAF People's Liberation Armed Force (aka "Viet Cong")

RF Regional Forces

RPG Rocket-Propelled Grenade

SIGINT Signals Intelligence

SLF Special Landing Force

TAOR Tactical Area of Responsibility

TF Task Force

TZ Tactical Zone

USAF United States Air Force

USAID United States Agency for International Development

USMC United States Marine Corps

USN United States Navy

VC Viet Cong

VMA Marine Attack Squadron (Tactical Bombers)

VMFA Marine Fighter Attack Squadron (Fighter-Bombers)

XO Executive Officer (second-in-command)

BIBLIOGRAPHY

Albright, John, John A. Cash, and Allan W. Sandstrum. *Seven Firefights in Vietnam*. Office of the Chief of Military History, United States Army, Washington, DC, 1970.

Bowman, David J. *The Vietnam Experience*. Gallery Books, W. H. Smith Publishers Inc, New York, NY, 1989.

Carland, John M. *Stemming the Tide: May 1965 to October 1966. The United States Army in Vietnam*. Center of Military History, United States Army, Washington, DC, 2000.

Fails, Lieutenant Colonel William R. (USMC). *Marines and Helicopters: 1962–1973*. History and Museums Division, Headquarters, U.S. Marine Corps, 1978.

Gilmore, Donald L., with D. M. Giangreco. *Eyewitness Vietnam: Firsthand Accounts from Operation Rolling Thunder to the Fall of Saigon*. Sterling Publishing, New York, NY, 2006.

Hayes, Roger. *On Point. A Rifleman's Year in the Boonies: Vietnam 1967–1968*. Presidio Press, Novato, CA, 2000.

Larson, Sarah A., and Jennifer M. Miller. *Wisconsin Vietnam War Stories: Our Veterans Remember*. Wisconsin Historical Society Press, Madison, WI, 2010.

Macgarrigle, George L. *Combat Operations: Taking the Offensive, October 1966 to October 1967. The United States Army in Vietnam*. Center of Military History, United States Army, Washington, DC, 1998.

Maraniss, David. *They Marched into Sunlight: War and Peace, Vietnam and America—October, 1967*. Simon and Schuster, New York, NY, 2003.

Melson, Major Charles D. (USMC), and (USMC) Lieutenant Colonel Curtis G. Arnold. *U.S. Marines in Vietnam: The War That Would Not End 1971–1973*. History and Museums Division, Headquarters, U.S. Marine Corps, 1991.

Moore, Lieutenant General Harold G. (Ret.), and Joseph L. Galloway. *We Were Soldiers Once . . . And Young: Ia Drang—The Battle That Changed the War in Vietnam*. Random House Publishing Group, New York, NY, 1992.

Morrison, Wilbur H. *The Elephant and the Tiger: The Full Story of the Vietnam War*. Hippocrene Books, New York, NY, 1990.

Murphy, Edward F. *Semper Fi Vietnam: From Da Nang to the SMZ; Marine Corps Campaigns 1965–1975*. Presidio Press, Novato, CA, 1997.

Pimlott, John. *Vietnam: The Decisive Battles*. Macmillan Publishing Company, New York, NY, 1990.

Rogers, Lieutenant General Bernard William. *Vietnam Studies: Cedar Falls—Junction City: A Turning Point.* Department of the Army, Washington, DC, 1989.

Shore II, Captain Moyers S. (USMC). *The Battle for Khe Sanh.* History and Museums Division, Headquarters, U.S. Marine Corps, 1969.

Shulimson, Jack. *U.S. Marines in Vietnam: An Expanding War 1966.* History and Museums Division, Headquarters, U.S. Marine Corps, 1982.

Shulimson, Jack, (USMC) Lieutenant Colonel Leonard A. Blasiol, Charles R. Smith, and (USMC) Captain David A. Dawson. *U.S. Marines in Vietnam: The Defining Year 1968.* History and Museums Division, Headquarters, U.S. Marine Corps, 1997.

Shulimson, Jack, and (USMC) Major Charles M. Johnson. *U.S. Marines in Vietnam: The Landing and the Buildup 1965.* History and Museums Division, Headquarters, U.S. Marine Corps, 1978.

Smith, Charles R. *U.S. Marines in Vietnam: High Mobility and Standdown 1969.* History and Museums Division, Headquarters, U.S. Marine Corps, 1988.

Stanton, Shelby L. *The Rise and Fall of an American Army: U.S. Ground Forces in Vietnam, 1965–1973.* Presidio Press, Novato, CA, 1985.

Telfer, Major Gary L. (USMC), and V. Keith Fleming Jr. *U.S. Marines in Vietnam: Fighting the North Vietnamese 1967.* History and Museums Division, Headquarters, U.S. Marine Corps, 1984.

Tolson, Lieutenant General John J. *Vietnam Studies: Airmobility 1961–1971.* Department of the Army, Washington, DC, 1999.

Tucker, Spencer C. *The Encyclopedia of the Vietnam War: A Political, Social, and Military History.* Oxford University Press, New York, NY, 2000.

West, Andrew (ed.). *Rolling Thunder in a Gentle Land: The Vietnam War Revisited.* Osprey Publishing, Oxford (United Kingdom), 2006.

MAPS

Corps Tactical Zones in South Vietnam

Macgarrigle, George L. *Combat Operations: Taking the Offensive, October 1966 to October 1967. The United States Army in Vietnam.* Center of Military History, United States Army, Washington, DC, 1998.

I Corps; USMC Operational Area

Shulimson, Jack, and (USMC) Major Charles M. Johnson. *U.S. Marines in Vietnam: The Landing and the Buildup 1965.* History and Museums Division, Headquarters, U.S. Marine Corps, 1978.

Operation Starlite Battle Map

Shulimson, Jack, and (USMC) Major Charles M. Johnson. *U.S. Marines in Vietnam: The Landing and the Buildup 1965.* History and Museums Division, Headquarters, U.S. Marine Corps, 1978.

Battle at LZ X-Ray

Carland, John M. *Stemming the Tide: May 1965 to October 1966. The United States Army in Vietnam.* Center of Military History, United States Army, Washington, DC, 2000.

Ambush at LZ Albany

Carland, John M. *Stemming the Tide: May 1965 to October 1966. The United States Army in Vietnam.* Center of Military History, United States Army, Washington, DC, 2000.

Battle of Minh Thanh Road

Carland, John M. *Stemming the Tide: May 1965 to October 1966. The United States Army in Vietnam.* Center of Military History, United States Army, Washington, DC, 2000.

9th VC Division Attack Plan

Macgarrigle, George L. *Combat Operations: Taking the Offensive, October 1966 to October 1967. The United States Army in Vietnam.* Center of Military History, United States Army, Washington, DC, 1998.

Operation Attleboro—Battle Map

Macgarrigle, George L. *Combat Operations: Taking the Offensive, October 1966 to October 1967. The United States Army in Vietnam.* Center of Military History, United States Army, Washington, DC, 1998.

Operation Cedar Falls

Macgarrigle, George L. *Combat Operations: Taking the Offensive, October 1966 to October 1967. The United States Army in Vietnam.* Center of Military History, United States Army, Washington, DC, 1998.

Operation Junction City Phase 1

Macgarrigle, George L. *Combat Operations: Taking the Offensive, October 1966 to October 1967. The United States Army in Vietnam.* Center of Military History, United States Army, Washington, DC, 1998.

Operation Junction City Phase 2

Macgarrigle, George L. *Combat Operations: Taking the Offensive, October 1966 to October 1967. The United States Army in Vietnam.* Center of Military History, United States Army, Washington, DC, 1998.

Northern Quang Tri Province

Shore II, Captain Moyers S. (USMC). *The Battle for Khe Sanh.* History and Museums Division, Headquarters, U.S. Marine Corps, 1969.

Khe Sanh Area

Shore II, Captain Moyers S. (USMC). *The Battle for Khe Sanh.* History and Museums Division, Headquarters, U.S. Marine Corps, 1969.

Battle of Hue

Shulimson, Jack, (USMC) Lieutenant Colonel Leonard A. Blasiol, Charles R. Smith, and (USMC) Captain David A. Dawson. *U.S. Marines in Vietnam: The Defining Year 1968.* History and Museums Division, Headquarters, U.S. Marine Corps, 1997.

Dai Do Area; Battle of Dong Ha

Shulimson, Jack, (USMC) Lieutenant Colonel Leonard A. Blasiol, Charles R. Smith, and (USMC) Captain David A. Dawson. *U.S. Marines in Vietnam: The Defining Year 1968.* History and Museums Division, Headquarters, U.S. Marine Corps, 1997.

Eastertide Invasion of South Vietnam

Melson, Major Charles D. (USMC), and (USMC) Lieutenant Colonel Curtis G. Arnold. *U.S. Marines in Vietnam: The War That Would Not End 1971–1973.* History and Museums Division, Headquarters, U.S. Marine Corps, 1991.

INDEX